SCOTT ANDERSON

The Man Who Tried to Save the World

Scott Anderson is a renowned war reporter
whose work has appeared in *The New York
Times Magazine*, *Harper's*, and several other
national publications. He is the author of the
acclaimed novel *Triage*, *The 4 O'Clock Murders*, and co-author of *War Zones* with his
brother Jon Lee Anderson. He lives in
Brooklyn, New York.

The Man Who Tried

to Save the World

*The Dangerous Life
and Mysterious
Disappearance
of Fred Cuny*

SCOTT ANDERSON

ANCHOR BOOKS

A Division of Random House

New York

For Craig and Colton

FIRST ANCHOR BOOKS EDITION, MAY 2000

Copyright © 1999, 2000 by Scott Anderson

Photos on Prologue, Parts One, Three, Five, and Afterword are by Stanley Greene/Agence
VU. Photos on Parts Two, Four, and Epilogue are courtesy the Cuny family.

The Library of Congress has cataloged the hardcover edition as follows:
Anderson, Scott, 1959–
The man who tried to save the world: the dangerous life and mysterious
disappearance of Fred Cuny / by Scott Anderson. — 1st ed.
p. cm.
Includes index.
1. International relief. 2. INTERTECT (Firm). 3. Cuny, Frederick C.
4. Philanthropists—Biography. 5. Disappeared persons—Biography. I. Title.
HV640.A615 1999
362.87'526'092—dc21
[B] 98-43936
CIP

Anchor ISBN 978-0-385-48666-8

Map copyright © 1999 by Jeffrey L. Ward
Author photograph © Peter Svensson

www.anchorbooks.com

146119709

CONTENTS

INGUSHETIA   CHECHNYA

to Moscow
1489 kilometers/925 miles

Northern road from
Sleptsovskaya to Grozny

"Shadow" Trans-Caucasus road

Samashki

Sleptsovskaya

Sunzha R.

Trans-Caucasus Highway

Mined and closed

M 29   ✕✕✕✕✕   ✕ ✕ ✕ ✕ ✕

Outpost 6

Assinovskaya

Atchkoi-Martan

Orekhovo

Nazran

Bamut

Stari-
Atchkoi

Arshti

Forest road between
Bamut and Orekhovo

Galashki

Fred Cuny route from
Galashki to Bamut

Vladikavkaz

C   A   U   C   A   S   U   S

A 301

0 MILES   5   10

0 KILOMETERS   10   20

to Tbilisi, Georgia
120 kilometers/74 miles

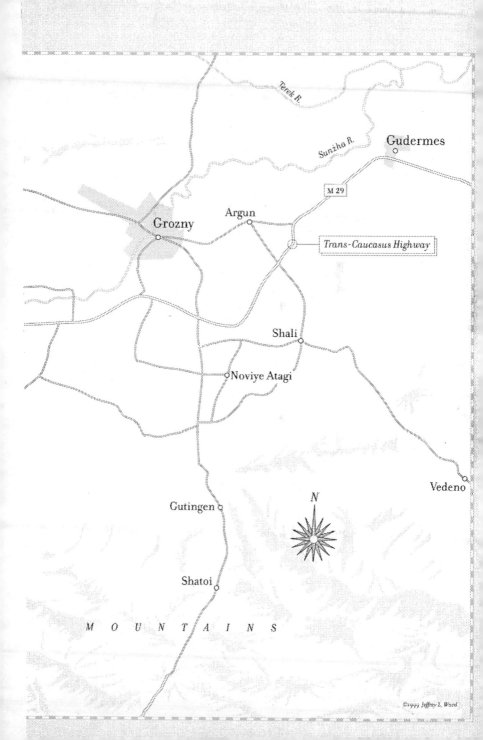

PROLOGUE

I AM STANDING at the edge of the war zone, trying to count off the artillery against the sky. Normally, this is not difficult—you see the flash and count off, five seconds to a mile, until you hear the blast—but on this night so many shells fall, their flashes are like sheet lightning against the low clouds, the roar rolling over the land, a steady white noise of war.

But I am patient and wait for my moment. I spot three quick, nearly overlapping pulses of light streak along the base of the clouds, and I begin to count. I count for a long time, but at fifty-five seconds I hear it: three soft knocks, little more than taps amid the avalanche of sound.

Fifty-five seconds. Eleven miles. They are shelling Bamut again. It is a small village up in the mountains, a place I think about so much I rarely refer to it by name anymore. They have shelled it every night I have been in Chechnya—just a few dozen rounds some nights, several hundred on others. The shelling has never been as heavy as tonight.

As I have done many times these past few days, I travel the path to Bamut in my mind. Not eleven miles by road, more like thirty-five. The paved road cuts across the broad plain until it climbs into the foothills. After a time a narrow dirt track appears, and it leads across a river and into the mountains. At some unmarked spot on this track, perhaps an hour or so past the river, neutral ground is left and the war zone begins. One is then quite close to Bamut, maybe just another half hour, but there are mines sometimes, and sometimes the helicopter gunships sneak in over the hills to destroy what they find.

The village is built along the exposed flank of a mountain valley, and the Russians are on the surrounding heights with their tanks and artillery batteries. Since this war began eleven months ago, a number of people have vanished in the area, and there are stories of torture, that some of those missing were buried alive. I have been frightened of Bamut since I first heard of it. On this night, its name sounds like death to me.

I have come to Chechnya to look for a middle-aged American man who disappeared here seven months ago. His name was Fred Cuny, and he was a hero.

This is not a word I use lightly; in truth, I'm quite sure I've never used it to describe anyone before. But Fred Cuny was a man who had dedicated his life to saving others, and who had done so; tens of thousands of lives over the course of a twenty-five-year career in disaster relief. He came to Chechnya to save more, and now he was gone. He was last seen alive near Bamut. I did not know Fred and he is almost certainly dead, but there is a part of me that has not accepted this, that holds to the fantastic notion that he is still alive and I might save him, and in the morning I will go into the mountains in hopes of finding him.

Fred Cuny was born in the last days of World War II, but the war zones he traversed over the course of his lifetime bore little resemblance to that conflict or any that had preceded it in modern times. It was those differences, in fact, that kept bringing him back to the fields of carnage.

Those who were once the traditional inhabitants of a battlefield—

soldiers, or journalists like myself—today represent only a tiny minority, their numbers overwhelmed by the purely innocent, the civilians who find themselves trapped in war's grip. On this modern battlefield, any comparisons to the Gettysburgs and Waterloos and Guadalcanals of history—ritualized slaughters between opposing armies—are largely useless. For a true comparison, one must reach back to man at his most primitive, to the time when barbarous hordes swept over the countryside laying waste to everything and everyone in their path, when a "battlefield" was defined simply by the presence of victims.

A few simple statistics chart this regression. In the American Civil War, civilian casualties were so low that no one even bothered to count them. From 1900 to 1950, civilians constituted roughly 40 percent of all war-related casualties. By the 1960s, that percentage had risen to 63, and by the 1980s, to 74. For every "conventional war," such as Desert Storm, that pushes the percentage down a fraction, there is a Bosnia or Rwanda that sends it ever upward.

The result is that today's "hallowed ground" is barren of the trappings of heroic folly that can be immortalized by poets and painters. Instead, this hallowed ground is a ditch or a filthy alley or a cluster of burned homes, and it is inordinately populated by the elderly, by mothers and their children, by those not quick enough to escape. These were the people Fred Cuny came to save.

. . .

Others have likened the sound of an artillery bombardment to the sky being ripped apart. I don't know. What I can say is that after a time it no longer even seems like a sound but like something animate. It travels through the ground, and you first feel the ache in your knees, then in your upper chest, and before long you can start imagining that it is inside you and will not leave. I wonder if this is why people go mad during bombardments; not the fear of a quick death, of a shell finding you, but the fear of a slow one, the sense that the constant thrumming through your body is inflicting violence from within. I wonder if Fred

Cuny had similar thoughts on that last night before he went into the mountains. He was in the same town where I am now, and they were shelling Bamut that night too.

The courtyard where I stand is an expanse of concrete enclosed by an eight-foot brick wall. Along the far wall is a fallow flower bed. I cross the concrete and step onto the bare earth. The vibrations are much softer here, barely noticeable. I lean my back against the wall, soothed by the stillness.

One night six weeks ago I sat on the back of a houseboat on a Texas lake with Craig Cuny, Fred's twenty-nine-year-old son. We sat there for many hours, drinking beer and talking—about women and football and Mexico, only occasionally about his father. At around 4 A.M., after a long silence, both of us staring out at the black water, he turned to me.

"I don't want you to go to Chechnya," he said. "It's not worth it. My father's gone. It's not worth someone else getting killed."

Craig had recently ended his own four-month search for his father in Chechnya, and over the course of a few days in Texas we had become close. Now he stared down at the beer can clasped in his hand, then took a gulp from it. "At least promise me you won't do anything crazy."

He was not used to talking to another man in this heartfelt way, and neither was I. I drank from my beer and looked out at the water. "I promise."

In the six weeks since that night I have offered a number of variations on this promise. To my family and friends, it was that I would be careful, that I would not do anything foolish. To those who knew the details of the story, it was more specific, that I would not attempt to go into the mountains. I was asked to make this promise so many times that I began to deliver it preemptively—"Well, I'm certainly not going to take any chances"—and the truth is, before I came here I believed my promises.

But I've come to realize that Fred Cuny probably made the same promises, and yet he went up that road anyway. His decision has presented me with a mystery greater than the one I was sent here to explore, not merely why he disappeared, but why he took such a terrible chance.

. . .

Every morning in Chechnya I awaken with a start, instantly alert, and this morning is no different. Out the window, I see the blue-black of dawn. I stare up at the ceiling and listen. Somewhere far off is the sound of a rooster. The shelling has stopped. I think of who will be making the trip into the mountains today, three of us in this house, two others sleeping a half mile away. I estimate the time to be 5 A.M. We are to leave at eight.

I go to the basin and throw water on my face, then walk through the house. All is bathed in the milky wash of first light. I pass Ryan, my interpreter, a twenty-two-year-old kid from Southern California I should not have brought here. He is sprawled on the bed, snoring. Nothing interrupts his sleep.

The front room holds a table with four chairs and the narrow cot where Stanley sleeps. He is on his back, perfectly still, his hands folded on his chest. Every time I've seen him asleep he is in this position, as if he doesn't move at all during the night. Stanley is forty-five, ten years older than I am, an American living in Paris, a gifted and brave photojournalist. He arrived in Moscow two weeks ago wearing an all-black outfit—black hiking boots, black jeans, black shirt, black jacket, black knit cap—and he has not changed out of it since.

Before we got to Chechnya I had no intention of trying to reach Bamut; the journey was impossible, insane. But, as often happens in these sorts of situations, there occurred a confluence of events, of coincidences, that began to make it seem possible—and then, quite quickly, what had seemed merely possible began to feel like destiny. I happened to meet a rebel liaison who said the journey could be arranged, who even wrote out a coded message of introduction for me to present to the Bamut commander, complementing my Russian government press card if Russian soldiers were encountered. Then I happened to meet Alex, a relief worker with a four-wheel-drive ambulance and a stockpile of medical supplies, who agreed to attempt a "mercy mission" into the village, with us—Stanley, Ryan, and myself—going along on the pretense of documenting the humanitarian effort. With such an extraordinary convergence of good luck, how could I not go?

Of course, riding this wave of good fortune meant overlooking certain details. Fred Cuny had also gone into the mountains with an interpreter and safe-conduct passes. He, too, had gone in an ambulance laden with medical supplies. And he had gone with an insurance factor I could not hope to arrange: two doctors who were well known in the region. None of it had helped; the doctors and the interpreter had simply disappeared as well.

As the days here pass, though, it has become increasingly easy to forget all this. A kind of resignation has settled upon us. Events are happening of their own accord, momentum has built to such a degree that there are no longer any decisions to be made. Whether owing to destiny or some kind of group psychosis, we are being propelled forward, the time for debate and reason having slipped away.

In the front room of the house I quietly pull a chair out from the table. It makes a creak when I sit, and I glance over at Stanley. He is a light sleeper, given to popping up at the slightest sound, but the noise doesn't rouse him.

My notebook is on the table, and I flip through the pages until I find the encoded letter of introduction from the rebel liaison. It's not really a letter but one word written in blue ink on a yellow Post-it note, with a couple of odd, Arabic-looking symbols at the end of the word and three quick dots above it.

It suddenly occurs to me that the code's meaning is unknown to us, that our "safe passage" note to the Bamut commander could actually say something very different, could even be our execution order. In this new light, I study what has been written. Why three dots? Maybe three dots mean "friend" and two mean "foe." Or maybe it's just the reverse. Maybe the liaison meant to make only two, but his hand slipped and left a mark that wasn't supposed to be there. Maybe the dots don't mean anything at all and what I should really be focusing on are the Arabic-looking symbols. And what happens if the Russians find the note? Or if the Chechens take offense at my press pass from the Russian government? The ugly scenarios are limitless and unknowable, but I find it both remarkable and a bit humiliating that my future might be decided by a cheaply laminated card, by a word hastily scrawled on a Post-it note.

I try to imagine what pieces of paper Fred Cuny was carrying with him to keep him safe, what assurances he was given, if they were more substantial than mine.

I turn to a blank page in my notebook and take up my pen.

Many years ago I developed a habit of trying to calculate the risks before going into a battle zone, to arrive at a percentage chance that something bad might happen. If it was above 25 percent, I wouldn't do it.

It wasn't a true equation, of course—just hunches and intuition, guesses contrived to look like math—and I'd never had much faith in my ability to weigh factors properly, but on this morning I try.

I try to imagine the chance that the Russians will attack the road while we're on it and decide on 10 percent each way: 20 percent. I try to imagine the chance that either the rebels in Bamut or the Russians on the surrounding hills will stop us and decide we are spies. Here, at least, there is some empirical evidence to work with—those who have gone uninvited into this tiny corner of the war zone and not returned. I decide on 50 percent.

Seventy percent. I have never done anything anywhere near 70 percent.

I decide these numbers are way too high. I cross them out and start again. Five percent for the drive each way, 30 percent for Bamut: 40 percent. Still too high. Five percent total for the drive, 25 percent for Bamut: 30 percent. Out of curiosity, I calculate the odds of being unlucky at Russian roulette—a little less than 17 percent—and then decide the whole exercise is a waste of time, that either something will happen or it won't.

But my fatalism wavers. I stare at the three pieces of paper in front of me, the laminated press card, the word in blue ink on the Post-it note, my calculations on the page. I turn in the chair and look at Stanley. Even though he is asleep, I am surprised that he cannot feel my stare, that some unconscious alarm doesn't trigger him awake. I slowly press against the chair back until it creaks. I wait for his eyes to snap open, for him to bolt up in the bed and meet my gaze.

I believe that if Stanley wakes up right now I will tell him we're not going to do it. I believe I will show him the numbers in my notebook, explain that we might die over what is written on the Post-it note, tell him that it was a crazy idea, that I am frightened. But Stanley doesn't wake up, and I lack the courage to make him.

Was there a time like this for Fred Cuny? Did there come a moment when he finally saw the full danger ahead but simply could not bring himself to act, a crucial instant when he lost the courage to say, "We can't do this, we have to go back"?

.   .   .

At 7:45 A.M., minutes before we are to set out for the mountains, I tell Ryan and Stanley that I am going to the town square for cigarettes and slip away from the house. The day has broken cool and the air is clear. By noon, the dust will rise to hover over the town like a shroud, but for now the earth is still wet with dew, and in the distance the snowcapped Caucasus Mountains shine like glass.

In the square the kiosk women are just setting up for the day, throwing open the wood shutters of their booths or laying out their wares on the sidewalk, blankets wrapped tightly over their shoulders. I buy three packs of Marlboros and push them into my coat pocket.

At one end of the square is a high school and, next to it, a small park, its entrance dominated by peeling portraits of men I do not recognize. I have passed the place often in the past few days, and on this morning I wander inside.

It is a very modest park and suffering from neglect—the paving stones of its path are shattered, and nothing has been pruned or trimmed in a very long time—but at its center I come to a massive marble monument, an eternal flame burning at the base. It is a memorial to the town's dead from World War II, and in the black stone are chiseled scores of names.

Standing before the flame and the list of war dead, I suddenly find that I am praying. I haven't prayed in twenty-five years and am not really sure anymore how it is done, if I'm supposed to preface it in some way or direct it to some god in particular. In any event, it is a selfish prayer; for the soul of my dead mother, for the safety of my companions and myself on this journey.

In my absence, the ambulance has arrived at the house, and my companions stand in the street, waiting for me. The relief worker, Alex, is a tall, rail-thin Hungarian in his early thirties, an Oxford divinity student, of all things, on leave to perform rescue work in Chechnya. There is something in his quirky, rather dandyish manner—his vaguely British accent and soft stutter, the long woolen scarf he habitually wears—that seems both charming and brave in its incongruity with this place. On this morning he appears to be in high spirits—clean-shaven and jaunty—and he bounds over the dirt road to shake my hand.

"Nice weather for it," he says, glancing up at the blue sky, "but I suspect we'll find mud in the mountains." He turns to me, still smiling his crooked smile. "In any event, perhaps we should take a closer look at this note from the liaison. Wouldn't want to walk into a trap of some sort, would we?"

Alex says this without any hint of real concern, and I take the Post-it note from my back pocket. He studies the single word for a moment, his fingers distractedly playing with the frame of his horn-rimmed glasses, then hands it to Aslan.

Aslan reminds me of other young men I have known in other wars, the native "fixer" hired by Western visitors—journalists, relief workers—to get them in and out of dangerous places. He is in his mid-twenties, with dark hair, sunglasses, and a black imitation leather jacket. Others have dressed differently, of course, have been Asian or African or Latin, but what unites them all is a cocky bemusement at our ignorance and bad ideas. Fred Cuny had a fixer, too, the only member of the group to make it back from the mountains.

Aslan glances quickly at the note and shrugs. "I don't know what it means. It's in code."

"Nothing for it, then," Alex says merrily. "We'll just have to go and find out."

And so we set off, the boxes of medical supplies—gauze bandages, glucose solution, antiseptic wash—jouncing and sliding in the ambulance bay. We follow the path of my imagination: over the plain, into the foothills, and then there is the dirt track, the river, and we are in the mountains. The day is bright, a blinding light reflecting off the snow-capped peaks to the south, but the small valleys below us are cloaked in morning shadow and fog. We are still on neutral ground, but that doesn't mean much here, and out of habit I watch the valleys, look for a flash of refracted light in a dark recess, a sudden swirl in a fog cloud, for some sign that a trolling gunship is rising out of the depths to meet us. But there is no flash or swirl, and the only sounds are those of the wind and the grinding of the ambulance engine.

At long last we come to some unmarked bend in the road and neutral ground is left, the war zone before us.

We are duplicating the journey of Fred Cuny and his lost companions to a degree I prefer not to dwell on. We are following the same path into the mountains. They traveled in a gray, Russian-built UAZ ambulance, as are we. There were five people in that group—five people thrown together by fate and circumstance—and there are five in this one.

We drive on, drawing steadily closer to the battlefront. We pass no one on the track—no cars, no homes—and we do not talk. It is as if each of us is making this journey into the mountains utterly alone, each in his own private ambulance on a ridge line at the top of the world.

• • •

When a person believes he is about to die at the hands of another, he does not look at all the way one might expect. He does not scream or cry. Rather, he becomes very quiet and lethargic, and his eyes fill with a kind of shattered sadness, as if all he wants to do is sleep. It is only like this with a certain kind of dying, I imagine, the kind where you have been given time to see what is coming, where you have tried to negotiate and reason and have failed.

In the front room of the farmhouse I see signs of this exhaustion in all my companions: Alex hunched forward on the couch, gazing miserably at the bare concrete floor; Aslan leaning against the wall, his arms wrapped about his middle, staring down at his white athletic shoes; Stanley's eyes fixed on the far white wall, distant and puzzled; Ryan seems chastened, his habitual grin gone, his eyelids heavy.

We were stopped as soon as we reached the outskirts of Bamut by a group of heavily armed men wearing Russian army camouflage fatigues, the preferred uniform of both sides in this war. Hustled out of the ambulance, we were led into the stone farmhouse that was their command post. For some time we did not know precisely whom we were dealing with. Were these Russian soldiers or Chechen rebels? Rebels, we finally decided, but were they part of the central command or "freelancers," one of those bands of gunmen that increasingly roamed Chechnya, alternately fighting and cutting deals with both sides? It was impossible to tell, and they were careful to give us no indication.

They were startled to see us—the area was closed to all civilians, the track in "restricted"—but at first we were treated more with curiosity than with suspicion; we drank tea and shared cigarettes, carried on a careful, desultory conversation. It was when the commander arrived that everything changed.

He was in his forties, wearing a black leather jacket and strange, ankle-high boots. He shook each of our hands without smiling, then sat on the edge of the broken-down couch and leaned onto his knees, and in the long silence that ensued he seemed lost in thought, methodically massaging his fingers, staring down at the floor. At last he sighed and looked up at me.

"You are not supposed to be here. No one is allowed here. How do I know you're not spies?"

Before the commander appeared, I had decided our captors were "regular" rebels, and had given the encoded Post-it message to the gunman who seemed most senior; even while handing it over, however, I wondered if I might be making a terrible mistake. Now, under his commander's impatient glare, this man made a great show of looking for the note, rummaging through the various pockets of his fatigues and turning up nothing.

"I must have given it back to you," he said to me. "You must have it."

He was lying, but I didn't know to what end. Was he protecting us or doing the opposite? It was impossible to know, and there was no time to ponder or watch for clues.

In the absence of the note, the commander began his slow, calm interrogation of us. He asked why we had come, who had sent us, and studied our passports as if they were weighty evidence. To his questions we gave the most innocent of answers—that Alex had come to deliver relief supplies, that I had come to chronicle the mission—but nothing swayed the commander. Instead, it seemed that everything we said, every insistence on our simple intentions, served only to convict us more, lead us that much closer to a bad end. Everyone in the room knew what was happening—the gunmen who a short time before had given us tea and cigarettes now looked away, refused to make eye contact—and it was the interminable slowness of our descent, our grinding inability to find an ally or the words that might save us, that finally led us into a crushing apathy, to this place where our strongest remaining desire is simply for the process to end.

And then I find the words that cut through. Or maybe it is not words at all but the way I look unblinkingly, guiltlessly, into the commander's eyes. Or maybe it isn't any of this but only a capricious shift in the executioner's heart—suddenly we find the interrogation is over and we are free. Still dazed by the speed and mystery of our deliverance, we are led to the ambulance. After the gunmen unload the medical supplies, they gather around to shake our hands, to slap us on the back, to wish us a safe journey, as if we are close friends they are sad to see leave.

While driving back through the mountains, I think of the man I had gone to find. Why had we escaped, found a way to free ourselves, but Fred Cuny had not? Far more experienced than I, he had also gone onto the battlefield with far more protection. He was well known—and well liked—by senior rebel commanders. His own prominence and the company of two Russian doctors should have safeguarded him from Russian reprisals. Yet, for some reason, none of this had been enough, neither he nor any of his companions had found the words that might have saved them.

What went wrong up there in the mountains?

PART ONE

The Disappearance

CHAPTER 1

*You have entered the wilderness of trees and mirrors. This is a
story with no obvious answers because that's how it was set
up, the way it's supposed to be.*
—Former U.S. intelligence officer
   on the search for Fred Cuny

SHORTLY AFTER eleven o'clock on the morning of March 31, 1995,
five people emerged from a building at the south end of the main
square of Sleptsovskaya, a small town in the northern Caucasus republic of Ingushetia. Crossing to the tree-lined curb, they climbed aboard
a battered gray ambulance and pulled away.

The two-story building they had just left housed a Russian government agency with a very long name: the Ministry of States of Emergency and Elimination of Consequences of Natural Disasters—or
"Emergency Situations" for short. There had been a number of "emergency situations" in the Russian Federation since the collapse of the
Soviet Union, but the most pressing one in Ingushetia that spring of

1995 was the war in neighboring Chechnya. At the end of March the conflict between the Russian army and Chechen separatists was only fourteen weeks old, but already tens of thousands were dead, whole towns and cities flattened, and the tide of battle had moved steadily westward to lap at the Ingushetia frontier. In Sleptsovskaya, a dusty, dull town less than a mile from the border, the fighting was now so close that on some nights its windows rattled from the concussion of Russian artillery, certain breezes carrying the sounds of combat so distinctly—the tap-tap-tap of machine-gun fire, even the soft, metallic clank produced by a tank moving over uneven ground—that it seemed the war had reached its own streets.

But it was at night that most of the killing in Chechnya took place, and when the Russian-built UAZ ambulance left the main square that sunlit morning all was quiet, as if Sleptsovskaya was still what it had always been: a sleepy agricultural town set amidst a beautiful and fertile valley, its bare trees and fields awaiting the first stirrings of spring.

The five people in the UAZ ambulance were bound for Chechnya, apparently planning to conduct a "needs assessment" tour of the war zone. In addition to the local driver, the party consisted of two Russian Red Cross doctors, an interpreter, and the leader of the mission, a fifty-year-old Texan named Frederick C. Cuny.

An already imposing figure at six foot three, made more so by his trademark hand-stitched cowboy boots with their two-inch heels, Fred bore a strong resemblance to the late actor Slim Pickens, a comparison accentuated by his somewhat paunchy frame and a soft North Texas drawl. While not strikingly handsome by traditional measure, there was about him an extraordinary sense of self-assuredness, an air of quiet authority and determination that most people found deeply charismatic; women, in particular, seemed to find him quite entrancing. With his close-cropped graying hair, habitual lopsided grin, and vaguely martial bearing, he gave the impression of an aging, slightly quirky ex-military man who was not taking very good care of himself, and he looked rather out of place for the wilds of the North Caucasus. Then again, Fred Cuny looked out of place in most of the forsaken spots he usually found himself in.

As founder and president of the Intertect Relief and Reconstruction Corporation, Fred was one of the world's most accomplished disaster relief experts, both a pioneer and an iconoclast in the field of international humanitarian aid. Operating out of a threadbare office in Dallas, he and his Intertect consultants had spanned the globe over the past twenty-five years to battle the catastrophes wrought by both nature and man—earthquakes in Guatemala, cyclones in Madagascar, wars on four continents. A man of astounding energy and will, he had repeatedly achieved what others deemed impossible, before quickly moving on to the next impossible task. On the strength of such accomplishments, he had earned an assortment of grandiose nicknames: "the Lone Ranger of emergency assistance," "the Red Adair of humanitarian relief"—and one he was especially fond of, "the Master of Disaster."

Along the way, however, Fred had fueled a fair amount of both resentment and suspicion. In recent years, many of his colleagues in the disaster relief fraternity, a fraternity where at least the appearance of neutrality was carefully maintained, had grown alarmed by his outspoken partisanship in different war zones around the world, as well as by his unusually cozy relationship with the American military. By the mid-1990s an increasing number of those who encountered Fred Cuny in the field began to suspect he might actually be an American intelligence agent. It was speculation Fred did little to discourage.

He had first come to Chechnya seven weeks earlier, in February 1995, at the behest of billionaire financier and philanthropist George Soros. Arriving amid the Russian army's "pacification" of the capital of Grozny—a scorched-earth campaign that was steadily reducing the city to rubble and killing hundreds of civilians each day—Fred had spent a week shuttling across the battle lines, meeting with both senior Chechen rebel commanders and Russian generals in an attempt to arrange a cease-fire, one long enough to evacuate the estimated 30,000 civilians still trapped in the city. In the end, the Russian high command vetoed his plan, and the shelling had resumed.

Professionally, that first brief sojourn onto the battlefield had been a bitter experience for Fred. In typical fashion, he had come to Chechnya with a number of bold ideas to salvage the place, but with the Russian military tightening their hold on the breakaway republic and openly contemptuous of any effort to ease civilian suffering, the "Master of Disaster" had been able to accomplish little. After laying the groundwork for a tiny emergency medical team that would operate out of Ingushetia, Fred had left the region, his far more ambitious goals indefinitely postponed.

But that trip had affected him in another, more personal way. Even for an eyewitness to some thirty conflicts over the previous quarter century, Fred had never seen a war to match the brutality or terrifying unpredictability of Chechnya. To friends and coworkers back in the United States, he called it "the scariest place I have ever been."

That reaction, however, simply served as a goad to greater action. Throughout March, Fred had waged a dogged—and increasingly public—campaign in the United States excoriating the Russian military for its brutal tactics in Chechnya. He had met with senior State Department officials in Washington, and testified before a congressional subcommittee. In early April a long article he had written in the same vein would appear in the New York Review of Books.

So prominent had Fred become on the topic of Chechnya that many of his colleagues worried that it made him a marked man in the eyes of the Russian military—and a dead man should he ever return to the region. Now he was back, having flown into the Sleptsovskaya airport on the afternoon of March 29.

Shortly after nine o'clock on that last morning of Friday, March 31, Fred called his assistant at the Soros office in Moscow, Elisabeth Socolow. Toward the end of the conversation he mentioned he was going into Chechnya later that morning on a quick "needs assessment" tour, but would return to neutral Ingushetia by evening or the next day at the latest.

Wary of the Russian telephones, Elisabeth did not press him for details on the trip, but she detected something strange in Fred's voice;

usually jocular and engaging, his tone that morning was flat, somber. "Is everything okay?" she finally asked.

There was a pause. "Just think about me," Fred said softly, then hung up.

. . .

Within minutes of leaving Sleptsovskaya's main square, it became clear that those in the UAZ had chosen a most unusual path into Chechnya. It was a decision that would lie at the heart of the mystery about to occur.

At the end of March 1995 there were two main routes into Chechnya from Sleptsovskaya, both under Russian control and both eventually leading to the capital city of Grozny some forty miles to the east. One was a patchwork link of back-country roads—some dirt, some heavily rutted asphalt—that led east through the Chechen lowlands. The other was a dirt road that first went north from Sleptsovskaya, winding over a range of low mountains before connecting up with a fast paved highway that led into the capital. Almost without exception, wherever the party was headed in Chechnya that day, the safest and fastest route to their destination would have led them to take one of these two roads.

But there was at least one more path into the war zone, one to the south of the others and so insignificant it did not appear on any maps. Beginning about fifteen miles below Sleptsovskaya, it was a rugged and windswept dirt track that snaked through the Caucasus Mountains before descending into the village of Bamut, a track that had already earned the reputation of being the worst road in Chechnya.

That worst-road distinction had been won in two ways. Traversing a high mountain ridge, the narrow lane was prone to slides and washouts, so littered with axle-bending boulders and gullies that even at the best of times a sturdy four-wheel drive like the UAZ might need two hours to cover its twenty-mile span; in bad weather, it was utterly impassable. By the end of March 1995 it was notorious for another reason: a back pathway into one of the newest vortexes of the war, the fierce battle for control of Bamut. Over the previous three weeks the

Russian army had virtually encircled the rebel-held village and begun pounding it with artillery and tank fire. The exposed path over the mountains was now the last western route into Bamut—a lifeline for the Chechen rebels, and a shooting gallery for Russian helicopter gunships. Incredibly, this was the route that Fred's party chose.

By noon of that day the UAZ had climbed through the southern foothills of Ingushetia to reach the outskirts of the small town of Galashki. There, the ambulance turned left off the paved road, onto a steep, gravel-strewn lane that led down to the Assa River and a low, one-lane metal bridge that forded it. Within minutes the ambulance began climbing again, up the muddy track that led into the mountains. At approximately two o'clock it crossed some unmarked spot on a barren ridge, and then it was in Chechnya. The ambulance, along with four of its five occupants, would never return.

As with every other aspect of the mystery about to unfold, the lost party's decision to take the Bamut road would be the object of intense speculation in the months ahead. The theories would range from the simple and innocent to the darkly byzantine.

One rumor circulating at the time held that several rebel leaders Fred wanted to meet were holed up in Bamut or another rebel-held village nearby. Or perhaps the decision was made to give as wide a berth as possible to any Russian army outposts—and no wider berth existed than the Bamut road. The simplest explanation of all was that Bamut was the hometown of Ruslan Muradov, the group's driver and guide; it is conceivable that he somehow persuaded the others this was the safest route into "liberated" Chechnya.

But there is at least one more possible explanation for the group's choice of paths that day, a rather more complicated one. That's because there was something about Bamut that set it apart from other mountain villages in Chechnya, a detail that may have explained why the Russians were intent on capturing it, why the rebels were intent on defending it, and why someone in the UAZ ambulance may have been determined to reach it. Behind a razor-wired fence at one end of the village was a vast underground complex, an old—and officially decommissioned—Russian nuclear missile base.

. . .

Late on the evening of April 4, four days after the group had set off, the driver, Ruslan Muradov, appeared at the Emergency Situations building in downtown Sleptsovskaya. He was alone and on foot, and carried a handwritten note from Fred Cuny. As Ruslan explained, there had been some small difficulties in the mountains.

From almost the moment they crossed into Chechnya, Ruslan recounted, the expedition had been beset with problems both natural and man-made: rain had turned roads into seas of mud, Russian bombardments were increasing, the group of travelers had come under the suspicion of local rebel commanders. For the past four days the party had been stuck in the Bamut area, barred from proceeding farther into rebel-held territory until gaining permission from the local counterintelligence commander, a procedure constantly delayed by both combat and bad weather. It had been only that morning, Ruslan said, that progress was finally made; when a squad of rebels arrived to escort the group to the counterintelligence commander, Fred had hastily dictated a note and asked Ruslan to take it to Sleptsovskaya.

Most of Fred's message was routine to the point of dull, explaining he would probably be delayed for two or three more days and instructing Elisabeth Socolow in Moscow to cancel or reschedule various meetings he had planned there. From the note's tone, he was clearly not worried about the situation.

Neither, initially, were Soros officials in Moscow. While frustrating, such bureaucratic obstructions as Fred's group was experiencing had begun to be common occurrences with both warring factions in Chechnya—and certainly the news that they were in Chechen hands was preferable to the alternative. The Soros Foundation was held in high regard by the Chechens, and Fred was well known to a number of top-ranking rebel commanders from his first visit. Just to be safe, however,

Ruslan Muradov was dispatched back to Bamut with instructions to find Fred's group and escort them back to Ingushetia.

By April 7 it appeared even this precaution would be a wasted exercise. That morning a Russian Red Cross worker in Sleptsovskaya reported making brief radio contact with one of the doctors on the mission, Sergei Makarov. "Everything is going okay," Sergei said, calling from one of the battery-powered field radios the group had with them. "We'll be back tomorrow or the day after tomorrow."

Before the Red Cross worker could learn anything further, the line went dead.

With Makarov's reassuring message, those waiting in Ingushetia spent the next day in anticipation of the group's imminent return. They did not. On April 9, another brief radio message was received from Makarov; again, he reported that all was well, that they would be returning soon. Then, at dawn the next morning, the Russians unleashed an all-out offensive on Bamut, effectively sealing off the area. When Ruslan Muradov finally made it out of the mountains, he explained that he had been unable to find the group, that no one in Bamut knew where they were.

Now Soros officials became concerned. They began quietly approaching potential intermediaries—high officials in both the Ingush and Russian governments—and spreading the word among Fred's disaster relief colleagues back in the United States that there might be a serious problem. As the days passed with still no sign of the group, the case of Fred Cuny was gradually taken up at the highest levels of the American government. By late April, the first of what would become many searchers began making their way toward the North Caucasus.

By then a steady trickle of conflicting accounts was coming in from the field. Most suggested that Fred and the others had been cleared by the rebels and let go—but let go onto a battlefield landscape that had worsened by the day. There were sightings of the group in a half dozen towns over the breadth of Chechnya, even in neighboring countries. One report held that the doctors were busy delivering babies in a rebel village in the southern hills, another that the four had been taken hostage by a gang of thieves, yet another that they had been picked up by the Russians and sent to an infamous military "filtration center" prison.

Of course, if there was one person uniquely qualified to sort through these contradictory reports, it was the sole member of the expedition who had returned from the mountains: the driver, Ruslan Muradov. Within days of the first searchers reaching Sleptsovskaya, however, Ruslan vanished as well.

In his absence, the searchers had only the smallest handful of facts to go on. That, and Sergei Makarov's haunting radio message. "Everything is going okay. We'll be back tomorrow or the day after tomorrow."

Through that spring and summer of 1995 the story of those lost in Chechnya would move governments and attract worldwide media attention. The case would draw the personal involvement of at least four heads of state, including the presidents of the United States and Russia. It would also lead to one of the oddest manhunts in history, one involving an array of private citizens as well as CIA and FBI agents, Russian intelligence officers, and Chechen rebel commanders.

Along the way there would be false sightings, extortion attempts, disinformation campaigns—even a "body double" recovered from a battlefield grave with a carefully destroyed face. There would also be a pattern of violent death among those reported to have firsthand knowledge of the missing four.

In the end, the searchers would find themselves back almost where they had begun, confounded by the same two mysteries that had haunted them from the outset. One was that strange last journey into the mountains, the five companions setting off into the very teeth of war on a mission known only to themselves. The other was the murderous terrain of Chechnya itself, a place where anything can be true and anything a lie, and where secrets are buried with the dead.

. . .

In early July 1995, I was approached by the *New York Times Magazine* to write an article about Fred Cuny and his lost companions. By then the group had been missing for nearly three months, there was no substantive lead, and the ongoing manhunt in the North Caucasus was beginning to wind down.

Like most Americans, my knowledge of the war in Chechnya extended very little beyond what I'd read in newspapers or seen on television network news. And, like most people, I had never heard of Fred Cuny until after his disappearance.

I was drawn to the story for several reasons. The first, quite frankly, was a rather mercenary one. In each of the handful of newspaper articles that had been written to that point, Fred Cuny was portrayed as a larger-than-life figure, a swashbuckling Texan with a renegade streak. For an investigative writer such as myself, the chance to explore that personality, together with the continuing mystery in Chechnya, had an almost irresistible pull.

There were more personal motives as well. As the son of a foreign aid officer for the American government, I had spent most of my childhood in Third World countries and watched my father pursue in an official capacity many of the same initiatives—agrarian reform, food distribution, disaster relief—that Fred had devoted his life to as a freelance consultant. From what I could superficially glean, there seemed to be certain similarities between Fred and my father: in personality and temperament, in how they had viewed their work. Both were politically liberal in a prairie-populist sort of way—which is to say a liberalism built on a bedrock of conservative values. Both had become deeply disenchanted with how the traditional humanitarian aid system worked and—with the impolitic streak common to would-be reformers—made few attempts to disguise it. Both had battled against that system, and both had paid a professional price for doing so.

Yet there was a big difference between Fred Cuny and my father.

At a critical juncture both had been forced to choose what would assume paramount importance in their lives—their families or their battles. Fred, divorced and with a young son, had chosen one path. My father, with a wife and five children, had chosen the other. In some ways, I felt Fred Cuny had led the life my father might have if he had chosen differently.

There was another reason I was attracted to his story. Throughout the 1980s, I had spent time traveling to and writing about various wars around the world. Ultimately a compounding of unpleasant incidents had led me to question my presence in such places, and I decided not to go to them anymore. I think what most gnawed at me was what I saw as the insignificant role of a journalist in a war zone—at best, a chronicler of atrocity and human suffering, at worst, a voyeur—and after a time the only people I admired on the battlefields were those actually doing something tangible to ease the cruelty: the doctors and nurses, the relief workers and volunteers, men and women who labored in horrible conditions, often at tremendous personal danger and always for little or no reward. Fred Cuny was certainly one of these, and if my writing about him only served as a reminder that there were still people who risked their lives in order to save others, I felt the effort would be worthwhile.

The original idea for the article was a kind of profile of Fred and his extraordinary life and work. I would go to Texas and Washington, D.C., to interview members of his family, as well as some of his friends and colleagues. I confidently told my editor that the researching and interviewing should take about ten days, two weeks at most.

But as I delved into the story of Fred Cuny in those early days I quickly became aware of some dissonant notes. Among his colleagues—and even some family members—there was a persistent pattern of veiled doubt, flickers of uncertainty about who Fred really was. I also discovered that the whispered speculations about a possible hidden agenda to his mission in Chechnya were not unique; Fred had been a figure of controversy in a lot of trouble spots around the globe over the span of his career. On separate occasions, two of his closest family members would quietly raise the possibility that he had been doubling as a spy.

Above all else, Fred Cuny was an enigma: a middle-aged man with health problems who compulsively returned to the world's most dangerous and fetid corners at an age when most in his field had long since settled into air-conditioned offices in government or private agencies; a warm and outgoing man who was nevertheless a loner with few real friends; a stickler for long-range planning and organization whose greatest joy was soaring in his beloved glider, carried off to wherever the winds took him; an adorer of women who yearned for family and stability, but who had walked away from a half-dozen potential marriages and left his only child to be raised by his parents.

And behind all these ironies an even larger one loomed. It seemed that what drove Fred Cuny—and what had, in fact, made both his personal and his professional life such cluttered, contradictory affairs—was an almost obsessive desire to bring order out of chaos, the dream of forging a unique strategy in tackling the messy problems of the world.

From his first exposure to it in the late 1960s, Fred had concluded that the international disaster relief system was pretty much a disaster itself, an opinion that had only strengthened with time. All too often, he contended, responses to emergencies around the world were crippled at every step of the process: by bureaucrats sitting in Washington or Geneva working from political agendas or unrealistic blueprints, by local governments that were obstructionist or thieving, not least by the lack of any coordination in the field, the sudden flood of poorly designed projects, inappropriate supplies, and incompetent volunteers—"do-gooders," he disparagingly called them—that often only made matters worse. What Fred dreamed of creating was a true system, an in-tandem approach in which all the various relief components—medical teams, food deliverers, reconstruction crews, perhaps at times even military units—worked in concert.

For nearly two decades Fred's calls, along with those of other would-be reformers, were largely ignored by the larger humanitarian aid community. What's more, his persistent willingness to criticize the status quo had led him to cross swords with officials at virtually every public and private organization involved in the field, whether it was the U. S. Government's Agency for International Development or the Red Cross or the United Nations; he'd even had a spat with Mother Teresa. The tricky part was that, since his Intertect consulting company was wholly dependent on outside contracts, these were often the same officials on whom his livelihood depended. So long as Fred remained a "bomb thrower," it had seemed he was destined to remain at the fringe of the profession, his often remarkable accomplishments always marked by a certain blemishing asterisk.

That had begun to change with the end of the Cold War in the early 1990s. With a speed no one could have reasonably predicted the Soviet Union had simply disintegrated, and the vacuum meant that a vast array of institutions and philosophies and assumptions were now suddenly obsolete. It also meant, Fred predicted, that a whole new range of dangers and potential disasters loomed just over the horizon. If ever there existed a golden moment to reform the humanitarian aid system—and to fashion the kind of disaster-fighting coalition he had long advocated—it was then. In the post–Cold War chaos Fred found the opportunity he had been awaiting his entire life.

Over the next few years he had managed to implement at least some aspects of his grand vision in the sad landscapes of the world— and he seemed to have particular success in gaining the ear of the American military. In 1991 he virtually took over a U.S. military operation in northern Iraq to resettle some 400,000 refugees fleeing Saddam Hussein's troops. The next year he produced a blueprint—the Cuny Plan—for the Marines' massive relief operation in starvation-wracked Somalia. In 1993 he embarked on a series of fantastically ambitious projects in the besieged city of Sarajevo, arranging to have huge amounts of supplies brought in by military transport. And increasingly, Fred had come to be regarded as he had always wished to be: as a valuable asset, a man to be consulted and listened to at the highest echelons of both the humanitarian aid establishment and the American government.

Not surprisingly, though, his growing prominence and close rapport with generals had been matched by a growing distrust, both among some of his colleagues and among combatants on the battlefields which he crossed. To many in the man-made disaster zones of the world, Fred and his bold initiatives represented an alarming new trend in the wake of the Cold War: the blurring of the once clear lines that had existed between what was governmental and what was private; the murky convergence of humanitarian relief, diplomacy, intelligence, and military operations; the difficulty in distinguishing between those who were there doing "mercy work" and those there for a more complicated and dangerous purpose.

Fred had regarded these deepening suspicions much as he had regarded those that shadowed him in the past: with a certain gleeful satisfaction. He had always rather enjoyed being the outsider, the mysterious Texan cowboy no one could quite figure out.

Those speculations had certainly been bolstered that summer of 1995 by the extraordinary degree to which the American government was involved in the search for Fred in Chechnya. Both President Clinton and Vice-President Gore had met with members of his family, and personally taken up the matter of his disappearance with their counterparts in the Russian government. The American ambassador to Russia had organized a special embassy task force to search for answers and had sent officials to the Caucasus to assist the manhunt. As the Deputy Secretary of State, Strobe Talbott, told a journalist that June, "Finding Fred Cuny is not just a concern for us. It is a preoccupation."

And it was a preoccupation that had quickly given rise to peculiar new levels of intrigue. By that summer, articles had begun appearing in Russian nationalist newspapers alleging that Fred Cuny was alive and well and working as a CIA adviser to the Chechen rebels. The ultimate source of those reports, investigators soon discovered, were some of the most senior officers in the Russian intelligence service.

At the outset I had envisioned my article for the *New York Times* as the portrait of a remarkable man who had gone to one war zone too many. I now saw I was grappling with a much larger story, and was confronted with not one mystery but two: What had happened in the mountains of Chechnya? Who was the real Fred Cuny?

Instead of a brief magazine assignment, my search for answers to those questions would turn into a three-year odyssey, one that would repeatedly take me back to Texas and Washington, as well as to Russia, Croatia, Bosnia, and Mexico. And despite my earlier vow, it would also lead me back to the battlefield, to retrace Fred's last journey in hopes of finding the essential clue that might finally lead to a grave or a hostage cell.

But amid this odyssey I would discover I was actually faced with a third riddle.

A year after Fred's disappearance, his coworkers in Dallas were cleaning out his office when they found a sealed envelope carefully taped behind the back panel of his desk. Inside was a single sheet of paper, a poem Fred had written to his son Craig. It began:

Do not mourn for me,
For I have lived as few men have,
With honor served
For those whom God forgot.

The refrain, "Do not mourn for me," was repeated four times.

In the year since he had vanished, many people had offered theories on why Fred had gone to Chechnya a second time. Most decided it was a kind of hubris, that the man who had witnessed and survived so many wars had simply concluded he was invulnerable, that bullets couldn't find him. The poem to his son suggested that this theory could not have been more wrong—and also raised a last mystery.

Why had he gone back? What possible lure had compelled Fred Cuny to return to the scariest place on earth?

The Man Who'd Save the World

CHAPTER 2

A Marine combat pilot, that's what he was going to be. Fred said that the first time I met him, and he never wavered.
—Beth Rabren, Fred Cuny's ex-wife

"I THINK one of the keys to understanding Fred," Allen "Tex" Harris said, "is seeing him as a true son of Texas—and part of that is that whole Texan tradition of storytelling. Fred was this wonderful, bigger-than-life guy who loved nothing more than to sit around and tell these long, fantastic yarns. And he had a lot of good ones."

For Harris, a senior State Department official who, like Fred, had grown up in Dallas, one of the best stories was about an incident that occurred during Fred's military flight training.

"They were doing aircraft carrier training," Harris recalled, "and apparently one of the things you did before taking off from the carrier was walk around your plane, check everything out—and you especially made sure there's no problem with the hook that hangs down in back and that catches you when you come in to land. Well, the way Fred tells it, the head of training was just the biggest asshole in the world, and this guy would come out, jump in his plane, fire up the engine, and take off, never even check the hook. So what Fred and some of the other guys did one day, they went out and cut the hook off. This guy takes off, comes back in to land, and they wave him off because there's no way to land without that hook. This guy's career is ruined because he's violated one of the cardinal rules of naval aviation, and he's sent in disgrace to the local National Guard air base off the coast of wherever they were."

Tex Harris chuckled, then shook his head with an appreciative sigh. "Well, that was Fred, just a born storyteller. And apparently he carried that hook around with him for many years as a symbol of how to get back at evil authority."

. . .

His very first word was "airplane."

"I remember that so vividly," Charlotte Cuny said with a smile, sifting through the manila folder of loose photographs. "Fred couldn't have been more than about a year old, and we were out back at my parents' house when a plane went over. Fred pointed up and said, 'Airplane.' I laughed, because I thought it was such an omen."

She found the photograph she was looking for and held it up. It was of a young Fred, maybe eight or nine, waving from the open cockpit of an old fighter with a broad grin, his hand framed against the sky as if he were already airborne. "Airplanes, pilots, he was just crazy about them."

Charlotte closed the folder and set it alongside the four others on the long dining-room table. It had been only recently that she could look at the photographs of her oldest son, especially those of Fred's childhood, without much emotion. Her husband, Gene, sitting at the head of the table, still had problems with it.

Theirs was a pleasant and modest ranch-style home, sparely decorated with artifacts collected from their own travels in India and East Asia, others brought back by Fred from more offbeat places. From the dining-room windows the lawn sloped gently down to the eastern shore of Lake Ray Hubbard, crisscrossed by boats and jet skis on that hot spring day in Rockwall.

They didn't really want to talk about Fred—the pain of not knowing precisely what happened to him, whether they would ever learn more, was haunting—but they had been far too polite to refuse. And so they did talk, patiently answering the questions they had been asked before, producing the five manila folders of photographs and newspaper clippings that, together, formed a chronological history of his life. The easiest folder for them was the last, the one filled with articles about Fred's accomplishments, letters of praise from diplomats and generals; as Charlotte leafed through them, Gene came down the table to peer over her shoulder.

"The funny thing is," she said, "and it's actually something I'm a little ashamed of, we really didn't know how important Fred was until he went missing, just how many people all over the world looked up to him as a kind of hero. I don't think anyone in the family had any idea."

Gene nodded. "Just hadn't a clue."

. . .

He was born on the forward cusp of the baby boom era, November 14, 1944, the oldest of Charlotte and Gene's four boys. To his everlasting dismay, Fred was not actually born in Texas, but in New Haven, Connecticut, the first of several embarrassing details in his biography that he would spend a lifetime trying to shield from others. His father was a thwarted Broadway producer who built a successful career as a television station general manager, Charlotte a vibrant, civically active schoolteacher, and Fred would eventually inherit their easy social grace and moderate politics. Eventually, but first he would be a rather awkward boy, and a militantly conservative youth.

Even as a child, according to his parents, Fred was earnest and driven, given to intense focus on matters that interested him and blithe disregard for those that didn't. Although clearly very bright, even placed in an advanced class in fourth grade, he remained a resolutely middling student until his teen years; especially in middle school, his mother recalled trooping to a series of parent-teacher conferences to hear the refrain that Fred was "not working up to his potential."

The one potential Fred spent quite a bit of time working on was becoming a pilot, a subject that obsessed him from earliest childhood and that he talked about constantly. For one long stretch, his mother even had to set an extra place at the table for his imaginary pilot friend. Part of the obsession probably stemmed from the fact that he had a particularly impressive role model to look up to, an uncle named Phillip Shutler. A fighter pilot who would be highly decorated in the Korean and Vietnam wars and make the Marines a career—he would eventually become a brigadier general—Shutler often did fly-ins to the military airfield outside Lake Charles, Louisiana, where the Cunys lived in the late 1940s and early 1950s. There, he would take his adoring young nephew on tours of the base and arrange to have him sit in the cockpits of planes. Through such experiences, Fred's knowledge of military aircraft became almost encyclopedic.

When Fred was eight the Cuny family—now expanded to five with the birth of two more boys—made the move to Gene Cuny's home state of Texas, when he was appointed general manager of a large broadcasting station in Dallas. At William Lipscomb Elementary School, Fred found at least one classmate with a similar fascination with flying, a slight, wiry boy named Carl Long. Living just a few blocks from each other in their eastern Dallas neighborhood of Casa Linda, the two became inseparable, developing a friendship that would be lifelong.

Fred also discovered a tangible outlet for his airplane fixation in Jim Hill, a neighbor who owned a small plane and kept it at an airstrip nearby. Taking a shine to the intensely earnest boy, Hill began bringing Fred along when he went out to tinker with his plane; before long he was teaching him the fundamentals of aviation during Saturday morning flights over the Texas countryside.

At the same time the oldest Cuny boy was emerging as something of a loner, with a preference for solitary pursuits. Other than his bond with Carl Long, he had few friends and often preferred to stay inside and work on models or read books on aviation than play ball with neighborhood kids. His withdrawing nature became more pronounced when he was transferred to a new school in sixth grade, and even more when he reached junior high.

Fred was considerably more outgoing and confident when he reached Bryan Adams High School in the autumn of 1958. If still quite shy—he would not start dating until he was seventeen—his circle of friends gradually expanded beyond Carl Long to include four or five other boys.

Then, of course, there was flying. Already anxious to earn his pilot's license by the minimum legal age of sixteen, Fred was barely fifteen when he began scouring the Dallas area to find the cheapest flight school around. He found it at a ramshackle airstrip where a retired fighter pilot—and severe alcoholic—had a two-seater Piper. After several sessions with the pilot, Fred was so enthusiastic he convinced one of his new high school friends, Michael Huston, to join up as well. Huston, now an investment adviser for Morgan Stanley in Dallas, vividly remembered his introduction to the "flight school."

"Fred had talked up how great it was," he said, "and he'd clearly given our parents this impression that it was a comprehensive training program, this school with classes and all. So I finally agreed to go out there, and it's just a hangar with a little room in the back of it, and the guy is completely passed out on the couch. But Fred is not gonna be denied. He grabs up his log book, gets the guy on his feet—his eyes are deep vermilion, not even fire-truck red, vermilion red—and out we go."

On Huston's very first day—and after what he estimated to be a full ninety seconds of flight instruction—he was ordered to take off while the barely conscious pilot slumped in the passenger seat. Once back on the ground, they were met by Fred, eagerly clutching his log book and awaiting his turn.

"This guy is clearly in a great deal of pain," Huston recalled, "just trying to get back to his couch and bottle, but he's cogent enough to realize Fred's gonna be an obstacle in that plan. So, as he goes by Fred, the guy mumbles, 'Solo.' Wow, Fred's off like a shot. And he did solo, just got in that plane and took off, started doing touch-and-gos and stuff—and this was after he'd been up with this guy maybe three, four times. Well, Fred was a natural pilot."

Early on the morning of November 14, 1960, Fred's sixteenth birthday, Gene and Charlotte Cuny accompanied their son to a small airstrip on the north side of Dallas. He passed his pilot's test with ease. His mother had a distinct—if not altogether accurate—impression of the day.

"It was the first time he soloed," she said, "and it was a real thrill. Fred was just beaming."

The early passion to fly would serve as a signal clue to the other passions to come in Fred's life, for in flying was the clean satisfaction of many of the desires he would endlessly pursue: autonomy, control, danger. In the years ahead he would pilot planes over some of the most breathtakingly beautiful landscapes of the world, as well as some of its most tragic.

. . .

They called it "the world's largest flying zoo," the bizarre assortment of characters—mercenaries, idealists, bush pilots, Catholic priests—who risked their lives to fly through enemy fire to deliver relief supplies to starving Biafra. By Fred Cuny's account, it was his first encounter with the world of disaster relief, as well as his first baptism of fire.

One of the bloodiest paroxysms to afflict Africa in its rocky transition from colonialism to independence, the Biafra tragedy began in mid-1967 when the Ibo ethnic minority of southeastern Nigeria declared their independence from the former British colony. Though vastly outnumbered, the Biafrans valiantly held off the Nigerian army for two and a half years, their enclave slowly dwindling as disease and starvation set in. By the autumn of 1969 one of the last relief supply lines into dying Biafra was an isolated and overwhelmed airstrip in the neighboring republic of Dahomey. It was there Fred Cuny showed up one day and presented himself to a harried Red Cross flight operations supervisor. As Fred recalled years later in a BBC interview, the man was close to desperation:

"He said, 'I've got a bunch of new airplanes coming in, I don't know how to use them, I don't know how to fly them. . . . My cargo systems are breaking down. Everything's a mess.' And I said, 'Well, that's interesting. I just worked on an airport, the world's largest airport in Texas, and I know a little about [cargo systems] and, furthermore, I'm a pilot. Maybe I can help you out.' "

Very quickly, Fred recounted, he was deeply involved in the Biafra airlift, first helping to coordinate relief shipments out of the Dahomey airfield, then going out on the mercy flights himself. This was no small step, for pilots making the Biafra run faced an incredible gauntlet of dangers: Nigerian and mercenary attack planes, ground fire from the rapidly enclosing government soldiers, and then the Biafran "airfields" themselves, often little more than wide spots on dirt roads. One story Fred was especially fond of telling—and which he repeated for the BBC—was of the time he took off from the main Biafran airport at the controls of a Red Cross plane.

"So I get in and strap into the seat, call up the [airfield] coordinator—'Red Cross 3 ready for take off'—and we're sitting there, and he says, 'Hold it, we've got another plane coming in.' And we looked out and sure enough here comes this guy in and he's been hit and his engines are smoking . . . and he just rolls over and the plane slides right past me and it cartwheels off the end of the runway, slides into a fuel tank, blows up, and there's flame all the way down the side of the parking ramp. [The tower then radios] 'Red Cross 3, clear for take-off.' " Fred laughed at the memory. "Nothing stopped. We just kept going."

When asked by the BBC how he had coped with living under such dire circumstances, Fred laughed again. "Drinking and chasing women!"

•   •   •

Although fashioning itself a city of the American West—what with its long history of cattle ranching and cowboy-hat-wearing business-men—Dallas has always had more the feel and manner of the Deep South. Socially and politically conservative, it is a place that boasts one of the highest church attendance rates in the nation, where upper-class girls still have coming-out debutante balls, and where a disproportion-ate percentage of young men enlist in the military. If still conservative today, Dallas was profoundly more so in the early 1960s, when Fred Cuny and his small circle of male friends came of age.

The core group consisted of six boys from two adjacent high schools—Fred and Carl Long, along with Mike Huston, Warren Mat-thews, and twin brothers, Don and Henry "Steve" Stevenson—and one of the main bonds that drew them together was that all aspired to careers in the American military. For the two closest friends in the group, Fred and Carl, the aspiration had long been very specific: both dreamed of becoming Marine Corps combat pilots.

To Mike Huston, one of the members of Fred's clique, their shared goal was rooted in a kind of old-fashioned patriotism and moral certitude.

"To understand the whole military thing, you've got to appreciate the mindset back then and what the military represented to us. We were young and pretty naive, and the world looked a whole lot simpler. The world was filled with good guys and bad guys, and the way to help clean it up was you were going to be a soldier and go take care of the bad guys. It was just that simple, so that's what we were gonna do. I can't recall questioning any of that for even a minute back then, and I very much doubt Fred did either."

In Huston's telling, he was usually the hapless foil swept up in his bigger and more forceful friend's schemes. The dubious Piper Cub training school wasn't the first of these. In 1958, when the two had been mere fourteen-year-old freshmen at Bryan Adams High School, it had been Fred's plan to head off to Cuba and join Fidel Castro's rebels in their war against the Batista dictatorship.

"To tell you the truth," Huston said, "I usually was reading one thing or another and not all that aware of my surroundings, and I'd get swept up in Fred's enthusiasms, and the Cuba thing, that was definitely one of them. But I was also conscious of our limitations. Fred I don't think was ever conscious of limitations. He wanted us to go down there and we'd become freedom fighters."

If joining Castro's guerrillas was one of Fred's passing fancies, becoming a military man was anything but; he worked toward the goal with the same single-minded devotion he had shown in learning to fly. During the school year he drilled and marched in the Bryan Adams ROTC program, and in summers attended ROTC camps established for Dallas-area high school students. The ultimate quest was admission into the military training program at Texas A&M University, one of the most prestigious officer training schools in the country, from where he would emerge as a commissioned second lieutenant in the U.S. Marine Corps.

At times the boys took their martial zeal to almost comical excess—and none more so than Fred and Carl Long. Finding the combination of high school and summer camp ROTC programs insufficient to sate their needs, the two teenagers organized an interschool program they called the Future Professional Military Officers Club. At regular meetings Fred and Carl tutored younger cadres on such prosaic soldierly skills as how to properly conduct inspections, roll sleeping bags, and fill out requisition forms.

But precisely what spurred Fred's militaristic ardor was not a simple thing to determine. Surely part of the attraction was the prospect of earning a living from doing what he loved—flying—but his streak of quiet willfulness suggested a difficult fit with military regimentation. With the notable exception of his uncle Phillip Shutler, his was not a family with a strong military tradition and, despite his fascination with explosives and firearms, he seemed to have little desire or capacity for violence. Although big even by Texas standards, he so avoided physical confrontation that friends couldn't recall so much as a schoolyard scuffle.

"Something that I think a lot of people didn't see about Fred right away," Mike Huston said, "was that he was a surprisingly sentimental and passionate guy, and I think a lot of the fascination with the Marines came out of that. I don't mean passionate in the normal sense, but the kind of passion where you're willing to make any sacrifice, pay any price. Fred's the only one I've ever met who really had that, and that was the credo of the Marines. It's a harsh world of violent men, but there is an impeccable code of ethics, an unyielding commitment, all this stuff that I think was extremely attractive to a guy like Fred. Sure, the surface glamor of the military, the thirst for adventure, that got all of us guys, but I think with Fred it was only 10 percent. The other 90 percent of Fred simply, passionately wanted to make things better. How do you do that in 1962? You become a Marine."

. . .

Kurt Schork has a very distinct memory of the first time he saw Fred Cuny. It was on the side of a mountain in northern Iraq in the early spring of 1991.

A reporter for Reuters news service, Schork was in the region to chronicle the mass exodus of Iraqi Kurds from their mountain homes in the wake of the Gulf War. On that particular day he was hiking into the hills after hearing reports of a group of stranded Kurds.

"There was a little village," Schork recalled, "and just beyond was a camp of about 125 Kurdish refugees. They were up above the tree line in the snow—just horrible conditions—and that's where I saw Fred. He was standing with a bunch of American officers who had just gotten out of a helicopter, this huge man—cowboy boots and blue jeans, a sort of Western shirt, and aviator sunglasses—and he was obviously in charge. After that, I kept running into him all over Kurdistan, this plainclothes guy in cowboy boots with his own military helicopter, and I just kept thinking, 'Who the hell is this guy?' "

Fred was in northern Iraq in hopes of mitigating the damage of a terrible miscalculation by the Iraqi Kurdish minority. In the last days of Operation Desert Storm the Kurds had risen up against Saddam Hussein and quickly liberated most of their homeland, only to fall victim to a ferocious Iraqi counteroffensive. Within days, and even as Allied forces stood by forbidden to intervene by the terms of the recently signed cease-fire with Hussein, some 400,000 Kurds had fled their homes before the Iraqi onslaught to huddle in squalid makeshift camps in the mountains along the Turkish border. As they began dying en masse from dysentery, cold, and starvation, American troops in the region launched a desperate rescue mission, code-named Operation Provide Comfort. Amid the crisis, Fred arrived on the scene.

Working twenty-hour days for the next three months, he assumed a leadership role in a bold plan to not only save the Kurds but allow them to return to their villages and avoid the grim limbo existence of permanent refugees. Ultimately, Operation Provide Comfort would be considered one of the most successful disaster relief missions ever carried out by the American military and, in Kurt Schork's opinion, a lot of the credit belonged to Fred Cuny.

"He gained the confidence and trust of the military commanders on the ground, and that was a very lucky thing because he was the one guy there who really seemed to know what was going on."

.   .   .

Bryan and College Station, Texas, home to Texas A&M University, are now joined cities of some 110,000 residents of whom 42,000 are students, their strip malls and subdivisions and faculty buildings sprawling out into the rolling fields and scrub-pine forests of central Texas. In 1962 they were still small towns and A&M more closely resembled a military base, its 6,000 all-male student population dressed in uniform, their days filled with rigorous training in the arts of soldiery.

Throughout this century Texas A&M has been regarded as one of the premier military officer training schools in the country, producing some of the most decorated soldiers in all four branches of the armed forces. For those seeking a career in the military, an appointment to A&M is nearly as coveted as one to West Point or Annapolis—and for young men in the state of Texas in the early 1960s, perhaps even more so. Among the freshmen arriving at A&M in the autumn of 1962 was a small group of teenage friends from the Dallas suburbs, including Fred Cuny, Carl Long, and Mike Huston. While Huston was entering A&M's regular Army program and was assigned to a different part of the campus, Fred and Carl remained together. Both were assigned to Company I-3 of the Sixth Battalion, a special hybrid unit composed of cadets from the Texas Maritime Academy and of cadets, like themselves, entering the Marine Platoon Leaders class.

From outward appearances, Fred seemed to adjust well to A&M, the very embodiment of the striving officer cadet. His father remembered watching him walk down the hill toward home during his first vacation leave.

"He looked like MacArthur coming down. Tall and thin and dressed in that uniform . . . like a new general. He was very, very proud to be in that uniform, part of that whole A&M tradition."

But appearances were deceiving. The gangly would-be Marine pilot from Dallas began having difficulties almost immediately. In high school Fred had been a steady B student, but at A&M his grades dropped to barely a C average in his freshman year.

One factor may have been the extreme degree of isolation that existed at A&M. With Company I-3 as their new home and identity, Fred and Carl had virtually no contact with their other friends in the regular Army program, who were housed on a different section of the campus, attended different classes, and ate in different cafeterias. For a young man who had always displayed a certain stubborn free-spiritedness, the exacting regimentation must have been a constant chafe as well.

Still, Fred struggled on, unwilling to admit that the dream that had propelled him for so long might have been a mistake. Then, in the fall semester of his sophomore year, an incident largely decided the matter for him.

In the early morning hours of December 9 a group of I-3 freshmen decided to carry out an end-of-the-semester prank against a rival dorm. With the apparent acquiescence of two upper-class "sergeants," they snuck into the rival dorm and set alight five tires in two bathrooms, a blaze that ruined some fixtures and caused smoke damage.

As could probably have been predicted, the A&M administration was not amused by the prank. Shortly, the dean of students announced three I-3 students were being placed on probation, the two sergeants who had approved the assault, and Cadet Fred Cuny, who "had knowledge of the planned 'raid' and advised the freshmen relative to the conduct of such action." Two days later the university commandant took even harsher steps, demoting the two sergeants to the rank of private, completely disbanding Company I-3, and scattering the cadets among a dozen units. Now the two boyhood friends from Dallas who had managed to stay together at A&M, Fred and Carl, were separated as well.

Although his probation was lifted at the end of the spring semester in 1964, Cadet Cuny was apparently now seen as a troublemaker in the eyes of the A&M administration, the sort of undesirable to be got rid of for any reason. They didn't have to look far, for in his sophomore year Fred's grades had continued their downward slide to barely above a D average. Within days of learning his probation had been rescinded, he was summoned to the administration building and "invited" to leave A&M.

For Fred, it was a crushing blow. Alone among his high school buddies, he had failed to make the grade at A&M, and now had a major black mark beside his name in the Marine Corps training system. With few other prospects, in the fall of 1964 he started classes at Texas College of Arts and Industries (A&I), a small state school in the South Texas town of Kingsville. About all that A&I had to recommend itself was a rudimentary ROTC program, but it kept alive the chance he might yet make the Marine Corps air wing. For Fred, that was still the only goal in life.

. . .

"What I can tell you," Ognen Samardcic said, "is that Fred Cuny was able to do very remarkable things in getting supplies into Sarajevo. In fact, impossible things."

During the long and bloody siege of Sarajevo, Samardcic was a program coordinator for the Soros Foundation, overseeing the logistical details on a variety of projects meant to sustain a city slowly being strangled by its attackers. It was an extremely frustrating task. With the Bosnian Serb besiegers surrounding Sarajevo on all sides, virtually all relief supplies, even basic foodstuffs, had to be flown in from neighboring countries aboard United Nations transport planes.

Lending the operation a slightly surreal edge was the fact that Sarajevo airport was under the joint administration of both sides in the conflict, with the Bosnian Serb "customs office" at one end of the terminal routinely grabbing 30 percent of all incoming emergency aid as a kind of war tax—when not refusing to let the supplies past altogether. For those relief agencies trying to save the Bosnian capital, this bizarre arrangement posed a constant headache. Not only could they never be sure if the Bosnian Serbs would let their supplies through or how big a cut they would take, but the agencies also had to vie among themselves for priority on the UN transport planes; without dogged persistence, one's "emergency" supplies might sit on the tarmac in Zagreb or Split, the two hubs for the Sarajevo airlift in neighboring Croatia, for months. To Ognen Samardcic's amazement, however, it seemed that one person was immune to all this: Fred Cuny.

"Whenever the Foundation was receiving goods under Fred's name," he recalled, "it got right on the UN planes [in Croatia] and the Serbs at the airport never took a percentage. Afterward, when a shipment was sent just in the Foundation's name, the Serbs always made problems for us, but during the Fred Cuny time, never. Just mention Fred's name, and without any problem you would get that shipment."

When asked his explanation for the phenomenon, Samardcic gave a wry smile.

"That I cannot say. I know he had a lot of good friends in the UN military structure, and with the American forces in Germany, too, but . . . ." Samardcic scanned his office wall for a moment. "There were a lot of stories about this, that he had very good connections with the U.S. Government. Which institution exactly, I cannot say."

. . .

In the summer of 1996 a former girlfriend of Fred's made an interesting observation of him. "It was very important to Fred," Sonja Vukotic said, "that he be seen as important."

In a variety of ways, this need appeared to be a driving force in Fred. In whatever disaster zone he happened to find himself, he always had to be the smartest, the bravest, the most tireless and accomplished. Ironically, this strong streak of egoism worked to the benefit of many thousands of people in his lifetime; Fred took success personally, and he took failure personally, and a lot of people around the world are still alive because he did.

On a personal level, though, this thirst for importance and affirmation made for a murky portrait. Seemingly compelled to present an already dramatic life as even more so, Fred constantly made up stories about himself and exaggerated others beyond all recognition. Most of these constructions were harmless enough and perhaps often not meant to be taken as literal truth, simply examples of the Texan story-telling tradition that his friend Tex Harris described.

Almost certainly, for example, the airplane-hook story he told Harris wasn't true; there's no record of Fred ever having undergone aircraft carrier flight training, and even if he had, the dangerous prank he claimed to have pulled would probably have won him a court-martial. Similarly, the depth of his involvement in the Biafran airlift, along with his "hot lead" adventures while there, appear to have been greatly enriched by creative license. To the best of his family's recollections, Fred used his vacation time from the Fort Worth engineering firm where he was then working to go to West Africa—a matter of two or three weeks at most—while researchers working on a documentary about Fred had great difficulty finding airlift veterans who remembered him at all. Although he certainly participated in the Biafran relief effort, it appears he was a very small—and very brief—cog in a much larger machine.

In one area, however, Fred's "stories" seemed to have more complex roots than mere self-promotion or a desire to entertain: his relationship to the military.

Under the "work experience" category on his 1994 résumé—a résumé that ran twelve pages—Fred Cuny's first listing was "U.S. Marine Corps (1961–66)." It was a most liberal interpretation of his service. What he had been, by virtue of his ROTC training in high school and college, was a member of the Marine Corps Reserve. In the summer of 1966 he was dismissed from that program for having failed to earn his undergraduate degree in the specified four years, without ever winning appointment to the regular Corps.

To many who knew him, the news that Fred had never been a full-fledged Marine would come as a startling revelation. While few could pinpoint an occasion when he explicitly lied about the matter, there's little doubt that he frequently "suggested" he had been one. A woman who worked alongside him for nearly twenty years was always under the impression that Fred had been a Marine combat pilot, a "fact" about his life that she often brought up in conversation because she found it amusing, and one that he never attempted to correct.

Also intriguing was the degree of spin he felt necessary to maintain even among those few people who did know the truth. Whenever relating his ignominious departure from A&M, for example, he focused on the tire-burning incident that had led to his probation, rather than on the far more prosaic problem of bad grades that had actually caused his leave-taking. Similarly, in explaining the final end to his Marine Corps dream, he usually didn't mention his academic disqualification and dismissal from the Marine Corps Reserve, but rather told of a car accident in Houston several months later in which he broke his leg in three places. That accident, so the myth went, dashed forever his chances of becoming a combat pilot.

Such biographical revisionism is hardly unique to Fred Cuny, of course, but what was truly remarkable in his case was the degree to which he could get others, even close family members, to accept the myths. Most of his immediate family members, for example, believed his departure from A&M was a result of the tire-burning incident. Even more telling was the account of his ex-wife, Beth Rabren, in describing his dismissal from the Marine Corps Reserve.

"When he got hit by that taxi in Houston," she said, "that just ended it for the military right there. With his leg so badly mangled, there was no way the Corps was going to make him a pilot."

Although they had been married at the time, Beth had apparently completely forgotten—or perhaps never been aware of—the Marine Corps' letter of dismissal that had come long before the car accident.

Yet however artfully he sought to give the impression of a military background, it would be unfair to dismiss Fred Cuny as a simple po-seur, or to place him in the same category as those bogus war heroes and Vietnam veterans who are periodically unmasked; even among those who believed he had been a Marine pilot, none recalled Fred telling war stories of personal heroism in Vietnam or elsewhere.

On one level, he might have considered it a clever strategy, one that paid dividends on the battlefields of the world. So long as neither the combatants nor his disaster relief colleagues could quite figure him out—was he truly a civilian or some kind of plainclothes American military operative—it might mean they trusted Fred less, but it also meant they were less likely to get in his way. Similarly, in disaster zones where the American military was active, commanders might be more likely to heed the advice of—and grant favors to—a crew-cutted man who acted and sounded like one of their own than one of the unkempt "longhairs" that seemed to dominate the disaster relief field.

On another level, though, the extent to which Fred felt the need to maintain a warrior persona—and to maintain a set of false histories even with his own family—suggest a motive that is a close cousin to the need for affirmation and importance: the refusal to ever admit personal failure.

More than anything else, the young Fred Cuny had wanted to be a Marine pilot and he had failed—and it was easier to attribute that failure to a vindictive college administration that had scapegoated him, or to a Houston taxicab that had shattered his leg, than to the more self-incriminating matter of his own academic shortcomings. And one doesn't have to look far to see why such an admission of personal failure might have been so painful an exercise: the experiences of his high school friends.

Alone out of his tight circle of boyhood friends, Fred flunked out of the military. All the rest graduated from their respective military academies, all received officers' commissions, and all shipped out to Vietnam. There, most paid a heavy price.

In a span of less than three months, August and November 1967, both Stevenson twins, Don and Steve, were wounded in combat in Vietnam—in Don's case, almost mortally. A little over a year later, Carl Long was severely wounded when his Marine platoon came under Vietcong attack. Steve Stevenson, now a retired Air Force colonel living in San Antonio, tried to describe the effect of that time on all of them.

"Here we'd all gone off together—twenty-one, twenty-two, starting our military careers—and here we all come back, one by one, wounded—in Don's case, with a good part of his stomach gone. It affected our families, and I know it affected Fred. You know, he'd always probably been about the most gung ho of any of us, and for one reason or another he didn't go in [to the military], and now all his buddies are getting shot. He must have felt . . . well, I don't know what he felt."

On the patio of his suburban San Antonio home, the taciturn, ramrod-straight former colonel slumped slightly, letting through the faintest trace of emotion.

"Well, and it affected us too," he said very softly. "There's a perverse mentality that happens if you're an officer and you've been wounded and come out. You feel like you let your men down. I went through it. Don went through it. Carl went through it. You have this impression that you let down the guys that you were there with, and you want to go back. And that's what Carl did. And, you know, those two were so close, Fred and Carl, growing up together, making all these plans together . . ."

Throughout his life Fred was a prodigious letter-writer. Probably none was more painfully honest than the one he wrote on August 26, 1992. It was to Veronica O'Sullivan, the daughter of Carl Long.

Dear Veronica: This is a letter that I should have written to you long ago and many times. I was one of your father's best friends. We grew up together, went to grade school at William Lipscomb Elementary in east Dallas and became best friends through our mutual love for camping and outdoor activities. . . . In 1962, I talked your father into joining the Marines.

After glossing over his own thwarted military career—"As luck would have it, I didn't continue with the Marines after I got out of college"—he described how he had become active in opposition to the Vietnam War, a stance that had caused some friction in his friendship with Carl.

After he was wounded and came back to the States, I visited him in the hospital in Corpus Christi. We had several long talks about the conflict, the tactics involved and where we were going. To a large extent, I think we both influenced each other's views on the matter. In the end, however, your Dad was a true patriot. My country, right or wrong, my country. And he felt obligated to return to try and bring the war to a successful conclusion.

The night before Carl was to return to Vietnam, his friends organized a going-away party at a Dallas steakhouse.

I can still remember everything about that night as if it were yesterday. The band was playing some Nancy Wilson hits (she

*was one of your Dad's favorite singers), your Mom was
wearing a turquoise dress and looked absolutely stunning. She
was trying to have a good time, but I am sure she had a
foreboding about him going off to war again. Your Dad was
sharp as a tack that night. He was telling all sorts of jokes.
. . . After the group broke up, my girlfriend asked me how it
felt watching my best friend go off to war, was I worried that
I might never see him again. In fact, the thought had never
occurred to me. He was so much bigger than life that not for
an instant did I ever believe that anything but a silver bullet
would get him.*

Because of the extent of his wounds from his first tour, Carl was
taken out of the field upon his return to Vietnam and given "light duty"
as an aerial observer aboard a two-man OV-10 scouter plane. On the
afternoon of December 20, 1969, while flying a reconaissance mission
over Vung Tan Province, the OV-10 was shot down and both the pilot
and Carl were killed.

*When your Mom called . . . and told me that he was
missing I couldn't believe it. Even today, I wouldn't be
surprised if he walked in the door. . . . I remember one night
about five years after he died when I suddenly woke up one
night, and wanted to discuss something with him. Without
thinking I went to the phone [sic] started dialing his old
number. I still have dreams about him. In most of them, we
are sitting somewhere talking about some major current event
of the day. He is always giving me advice (most of it good). I
can't tell you how much I have missed him over the years. I
know you never had a chance to really get to know him, and
you may not even be able to remember him, but he was really
a great man and would have done great things if he had had
the chance.*

In the letter, Fred then went on to describe his first visit to the Vietnam Memorial in Washington, some ten years earlier.

I arrived on a cold, drizzly night and after checking in to my hotel I decided to walk down to the memorial to try and find your Dad's name and pay my respects. Even at the late hour I arrived, there was a long line waiting to get to the book that tells which panel a person's name is on, so while I was waiting I decided to go down to see the memorial. I walked down the long rows of names and suddenly felt a very powerful pull towards the center middle section of the left wall. I can't explain how it happened, but I stopped on the very panel that your father's name was on and with the help of another person who had a candle, I found his name immediately. For the first time I realized that he wasn't coming back and I sat down there and cried for half an hour.

Veronica, have you ever visited the memorial? If not, I would like to take you there and spend some time telling you more about your father. If you are game, I will send you a ticket.

On a hot, muggy evening in late June 1994, Fred, formally attired in a tuxedo, arrived at the entrance to the Marine Commandant's House in downtown Washington. He was ushered inside by a Marine Corps dress guard. The occasion was a reception, hosted by the Marine Corps Commandant, honoring the Secretary of Navy and a number of Marine officers who had been involved in the Bosnian relief mission, and a special invitation had gone out to the man who had made that mission a personal crusade: Fred Cuny.

For a man who had once dreamed of nothing else than becoming a Marine, and then seen that dream crushed, it was probably one of the proudest days of Fred's life; his escort for the evening was Carl Long's twenty-eight-year-old daughter Veronica.

The next morning they went to the Washington Mall to see Carl's name inscribed on the Vietnam Memorial. "Fred knew exactly where it was," Veronica recalled. "He had me pose for a photo next to Carl's name, and then he asked me to take one of him next to it. It was really a very emotional experience for both of us."

Veronica's visit to Washington was a whirlwind two days, but her most distinct memory was Fred's endless stream of stories about her father.

"We were constantly running around, seeing lots of people, but every time there was a pause, Fred would talk about Carl—something they'd done together, some conversation they'd had—and it was like he recalled every detail."

Along with whatever other motives were at work in Fred's construction of a "shadow" military background for himself, it would seem that it was at least partly rooted in a yearning to somehow keep a dead comrade alive, a way to pay homage to a friend who had succeeded where he had failed, who had died in a war that he had not gone to— that he had, in fact, ended up protesting against. And in the clash of emotions he so clearly felt over that first combat death to touch him— shame, sorrow, anger, guilt—was born one of the fires that sent Fred out into other combat zones time and again, as if trying to avenge that first wasted life by saving others.

But, of course, that shadow background also made him an enigmatic figure on the battlefields of the world—and in modern wars, enigmas make enemies.

In the end, the boyhood friends from Dallas would be joined again, this time by eerie coincidence. When Fred disappeared in Chechnya, it marked twenty-six years since Carl had been killed in Vietnam. In 1993, American investigators in Vietnam found his wallet and identification papers, but his body has never been recovered. Today, Carl Long is one of the approximately 2,000 American servicemen still listed as missing in action in Southeast Asia.

CHAPTER 3

If it be a sin to covet honor,
I am the most offending soul alive.
—From the King's St. Crispian Day speech,
  Shakespeare's *Henry V*; Fred Cuny's favorite speech

BETH RABREN couldn't help but laugh thinking of the first time she met Fred Cuny. "I was sitting in some class and he walks in wearing that Marine uniform, and it was like, 'Hello, who are you?' It was really kind of funny, because he just seemed so out of place for A&I."

A thin, dark-haired woman in her early fifties, Beth sat in a dimly lit diner in the small town of Alvin, Texas, a diet soda and pack of Virginia Slims cigarettes before her. Taking a puff on a cigarette, she shook her head in amused disbelief.

"And, boy, was he right-wing, right-wing to the max. I'm telling you, Fred was kinda spooky there at the beginning."

Indeed, it would be hard to conceive of two more radically different people in the fall of 1964 than Fred Cuny and Beth Rabren—then Roush Fernandez—of Falfurrias, Texas. Where he was a conservative Marine Corps cadet, she was an avowed liberal. Where he was shy and serious, she was gregarious and fun-loving, with a wide circle of friends—and where he was still yet to have a serious girlfriend at the age of nineteen, Beth, only two years older, had already been married, had a baby, and been divorced.

There was one more intriguing detail in Beth's background. Her father, Clyde Roush, had joined the air wing of the U.S. military, serving as a bombardier aboard a B-29 in World War II. In the waning days of the war, when Beth was not yet three, his plane had been shot down over Japan, and his body had never been recovered.

Yet, despite their differences—perhaps because of them—Fred and Beth soon began dating, and in little over a year would be married. Almost as quickly, Fred's politics began to change radically.

After his departure in disgrace from Texas A&M, Fred had transferred into Texas College of Arts & Industries (A&I) at Kingsville in the autumn of 1964; its ROTC program at least preserved the possibility that he might yet make the Marine Corps. Instead, in that dusty, dull town, Fred was exposed to a world that would begin to steer his life in a wholly different direction.

Sprawled over the scrubland of South Texas, Kingsville in 1964 was a backwater town of some 10,000, where wild boars, or *javelinas*, still occasionally came down from the arroyos to prowl the streets. Its most striking feature was the sharp economic divide between the haves and have-nots, specifically between the Anglo and Hispanic segments of the population. While most Anglos lived on pleasant, tree-lined streets, virtually all the town's Hispanics were in tightly packed slums of tarpaper shacks, barely scraping out a living as hired hands on the mammoth, million-plus-acre King Ranch or as day laborers on the surrounding farms.

For Fred, this deep divide was an eyeopening experience. In Dallas he had grown up in one of the most rigidly segregated cities in America and, to a degree that might seem incredible today, it had been quite easy for a middle-class white youth to have virtually no contact, or even conception, of the city's black and Hispanic populations. In a town the size of Kingsville, such insulation was simply not possible.

"I think he'd been pretty sheltered all his life," Beth said, "and he'd just never seen the kind of poverty and overt prejudice you saw in Kingsville at that time. For instance, on the college campus there, Mexicans and blacks were not allowed to live in the campus dormitories. All the minorities had to live in off-campus housing, which at the time were just old rooming houses that were falling apart. Those kinds of things Fred was truly shocked by."

But by the autumn of 1964, even a place like Kingsville was beginning to feel the ferment of social change sweeping the country in the wake of President Johnson's declaration of War on Poverty and the passage of the 1964 Civil Rights Act. Fueled by his own sense of outrage—and prodded, no doubt, by his activist girlfriend—Fred quickly found himself immersed in the passions of the day. Strongly influenced by a group of young, liberal professors, he and Beth were soon helping to organize demonstrations against the institutionalized racism on campus, and volunteering as field organizers for the upstart United Farm Workers union. The couple helped create the Kleberg County Head Start program and, at the prodding of an A&I political science professor, Fred began spending time down in the *colonias* along the Mexican border, digging wells and latrines in the squalid "brown ghettoes."

This sudden burst of social activism seemed to spark an academic blossoming in Fred as well. Away from the rigid curriculum of a place like A&M and free to choose classes that interested him, he took a range of courses in political science and Latin-American studies; by his second semester, his grades had improved so markedly that he was placed on the A&I honor roll.

But the conversion of Fred Cuny from conservative militarist to liberal causist was not without its apparent contradictions. Still nurturing his Marine Corps dream, he remained a diligent cadet in A&I's ROTC program and attended Marine training classes at the Quantico training facility in northern Virginia during school breaks. And despite his antiestablishment leafleteering on campus on other issues, he remained an outspoken supporter of the growing American military involvement in Vietnam. Certainly one indication of where his heart still lay was made clear at his wedding to Beth in January 1966. For the occasion, Fred wore his Marine cadet uniform, and all his old Dallas buddies—themselves in various officer training programs around the state—wore full-dress uniforms and gave the traditional raised-sword salute as the couple left the university chapel.

Of course, Fred had strong personal reasons to support the war effort. By the summer of 1966 all his high school friends would be coming out of their various officer training programs, and most would be shipping out to Vietnam; Fred was anxious to be there with them.

. . .

On New Year's Day, 1967, Fred Cuny was living in a small "student ghetto" apartment in Houston, Texas. It was probably the bleakest New Year's of his life.

The previous summer, he and Beth had made the move from Kingsville so that he could finish out his undergraduate studies in a specialized international development program jointly offered by Rice and the University of Houston. No sooner had the newlyweds settled in, however, than Fred received his letter of dismissal from the Marine Corps Reserve for having failed to graduate on time. In an attempt to be reinstated, he had launched a desperate letter-writing campaign, even appealing to the commandant of the Marine Corps himself, but it had been for naught. Shortly after, his left leg had been broken in three places when he accidentally stepped out in front of a Houston taxi, and whatever thin hope he had continued to nurture of somehow becoming a Marine was gone forever. Now, nursing a leg so badly damaged it had to be held together with a permanent metal implant, Fred had to find a whole new life goal for himself.

There was considerable urgency to this. In the space of less than a year Fred had gone from being a young bachelor to a husband with two young children to provide for; along with three-year-old Shemin, Beth's daughter from her first marriage, there was also five-month-old Brandon Craig Cuny, born to Fred and Beth the previous August.

Initially, he saw his new future in politics. Joining the student association at the University of Houston, he soon became its executive secretary, and both he and Beth became active in the city's Democratic Party. By the autumn of 1967, and with little more than a new bachelor's degree in political science from the University of Houston to put on his résumé, Fred felt ready to make his move when a special election was called for an open seat in the Texas state legislature. On the day he announced his candidacy, he was not yet twenty-three, and had been a resident of Houston for just a year.

It wasn't a particularly auspicious beginning. Running as a Liberal Democrat with the campaign slogan, "Democracy is the worst form of government . . . except for all the rest," he struggled to be noticed in a field of fifteen candidates. What he lacked in name recognition he tried to make up for in ambition; among his platform planks were calls for expanding world trade, making poverty programs more responsive to people's needs, tightening controls on air and water pollution, placing more emphasis on rehabilitation in the state's prisons, and dramatically increasing state funding for education. Voters in Houston's twenty-second legislative district were clearly being offered a most energetic representative. Perhaps a bit too energetic; skeptics perusing Fred's campaign literature might well have wondered how even a very precocious young man had managed to be both a Marine Corps "veteran" and an "educator" at the age of twenty-two. Considering his entire campaign war chest consisted of $50 in contributions, Fred's 423-vote total wasn't so bad, though well behind the winner's 8,354.

It was in his next enterprise that he began to find his truer calling. From his time working in the *colonias* below Kingsville, Fred had discovered he had a certain knack for engineering—not perhaps in the highly technical "hard science" areas of the field, but in the more generalized sphere of planning, of identifying specific problems and devising simple, practical solutions to them. In the autumn of 1967, even as he launched his run for the state legislature, he began taking graduate-level classes in public administration and planning at Rice University.

But, as evidenced by his improbable bid for public office, it was hard to imagine Fred having the patience to spend the next three or four years studying theory in a classroom. Shortly after losing the legislature race, he signed on with a new federal initiative, the Model Cities Program, for a three-month stint as a planner.

Started in 1966, Model Cities was an outgrowth of the Johnson administration's much-touted War on Poverty, an innovative pilot program designed to tackle intractable social ills in some seventy urban centers around the nation through grassroots involvement and comprehensive planning. Just how much comprehensive planning had gone into devising the Model Cities Program was open to question, however, when considering Fred's assignment; rather than to an "urban center," he was sent to one of the most remote small towns to be found in the continental United States.

. . .

Travelers don't visit Eagle Pass, Texas; they drive through it. One hundred and forty empty miles southwest of San Antonio—and many more hundreds of empty miles from any other American city—it is a low-slung, dilapidated community of some 20,000 dominated by its much larger and more prosperous Mexican neighbor, Piedras Negras, just across the Rio Grande. For eight months of the year the town bakes beneath a searing sun, and at all times of the year it wears a coat of dust from the winds blowing over the surrounding, scrub-filled plains. So pronounced is Eagle Pass's desolate, end-of-the-road feel that in recent years it has come to the notice of Hollywood directors; large portions of both Alfonso Arau's *Like Water for Chocolate* and John Sayles's *Lone Star* were shot on location around the town.

But as dreary as Eagle Pass might be today, it is much improved from three decades ago. In the late 1960s few of its overwhelmingly Hispanic residents—then numbering about 10,000—had either electricity or running water. With nearly half its population living below the official poverty line, its paucity of medical and social services also ensured one of the highest infant mortality rates in the nation. Perhaps the cruelest irony, given its arid location, was the town's endemic mosquito infestation, a result of the large pools of standing water that formed in the dirt streets after every rainfall. In the autumn of 1967, Fred Cuny arrived in Eagle Pass to begin his three month stint for Model Cities. For both the town and Fred, there could scarcely have been a more perfect fit.

Enjoying a remarkable degree of autonomy and local cooperation, Fred quickly set to work on an impressive array of projects in Eagle Pass—paving roads, digging water lines, erecting streetlights, repairing *barrio* homes—and so profound was the poverty that the benefits were both immediate and dramatic. As he related to his father, the long-standing mosquito plague was virtually eliminated simply by getting rid of the standing water, a task accomplished by cutting drainage ditches and grading the roads.

"Fred was just amazed that no one had thought to do these things before," Gene Cuny said, "and I think that was really the big turnaround for him. In Eagle Pass the problems were so great, but also so basic and fixable, that he saw he could have this huge impact."

But the extent of his impact was also aided by a key personality trait of Fred's: bedrock practicality. Largely unfettered by formal training in "development models" or "assistance strategies," he was uniquely adaptive and creative, willing to try whatever approach might produce the best results. Just as important, he listened closely to the local people and involved them in every aspect of a project, from planning to final execution. Such grassroots participation was, again, basic practicality. From Fred's viewpoint, even the most sophisticated and well-funded development scheme was doomed to fail if the wishes of the people it was designed to help weren't taken into account—and if that was hardly a profound concept, the world was littered with well-intentioned development projects that had overlooked it.

It was this elementary approach, first learned and applied in Eagle

Pass, that would become the defining feature of all Fred's development and humanitarian aid projects over the coming years—as well as the source of some of his most intense battles with the field's old guard. As it was, the Eagle Pass experience was a tremendous satisfaction to Fred, one he would recount with a trace of nostalgia for the rest of his life.

Part of the nostalgia no doubt stemmed from the fact that it was during his Eagle Pass interlude that his personal life came the closest it ever would to idyllic. Just before signing on to the Model Cities Program, Fred had bought an old biplane with no navigational instruments, and every other weekend he took off from Eagle Pass to fly across the state, using highways and power lines as his guide, to visit his young family in Houston. On alternate weekends Beth loaded Shemin and Craig into their old Volkswagen bug and drove the 350 miles to Eagle Pass. So perfect was the arrangement that Fred's three-month assignment stretched into nine.

Perfect from his vantage point, perhaps, but less so from Beth's. From the beginning, she had wanted the whole family to move to Eagle Pass, but Fred had insisted she and the kids remain in Houston.

"At that point, he was still thinking about a future in politics," Beth said, "still very involved with the Democrats in Houston, so he wanted me to stay back and keep all that going. That was going to be his base of operations for the future."

With each new extension of Fred's tour in Eagle Pass, done with little or no consultation with her, Beth's disappointment grew. Matters came to a head soon after his return to Houston, when he was offered a one-year contract with a Fort Worth engineering firm, Carter & Burgess, to work on a low-income housing project in Philadelphia. Once again, Fred's idea was that his wife would stay in Houston with the children to keep the political fires burning but, to Beth, there was a big difference between the 350-mile separation of Eagle Pass and the 1,500-mile one of Philadelphia.

"He just came and presented it to me like it was a done deal," she recalled, "that he was going on, flying on, and I was staying put. And, you know, looking back on it even not much later, I could see there was a lot of blame on my part—I was very immature, very selfish—but at the time I just wasn't going to be dictated to like that. Marriage, the institution, I never thought that much of it to start with, and if we couldn't be together and do things together, I just didn't see any point in it. So that was pretty much the end of it right there."

After just two years of marriage Fred and Beth separated—and would spend nearly as long settling on the terms of a divorce. Eventually Beth agreed to give Fred permanent custody of Craig, while Shemin stayed with her in Houston. For at least one of Fred's old high school friends, Mike Huston, the dissolution of the marriage didn't come as a shock, more as a sad premonition fulfilled. He remembered a peculiar conversation he'd had with Fred when they were still in high school.

"This is gonna sound real strange," Huston said, "but we were riding along one night, and Fred was very depressed. And that was very out of keeping with him—he was rarely down—but this one night he was really depressed. So I finally asked, 'What is it, Fred?' and he said, 'I had a terrible dream last night. In the future, you're gonna get married to a real pretty blond girl and you'll be real happy'—which proved true—'and I'm gonna get married and I'm not gonna be happy.' And the thing is, we didn't talk like that back then, about dreams and omens, that wasn't normal for us. But I can still see the stretch of road we were on and hear Fred. 'You're gonna be happy, but my future's gonna stretch out horribly because I'm alone.' "

.   .   .

As the 1960s drew to a close, Fred stood at a crossroads. His brief attempt at marriage, like his youthful dream of being a Marine, had ended in failure. While his experience at Eagle Pass had been fulfilling and opened up a new range of possibilities, it was hard to see how he might make a living from them; there wasn't a lot of money to be made in "volunteer work," and he was now a single parent. Forgoing the Philadelphia project, he moved back into his parents' Dallas home with Craig in mid-1968 and accepted a different Carter & Burgess assignment, going off to work each day at the construction site for the massive new Dallas–Fort Worth International Airport then being built. If it wasn't exactly what Fred wanted to do, it at least paid the bills until he figured out what came next.

But already Fred was becoming restless, and his basic nature—his desire to stand out in a crowd, his chafing at having to follow orders—suggested he was probably as ill suited for a career at an engineering firm as he had been for one in the military. On the Dallas–Fort Worth Airport project—at the time, the largest construction site in the world—he was one tiny cog in a vast machine, and if a stint as a systems engineer at a New Orleans housing project was more to his tastes, he still played little more than a bit role in its development.

He was also starting to set his sights much broader afield. Even as a child, Fred had loved to travel—his parents had once bribed him with a trip to San Antonio if he improved his grades—and age had only increased his ardor. In the summer between his freshman and sophomore year at A&M, he had obtained a merchant marines card and shipped out on a freighter for the west coast of South America, the appointment finagled by one of his father's friends in the shipping line office. Together with his exposure to the Mexican border area during his time in Kingsville, that voyage had made Fred realize there was a vast world beyond Texas, and he was impatient to explore it. In September 1969 he took his Carter & Burgess vacation time and, leaving his son in the care of his parents, headed off to Dahomey in West Africa, one of the staging grounds for the emergency airlift into starving Biafra.

However brief the experience, this first foray into a disaster zone had a profound effect on Fred, and it provided much of the political and philosophical underpinnings of the problem-solving tactics he would employ in the future. As would become clear in subsequent years, the catastrophe in Biafra marked an evolutionary moment in the history of both warfare and disaster relief. Without precedent in the modern era, a government was openly using mass starvation as an instrument of war, and virtually annihilating a civilian population in the process. In the face of the West's abject failure to respond to the

Biafra "genocide," the International Committee of the Red Cross had, for the first time in its history, overtly violated the territorial laws of a sovereign nation and defiantly launched an emergency airlift of relief supplies into the starving secessionist state, decreeing that the moral responsibility to save lives outweighed the conventions of international diplomacy. When the Red Cross had finally been compelled to end their airlift, the "illegal" effort was continued by a consortium of religious relief agencies. Beyond the revolt of the Red Cross, the Biafran tragedy gave rise to a range of "rebel" organizations—like the French medical group Médecins sans Frontières (Doctors Without Borders)— that would openly flout the old "rules" and take an activist approach in the world's future man-made disaster zones. Even if Fred later exaggerated his daredevil exploits on that trip to West Africa, the experience certainly exposed him to this maverick wing in the relief community, the men and women with whom he would later work most closely and whose renegade approach he would share.

In the short term, however, the trip to Dahomey only served to remind Fred how far away he remained from the playing fields where profound events were taking place. When the housing project in New Orleans ended in the summer of 1970, he moved back to Dallas and a desk job at the Carter & Burgess main office. Within a few weeks he quietly set up a moonlighting operation, a new urban-planning consulting company called Fred Cuny & Associates.

Just who these "associates" might be was not an easy matter to determine, and it's unlikely that any prospective client would have been impressed by the company's headquarters: a small desk in a corner of the North Dallas apartment that Fred shared with his young son. The consulting business also seemed quite a leap for a young man who had spent less than three years in the planning field, but Fred seemed to have already adopted the basic tenet—that self-confidence was everything—which would guide him throughout his life.

Clearly, the future he envisioned for Fred Cuny & Associates was a bit more grand than just another North Texas consulting firm. Rather, it was to be the springboard toward a more dramatic life, one that would enable Fred to combine his growing adult passion—to be a player in the arena of sweeping social change—with those of his childhood: his thirst for adventure, his love of travel, the desire to make the world a better place.

But how that vision could be converted into reality—how, specifically, Fred Cuny & Associates might expand out from a small apartment in North Dallas to wage battle against the poverty and social ills of the planet—was not altogether apparent.

In November 1970 the answer was revealed. It started with one of the deadliest days in the history of mankind.

• • •

In the very early morning hours of November 13, 1970, a massive cyclone moved north up the Bay of Bengal to close on one of the flattest and most densely populated corners on earth: the South Asian enclave of East Pakistan.

Since the beginning of time, the region at the mouth of the Ganges River had been ravaged by cyclones, but there had never been one quite like this. Whipped by winds of over 150 miles per hour, the storm made landfall just at high tide and under a full moon, sending a twenty-five-foot-high wall of water over a land that averaged just a few feet above sea level. In minutes, hundreds of small towns and fishing villages along the coast simply disappeared, while many more were buried beneath an avalanche of water and mud. By dawn of that day an estimated 300,000 people were dead, and millions more left homeless. Yet, for the people of East Pakistan, even worse trouble lay just ahead; within months, the desperate survivors of the cyclone who had streamed into refugee camps would be joined by some 10,000,000 more as a brutal civil war set their land aflame.

As the civil war in East Pakistan intensified through that winter and spring, Fred Cuny energetically lobbied a variety of relief agencies for a job—any job—that would take him to the war zone. It wasn't until June that he finally managed to line up a low-paying position as an engineering adviser for the British relief agency, Oxfam. On July 5 he arrived in Calcutta and made for the refugee camps that had sprouted up all along the India–East Pakistan border. As he noted in his cheap little travel diary, it marked his first day as a refugee worker. It was also the beginning of an experience that would change his life forever.

Although Fred had seen aspects of the international disaster relief system in Biafra, that had largely been a guerrilla operation working outside the norm and, as disorganized and accident-prone as that effort had been, its shortcomings could largely be attributed to overtaxed and woefully equipped agencies trying to work in a fiercely hostile environment. On the Indian subcontinent, Fred would have his first contact with the vast machinery of the disaster r lief system—an array of governmental agencies, nonprofit organizations, and religious charities—operating at full throttle. The problem was, the machinery didn't work.

At the beginning of the 1970s much of the Western world's standard procedure in coping with large-scale disaster was still based on models and practices first developed in the 1940s during the reconstruction of war-torn Europe. In dealing with the catastrophe in East Pakistan, Fred would observe, a less applicable model could scarcely be found.

In the 1940s the flood of refugees in Europe had been a "slowmotion" disaster, one that rebuilders had been able to plan for well in advance; even before World War II ended, a vast network of displaced persons camps under Allied army supervision was being established throughout the continent. In contrast, the first phase of the disaster in Bengal—the cyclone—had struck in one night and without warning. What's more, the vast majority of Europeans in the DP camps were anxious to return to their original homes, and in all but the most devastated towns and cities there still existed at least the semblance of an infrastructure that could be repaired. In Bengal, however, there were millions of people who had no place to go back to, their communities either obliterated in the cyclone or their return made impossible by the horrific "ethnic cleansing" accompanying the war (in fact, even in 1999, twenty-eight years after the secessionist war in East Pakistan that led to the creation of Bangladesh, tens of thousands of refugees continue to live in "temporary" camps).

Most crucially, there was the very basic issue of organization. In Europe rebuilders and relief agencies had a vast and fairly efficient distribution network already in place to assist them—the occupying Allied armies—a network that could move supplies, provide security, and ensure a modicum of coordination. In Bengal there was nothing remotely like that. Instead, there was a United Nations hierarchy that remained so oblivious to the steadily worsening catastrophe that it failed to disburse even the woefully inadequate aid pledged to it by donor nations. Attempting to fill the void was a chaotic mélange of private groups and government agencies operating in near total autonomy, each with its own set of guidelines, each struggling to establish its own distribution system, each attempting to pursue its own mission—and, often, directly competing with the agendas of others to do so.

For Fred Cuny, the young planner from Dallas, the spectacle was astonishing. From his vantage point, mismanagement seemed to be the rule at virtually every level of the aid effort, an incompetence magnified by the lack of any central coordination. Most relief workers and volunteers, no matter how altruistic their intentions, seemed to have little or no idea of what they were doing. For lack of trucks or road repairs, emergency supplies rotted in warehouses while people starved a few miles away. Refugee camps were constructed with no discernible thought to such basic matters as location or sanitation, with the result that some had scant access to water, others were washed away in the first rains, while still others were turned into death camps by cholera epidemics.

Especially galling to Fred—the consummate studier of local conditions—was that many relief groups seemed oblivious to the most basic facts about the region and its cultures. One relief agency had distributed heavy woolen jackets, apparently not realizing that East Pakistan was in the tropics with a median annual temperature in the high-seventies. Another handed out cans of pork and beans to the hungry, seemingly unaware that the refugees had no way of opening the cans, no way of heating the contents, and that neither Muslims nor Hindus ate pork.

While Fred had no doubt encountered technical foul-ups or design snafus during his planning career, those accompanying the Bengal relief operation were in an altogether different category. Here, the end result was not cost overruns or delayed projects, but people dying—and dying en masse. And no matter how many excuses could be offered up—that the double disaster of cyclone and war would have overwhelmed even the most efficient relief system, that the mistakes made had been committed by selfless people working under extremely difficult conditions—the final message was the same: the world had been presented with its greatest emergency challenge in a generation, and it had failed very badly.

As Fred wrote in his diary on August 7, 1971, the day after he had left the disaster zone:

> And as same [sic] as Bengal's future is now in doubt, so is mine. The events of the past few weeks have altered irreversibly the course of my life. The internationalization of F. Cuny has begun.

By the time he returned to Dallas that summer Fred had a very clear idea of what he was meant to do with his life, and he would never waver from it. Within weeks he announced the creation of a new disaster relief consulting company, initially called the International Technical Consultants in Emergency Management—or Intertect for short—with himself as its executive director.

As might have been predicted, Fred's goal for Intertect was not a modest one. His ultimate aim was a radical restructuring of the way the disaster relief system operated throughout the world, with himself as one of the leaders of change. He was twenty-six years old.

CHAPTER 4

*Fred's whole approach was, "Think big, very little is
impossible." He raised the threshold of impossibility, and
being around him, you either got fed up and thought he was
bullshit, or he made you raise your own threshold of
impossibility. "What would Fred do in this situation?" You ask
yourself that, and it immediately pushes you forward,
because you know he wouldn't ever quit.*
—John Fawcett, International Rescue Committee
   director in Bosnia

ONE DAY right around his thirtieth birthday—November 14,
1974—Fred Cuny sat down with a yellow legal pad and a black felt tip
pen to make a list of the things he wanted to achieve in his life. The
list, divided into fifteen separate categories, ran for five pages.

MAJOR GOALS
Be selected for a high political or decision-making office in
   or near the executive office of the govt.

To be a part of a major policy decision(s) affecting the
course of a nation.
To gain the respect of my contemporaries as a man of the
people.
To build Intertect into a major center of technical assistance
for developing nations.
To serve in the UN.

He then tucked the list away in a filing cabinet at his Dallas home, where it remained for the next twenty-one years.

When discovered, the papers provided two remarkable insights into Fred Cuny. The first was how relentlessly he had pursued those "major goals" over the intervening two decades, and how close he had come to attaining many of them. The second was how, given Fred's lowly status at the time the list was written, those goals spoke of an optimism that bordered on the delusional.

But perhaps it was not optimism at all, but something quite different. For most people, life's disappointments have a way of tempering youthful dreams. For Fred Cuny, they appeared to have the opposite effect. With each setback—and there would be many over the years—his dreams had a way of growing simply more grand. Rather than optimism, it suggested a burning desire for relevancy, a need to place himself at the center of events and place his own imprimatur upon them. In short, a kind of hunger.

CLIMB
1. Mt. Kilimanjaro
2. Matterhorn
3. Mt. Aconcagua
4. Mt. McKinley
5. Mt. Cook
6. Mountain in Himalayas
7. Climb and name Mt. Cuny

. . .

Jean "Jinx" Parker is an affable, athletic woman in her early fifties, her words tinged with the soft accent of her native Virginia. Since 1989 she has run her own Third World development consulting company from a small office outside Washington, D.C., drawing on nearly thirty years' experience in the field. Chances are, she never would have entered that field if not for a chance meeting she had in the lobby of the Dallas apartment building where she was living in the summer of 1970.

"I had my little girl with me, who was four," she recalled, "and there was this big, tall man on the elevator, and he started talking. He was very genial, very nice, and he said he had a little boy the same age as my daughter and we ought to get the kids together. Well, I was newly married and very sensitive to guys hitting on you, so I just didn't tell him where I lived, and thought, 'Well, that's that.' "

A week later Jinx responded to a knock on her apartment door to find the man from the elevator, Fred Cuny, standing in the hall with his four-year-old son Craig.

"It turned out he lived just two floors up, and the kids really hit it off. And Fred was a very outgoing person and loved to talk—just loved to tell stories—so we'd get together for the kids to play, and we became good friends."

By the summer of 1970, Fred had already started moonlighting from Carter & Burgess with his Fred Cuny & Associates consulting company, and occasionally needed help typing reports. He also would love to have a place to spread out his papers, he pointedly told Jinx and her husband Cole. Quite quickly Fred became a semipermanent fixture in the Parkers' lives, moving into a corner of Cole's private practice law office and wheedling Jinx into typing up his handwritten reports at the rate of twenty-five-cents a page. When he headed off to East Pakistan in the summer of 1971 he moved most of his furniture into the Parkers' apartment so he wouldn't have to pay storage. Upon his return, flush with a bold new idea, it was to Jinx Parker that he first turned.

"He would come and sit in the office and have a cup of coffee," she remembered, "and start telling stories about what he'd seen over there, just the horrible conditions, and his ideas for establishing a disaster relief company. And, you know, you begin to get caught up in all these things, and so, slowly but surely, I began to do some work with him, to help him do all that."

Finally leaving his job at Carter & Burgess altogether, Fred printed up new business cards. While still the president of Fred Cuny & Associates, he was also now the executive director of a new company, Intertect, with Jinx Parker as his second in command. Tapping into his network of contacts, primarily relief specialists he had met in Biafra and East Pakistan, he managed to compile a rather impressive list of young consultants for inclusion on the Intertect masthead.

"It was wonderful," Jinx said, "because all of us were like sixties kids in the sense that we were idealistic. We all thought we could accomplish something out of the goodness of our hearts—in a sense, we could starve—because we had a goal in mind and were willing to put our time and effort into doing that and take very little money back. So we shared a lot of that, and Fred had no hesitation in encouraging any of us to do as much as we possibly could."

The problem was, there wasn't an awful lot to be done. For six months Fred vainly worked the hustings in search of Intertect's first contract, before finally heading off to Israel to work as a volunteer on a kibbutz. His exposure to the kibbutzim movement, then in its heyday, reinforced the basic philosophy he had adopted in Eagle Pass—that with collective will and grassroots participation extraordinary things were possible—but it was questionable whether he'd ever have the chance to apply that philosophy elsewhere.

"I know that was a very frustrating time for Fred," his mother said. "Here he had all these ideas and things he wanted to try, and he just couldn't get people to take notice."

The fledgling company's first big break came in late 1972, in the wake of another major natural disaster. On December 23 a powerful earthquake all but leveled Managua, the capital of Nicaragua, killing some 6,000 and leaving tens of thousands homeless. Contracted by Oxfam, the same relief agency that had hired him on in East Pakistan,

Fred and a small team of his Intertect consultants headed off for the devastated Central American country.

In the year and a half since starting Intertect—and in lieu of any actual consulting assignments coming his way—Fred had been at work on a series of slim handbooks on refugee camp planning and design. Drawing largely on the mistakes he had seen being made in Bengal, he had come up with a number of novel approaches, as well as one very attractive premise. According to Fred's thesis, the well-designed refugee camp—and design meant not just good engineering but working with the camp population and taking their cultural mores into account—could actually save a great deal of assistance money in the long run, for it would head off the sort of secondary emergencies, like sanitation breakdowns and infectious disease outbreaks, that required a whole range of remedial services in poorly designed camps. In Nicaragua he finally had the chance to test out the theory. In early January 1973 he and his Intertect and Oxfam colleagues broke ground on a new refugee camp, Coyotepe, just outside the town of Masaya.

The cornerstone of Fred's concept was very simple. In every major disaster zone of the previous half century, including Bengal, almost all refugee camps had been built in a square grid pattern, with large, high-occupancy buildings—Quonset huts, usually—lined up in neat rows much like a military barracks. While arguably more convenient for laying water lines and cutting drainage ditches, the square grid was also the most alienating for the camp's residents, providing them with no sense of community and little open space. And much as expanded highways usually mean expanded traffic, high-occupancy refugee buildings tended to become simply higher-occupancy. With more people constantly moving in, every aspect of the camp's infrastructure—from its water supply to medical service to food distribution—was constantly stretched to the breaking point, reducing camp workers to "firefighters," all their energy expended on simply trying to stay abreast of a steadily worsening situation. At one such high-occupancy camp designed for 35,000 in Bengal, for example, three times that many refugees had moved in on the first day, a number that swelled to 700,000 within weeks. In such an environment the phrase "camp planning" quickly became an oxymoron.

At Coyotepe, by contrast, Fred used single-family tents and arranged them in what was called a "cross-axis" plan, clustering twelve to fifteen tents around a common open area to form a communal unit. Each communal unit had its own basic services—latrines, bathing and cooking areas—while the more advanced facilities, like medical services, were congregated at the center of the camp and set off by a "greenbelt" vaguely reminiscent of a plaza.

The result was nothing short of astonishing, especially when compared to two refugee camps that the U. S. Army had built nearby using the traditional square-grid design. At the Oxfam-Intertect camp the population level quickly stabilized, which allowed for long-range planning; at the U. S. Army-administered camps the populations constantly fluctuated, setting off an alternating cycle of supply shortages and surpluses. At Coyotepe there were no mass inoculations because there was never an outbreak of infectious diseases; the U. S. Army camps were so plagued with health problems that, at one, nurses had to administer full-population inoculations on six different occasions. In the Oxfam-Intertect camp a communal spirit quickly developed, with refugees starting up a number of cottage industries and self-help organizations. In the other camps thievery and tension were rife; at one, American soldiers had to be called out to forcibly segregate feuding factions. Best of all, in view of the cold economic realities that governed humanitarian aid, Coyotepe cost nearly 40 percent less to operate than the other camps.

On his first big test, Fred Cuny had scored a major success.

DESIGN
1. City for Spacemen.
2. Racing Yacht.
3. Regional Plan.

•   •   •

But if Fred understood the economic considerations of his new vocation, it appeared he had a less firm grasp on its political ones. The old adage about invention—"Build a better mousetrap and the world will beat a path to your door"—just didn't apply to the builder of a better refugee camp in the traditional humanitarian aid establishment. Even after Fred's remarkable success at Coyotepe, the services of Intertect were rarely called upon.

Part of the reason, no doubt, was the tendency toward inertia common to any bureaucracy and by the early 1970s humanitarian aid, with its complex network of private, governmental, quasi-governmental, and supranational organizations, had become a very large bureaucracy. In the nonprofit realm, the system was still dominated by a dozen or so very large organizations—outfits like the Red Cross and Save the Children—that had been working in the field for decades and saw little reason to suffer the advice of upstarts from Texas. In such a codified environment, rife with blueprints and models and standard operating procedures, it took a great deal of patience and persuasion, as well as a certain amount of chutzpah, to convince the authorities to try something new.

There were also more cynical explanations. By the early 1970s many of the large nonprofits had carved out very cozy existences for themselves over the years, deriving a steady income from both government contracts and public donations.

Even more extravagant were the salaries and lifestyles of those in the employ of the American government, notably the Agency for International Development (USAID), or any of the branches of the United Nations. Throughout the Third World, USAID employees were provided pleasant homes and cars with drivers, the cost of a retinue of servants making barely a dent in their 75 percent "hardship" pay bonus, while everyone regarded the UN agencies as incompetent, overpaid, and corrupt. The last person the administrators of these charities and governmental agencies wanted to hear from was someone like Fred Cuny with his argument that there was a better and cheaper way of doing things. Likewise, even the most progressive in-country director had to think twice before adopting a cheaper method, for the most immediate result could be reduced project funding during the next budget allocation.

A similar set of concerns could be found away from the field, at those governmental agencies which doled out aid contracts. In the reverse-logic mindset endemic to government bureaucracies the world over, such cost-cutting innovations as Fred was advocating carried the unpleasant implication that the traditional approach had been inefficient and wasted taxpayers' money. And at government agencies, just as at the blue chip charities, a cheaper way of doing things raised the alarming specter of budget surpluses at the end of the fiscal year, an affront to the system sure to be avenged in the next appropriations bill. Quite simply, if those holding the purse strings had been convinced to cough up $5 million for the construction of a refugee camp last year, it damn well better cost at least as much this year. Added to this was the great deal of employment cross-over that occurred throughout the system, with many specialists earning their humanitarian aid stripes in the lower-paying nonprofits before moving over to the better-paying government sphere. For such careerists, there was little to be gained by rocking the boat.

And certainly any departure from the status quo was likely to meet resistance from the third element of the disaster-response triangle: the private sector. For a number of American companies, foreign disasters represented a windfall source of revenue, since they generated a rush of purchase orders from both private organizations and the government: for tents and sheeting, specialized vehicles, piping and construction material. For other companies—most notoriously, pharmaceuticals—such emergencies presented a golden opportunity to unload obsolete or outdated goods stockpiled in warehouses, so-called "junk aid," that could then be turned into a profit by claiming a charitable deduction on corporate tax returns. Put most cynically, Fred's ideas for rebuilding after disaster—adopting simple technology, harnessing local manpower, using indigenous materials whenever possible—was bad for business. On the flip side, and taking the cynicism to its most venal, the very inefficiences of the traditional disaster-response system was good for business, not only for the original surge of purchase orders it generated but for all the secondary and expensive-to-fix problems those inefficiencies created. For many of those with a stake in the status quo, then, reformist ideas like those being put forward by Fred Cuny were about as welcome as rattlesnakes.

Yet the disaster-industrial complex was not solely to blame for the dearth of contracts coming Fred's way. In establishing Intertect, he had made the somewhat novel decision to operate it as a for-profit company rather than as a nonprofit organization. As he often explained, to Jinx Parker and many others, experience had taught him that people only took advice seriously when they paid for it, while even the best free advice was routinely ignored. There were also a lot more paperwork and rules involved in operating a nonprofit, and Fred had little tolerance for either.

Although Intertect wasn't the first for-profit consulting company in the disaster relief field, it was rather unusual for the time, and in some potential hirers' minds it raised the question of whether the Dallas-based outfit was somehow trying to make it rich off others' misery. The reality could hardly have been further from the truth. In the field, Fred and his Intertect consultants most often lived in tents and sleeping bags, for a salary that was a pittance when compared to what they could earn in the mainstream economy. Nevertheless, Intertect's for-profit label was one that would continue to arouse suspicion—and, in some quarters, animosity—for the next two decades.

At least as great a factor, though, was Fred's own personality. While he could be extremely genial and charming, his supreme self-confidence always flirted dangerously close to the border of arrogance. Like any visionary—and Fred most certainly saw himself as one—he had little patience with those who didn't see things his way or competed with him for authority. Over the quarter-century span of his career and the hundred-odd projects he would eventually work on around the world, there would be many disaster relief colleagues who, while deeply admiring of his energy and ingenuity and ability to get things done, would vow never to work with Fred Cuny again.

For whatever combination of these reasons, the grand splash Fred had hoped to make with Intertect failed to materialize. Through the early seventies, the company existed in little more than name, limping along on barely a handful of small-scale consulting projects. For a long time Intertect headquarters consisted of the same corner desk at Cole Parker's law office that Fred Cuny & Associates had occupied, and even when Fred did finally rent a small office of his own there wasn't enough money for a telephone. In the summer of 1973 came what must have been a disheartening moment even for Fred: just a little more than a year after his triumph with the Coyotepe refugee camp, he was so broke he had to take a crop-dusting job in West Texas.

But if others associated with Intertect began to wonder if it would ever get off the ground, Fred was not among them. In fact, through those early lean years, he simply continued to broaden his vision, driven on by an ambition and yearning that seemed as desperate as it was implacable.

PERSONAL ACHIEVEMENT GOALS
1. To sail a Chinese junk or sampan across the Pacific.
2. To win a major yachting event (as captain).
3. To spend a year sailing the rivers of Europe on a houseboat.
4. To achieve an ATP [Airline Transport Pilot] type rating for: helicopter; 4-engine aircraft; glider; jet; gyrocopter; crop duster; balloon.
5. To visit every country on earth.
6. To teach at a major college or university.
7. To attain a PhD.
8. To develop a floating school for planners.
9. Learn to speak 5 languages other than English.
10. Cross Asia overland.
11. Cross South America overland.
12. Cross the Sahara overland.
13. Cross Africa north-to-south.
14. Write a book.
15. Learn to play a musical instrument.

16. Become proficient in a competitive sport.
17. Become member of explorers and adventurers clubs.

· · ·

Just before dawn on the morning of February 4, 1976, the heartland of Guatemala was rocked by an earthquake that measured 7.5 on the Richter scale. By the time the aftershocks ended that afternoon, a vast stretch of the small Central American nation lay in ruins, with some 28,000 people dead and as many as a million—nearly a quarter of the national population—left homeless. Especially hard hit were the Mayan Indian communities of the central highlands; on that morning, dozens of their villages, clinging to the steep banks of mountains, had simply ceased to exist.

For those in the disaster relief business, there was suddenly work enough for everyone in Guatemala. Within days, Fred Cuny and his Intertect colleagues had been hired on by Oxfam and a smaller relief agency, World Neighbors, and were on their way to the disaster zone.

A few weeks later an American journalist named Gerry Nadel was touring the devastated country when he dropped in at Oxfam's field headquarters in the town of Antigua. He discovered an impromptu training seminar for relief workers was about to begin, one led by "a thirty-one-year-old Texan, a Good Ol' Boy, but brainy," named Fred Cuny. As Nadel wrote in *East West Journal*, more relief workers kept arriving at the Oxfam headquarters, "until there are more than a dozen clumped in a circle around Fred in front of the fireplace. They are all CARE fieldworkers, and they have come for advice from Fred Cuny. . . . The CARE people had been following their organization's standard policy, which seems to be 'act first, ask questions later.' Then one of them met Fred."

Fred's mission for Oxfam and World Neighbors was not just to replace homes destroyed in the February earthquake but to employ building techniques that would make those replacements much safer; Guatemala lay at the center of one of the most earthquake-prone regions in the world, and it was only a matter of time before another struck. As Nadel discovered during that evening's seminar, Fred was approaching the task in a rather clever—and by the traditional practices of the disaster relief community, highly unorthodox—manner.

"[He] has been training *albaniles*, the local masons and builders, to pass on the [improved reconstruction] knowledge to others who will then pass it along again, in ever widening circles. Tonight, he is trying to convince the CARE workers to do the same. All they have been told to do, so far, is build houses. All they will leave behind, if they do so, will be buildings. By teaching instead of building they would leave behind the knowledge which people could then use to help themselves instead of being forced to depend on Yankee technology and Yankee charity."

In Guatemala, Fred, the guru of practical solutions and grassroots involvement, was finally commanding attention.

That process had actually begun a few months earlier. Expanding from the thin handbooks he had written on refugee camp design after Bengal, he had spent much of the previous two years laboring over his first magnum opus. The result, the four-volume *Relief Operations Guidebook*, was a virtual encyclopedia of knowledge on nearly every imaginable aspect of disaster relief: some three hundred single-spaced pages divided into forty chapters, covering everything from "Waterborne Operations" to "Handling and Disposal of the Dead." Needed to know how to signal in a helicopter for an emergency landing, or the best urinal design for the tropics, or how to thatch a roof when only short-stem palm fronds were available? The *Relief Operations Guidebook* told you in exacting detail.

Above all, the guide pointed up one of Fred's greatest talents, that of an extraordinary collector and synthesizer of new ideas. Having not worked his way up through the ranks of either a governmental agency or one of the nonprofits, he had never been inculcated with a "standard operating procedure" or an institutional bias, leaving him receptive to whatever innovations came along, whether it was how to make houses more hurricane-resistant or a more efficient way to distribute food. In putting together the *Relief Operations Guidebook*, Fred had gathered up and evaluated every new idea he could find.

"I think he probably corresponded with everybody he had ever met in the relief world," Jinx Parker said. "He would draft a chapter and send it out and say, 'Give me your info and comments back,' and then we'd revise it. And this was in the days before computers, so every time it would have to be retyped."

But the *Guidebook* was also something of a manifesto, a reflection of both Fred's personality and his self-appointed mission; he wasn't there to ingratiate himself with the disaster relief fraternity, but rather to give it a good spanking and then reform it. As a result, many parts of the guide read less like a neutral, just-the-facts reference tool than a highly opinionated *Consumer Reports*, and just about every nonprofit group or governmental agency involved in relief operations could point to places where their established practices came in for criticism. By virtue of the book's comprehensiveness, those criticisms were aimed both high and low.

The U.S. government's Agency for International Development (USAID), for example, was unlikely to be pleased to learn of Fred's assessment of the four-person tent it had been buying and distributing to refugee camps in great quantities for many years:

> The tents are not suitable for large families, a tropical climate, heavy use, or a refugee camp environment. They are poorly designed, cheaply sewn, inadequately ventilated, and not weatherproofed. The plastic floor is useless and prevents modification of the living space. In many native populations, the colors are offensive. . . . A minor twist of the pole could bring the whole unit down.

In the early days of Intertect, Fred's greatest frustration had been simply getting the disaster relief establishment to notice him. With the publication of the *Relief Operations Guidebook*, they noticed him; the problem now was that they didn't care for a lot of what he was saying.

In Guatemala, however, he was being given a new chance to apply his ideas in the field, and the efficacy of those ideas was winning him converts among the younger fieldworkers. As one of those attending Fred's ad hoc seminar at the Oxfam headquarters told Nadel, what was taking place was "a palace revolution."

If not quite a revolution, the Oxfam approach certainly represented a departure from that of most other relief agencies in Guatemala. Where other relief workers were being housed in hotels in the largely unaffected capital, visiting their project sites by car or even helicopter, the Oxfam workers were living in the field, enabling them to quickly assess what the most pressing needs were. Rather than simply handing out rebuilding supplies, they were organizing salvage crews to find reusable materials amid the ruins. To overcome the obstacle of teaching better construction techniques to a largely illiterate Indian population, Fred devised a system of "pictographs"—simple diagrams printed on old coffee sacks—to show how and where they could rebuild most safely.

"Guatemala was really the breakthrough," Jinx Parker said, "both for Intertect and for Fred. It was like we'd finally won some respect. After that, we started getting projects coming our way."

In the three years that had elapsed between the creation of the Coyotepe camp in Nicaragua and the earthquake in Guatemala, Intertect had landed a mere four, very small-scale contracts. In the four years after Guatemala, there would be some fifteen projects spanning five continents, everything from helping devise a flood recovery program in Jamaica to mapping out a reconstruction plan in war-torn Lebanon. The Dallas outfit was still an outsider, its director still a wave-making renegade, but even the powerbrokers of the disaster relief industry were beginning to have a hard time arguing against success.

And Guatemala also marked the beginning of the Fred Cuny myth, one that would steadily expand over the coming years. In describing the background of the "Good Ol' Boy" from Texas in his 1976 *East West Journal* article, Gerry Nadel had apparently relied on information supplied to him by Fred:

> In engineering school, he specialized in problems of underdevelopment. His post-graduate field-work in Nigeria turned into the relief plan after the [Biafra] civil war and he found himself with an international reputation in disaster work. With colleagues, he formed his own company, Intertect of Dallas, and now he spends his life circling the globe; the Mideast, Africa, Asia, the Subcontinent—wherever nature or mankind has done its worst most recently.

In 1976, virtually every detail in that description, save for the mention of Intertect, was in error.

.   .   .

"I think Fred was probably the most creative, original thinker I've ever met in this field," Don Krumm said. "The mastery of the tiniest details, while at the same time having this grand, strategic view—I can't think of anyone else who had it like he did. At the same time, there was a certain brand of existential struggle about him, and one big way it showed itself was this absolute refusal to sidle up to authority. It was almost a badge of honor with him, and it cost him."

A tall, thin man in his early fifties, Krumm has spent his professional life as one of those authorities, most recently as a State Department official dealing with refugee crises. Despite the differences in their personalities and career paths—Krumm, a soft-spoken Foreign Service officer, Fred, the brash Texan maverick—the two became fast friends almost from the day of their meeting in 1982. Sitting at a table in the State Department cafeteria, Krumm reflected on the hard, lonely path Fred chose for himself.

"At one time or another, he offended or was on the wrong side of just about everybody in this town and just about everybody at the UN organizations—which meant most of the people who could employ him. He got long in the tooth. He was always telling it like it was, not what everyone wanted to hear. He was unbought and unbossed." Absently turning a Styrofoam cup of coffee on the cafeteria table, Krumm slowly grinned. "But I think it got to a point where he was simply too good, too important, to be ignored. Some crisis would come along and people would be scrambling around trying to figure out what to do, and they'd come across some report Fred had written ten years before that gave them the answers to questions they didn't even know they had yet. I think it probably rankled a lot of people, because they really wanted to keep him frozen out; they just couldn't do it anymore."

By the early 1980s, Intertect was finally breaking out of its "guerrilla" status, the relief establishment increasingly forced to recognize Fred as a leading expert on postdisaster reconstruction. Invitations to speak at seminars on refugee camp planning and emergency preparedness filtered in from around the world. At the same time the Intertect client list was growing to include many of the same organizations Fred had so energetically lambasted in the past, nonprofit groups like Save the Children, as well as governmental agencies like USAID, the Peace Corps, and the United Nations High Commission for Refugees.

"Of course, people still grumbled," Don Krumm said. " 'Oh, Fred's got such an ego, he always has to be right.' Well, damn right he had an ego. I don't know that you can find a man or woman who does great things who doesn't have an ego. But you've also got to look at the kind of work Fred was doing. This wasn't the ego of some trial lawyer who has to win the big case, or some businessman trying to outdo a competitor. This is a guy who was in the business of saving lives. When he saw someone doing something stupid, something that could get people killed, of course he was going to raise hell."

STUDY AND DOCUMENT
1. A primitive culture.
2. Military power in world politics.
3. Decision-making in government.
4. A vanishing species.
5. The life of Sam Houston.
6. Refugees in world politics.

. . .

If Fred was finally beginning to find the success and recognition he had always sought, it came at a high cost. His routine had become a blur of airports, hotel rooms, and time zones, a near constant shuttle from one disaster zone or disaster assessment symposium to the next. While it was obviously a situation of his choosing—and far preferable to the old days when he had been scarcely acknowledged by others in the field—there was at least one major casualty to his peripatetic life-style: his young son Craig. Yet "casualty" is certainly not the term Craig himself, twenty-eight when Fred went to Chechnya, would choose.

"I always thought my dad was the greatest," he said, sitting on the deck of his houseboat on Lake Travis, outside Austin. "And I always really looked forward to seeing him because it was such a special occasion."

In the late 1960s, Fred had waged a bitter custody battle for Craig with his ex-wife Beth, and he had ultimately won that battle. In the early years he had managed to strike something of a balance between the demands of his fledgling career and those of being a single father; when he'd been sent to New Orleans by Carter & Burgess, for example, he'd simply taken Craig with him. He'd also had a convenient support network in place for the boy during his first, brief sojourns abroad. Fred's parents, Gene and Charlotte, had moved to the town of Rockwall, some twenty-five miles northeast of downtown Dallas, and their small ranch-style home on the very shore of Lake Ray Hubbard came complete with a dock and fishing boat. What's more, after having three boys in quick succession in the 1940s, Gene and Charlotte had had a "surprise" fourth one, Chris, in 1960, just six years older than Craig.

"Well, having two little boys around isn't much different than having one," Charlotte Cuny said with a laugh, "and it was like we were starting a second family. Pretty quick, we just started thinking of Craig as our fifth son."

As Fred's trips abroad grew more frequent and of longer duration, so did Craig's stays with his grandparents. By the time he was ready to start school, the arrangement became permanent, Craig moving into the bedroom next to Chris's and attending the local Rockwall elementary school.

Almost at once Fred adopted a detached attitude toward his son—curiously so, considering the fierce battle he had waged for his custody. In early January 1973, while en route to the earthquake disaster site in Nicaragua, he sent a postcard of the Panama Canal to six-year-old Craig. In its entirety it read:

Dear Craig—This is the Panama Canal which divides North and South America. This canal was built 70 yrs. ago to make going from the Atlantic ocean to the Pacific much easier. See you soon, Daddy.

Throughout his growing up, Craig decorated his bedroom with the artifacts Fred brought back from his travels, and carefully saved the postcards he received during his father's absences. As the contracts started to roll into Intertect in the late 1970s, Fred's return visits to Texas became more sporadic, Craig's collection of postcards ever larger. If it was a situation that weighed on Fred, it was one he was either unwilling or unable to change.

"I think he was really kind of stuck," his old high school friend, Mike Huston, said. "You know, every parent faces these situations where they have to choose between their career and their family, where they have to look at themselves in the mirror and say, 'Well, am I going to do what's right for my kid, or what's right for my job?' But for Fred it was a lot more complicated, because if he didn't go back, people were going to die as a result. So what was he going to do? He was constantly placed in situations where he had to make that choice. 'Do I stay to watch my son's basketball game, or do I go back out there where people are counting on me, where if I don't go another five, six, one thousand—pick a number—people are going to die?' What a terrible choice.''

Dear Craig, I'm now in Bangkok for a few days working on plans for the refugee camps along the Thai border. Bangkok is not a very pretty city, but the canals are nice and quite interesting. The work is a bit overwhelming but for the first time we have tremendous resources for helping the refugees and the staff to do the work. I expect to be home about Feb. 5. I hope you are having a good X-mas. I miss you greatly and wish you were here. Love, Dad

—POSTCARD FROM THAILAND
JANUARY 1980

While that life-and-death aspect was certainly true, Fred also relegated his son to second fiddle in far less pressing situations. In the early 1970s he had begun a steady relationship with an English nurse living in Dallas, and on his returns to Texas would frequently stay with her for several days before even calling out to Rockwall.

"I remember sometimes wondering when my dad was going to be back in town," Craig said, "and then come to find out he'd already been back for quite a while." He laughed good-naturedly. "He'd try to hide it—'Yeah, just came in from the airport'—but he'd always screw up his alibi somehow."

Handsome and charming, and at least as tall as his father, the adult Craig preferred to recall those occasions when Fred did spend time with him.

"He was very effective at finding a special connection between himself and another person, and then keeping that connection unique.

For us, it was flying. I obviously got the flying bug from him, and that was our special bond. Sometimes when he came back, we'd go camping—went down to Big Bend a couple of times—but flying was the big thing. We'd hop in a plane and head off somewhere, just the two of us."

Fred also arranged to have his young son join him on several of his overseas assignments, first in Guatemala in 1976, and again in Peru in 1979.

"I guess I was about nine when I went down to see him in Guatemala," Craig recalled. "It was really eye-opening for me to see the kind of work he was doing, how important it was. Before that, there'd been some times when maybe I was a bit resentful that he wasn't around more, but that trip made me realize that I was being pretty selfish."

Dear Craig—This will have to do for your birthday card till I return. I hope it's a nice day and the strain of recent events and the return to school hasn't clouded it up too much.
I love you a lot and only wish I could be there to help you celebrate—or that you could be here so we could do it Jamaican style. Love, Dad.

—POSTCARD FROM JAMAICA
AUGUST 1981

Through Craig's growing up, a poignant pattern developed between father and son, Fred ending most every postcard with some variation on the vague promise that he would be home soon, Craig scrawling out long, handwritten letters designed to engage his father's interest. As early as eleven and twelve, Craig developed the habit of giving his father comprehensive updates on what was happening back in the United States—in his school or in American politics or with his beloved Dallas Cowboys—as well as reading up on whatever disaster zone Fred happened to be in at the moment so as to ask him detailed questions about his work. Craig also zealously maintained the "special connection" they had between them: flying. At fourteen, he started working as an errand boy at the airstrip outside Rockwall, and took up gliding. He was also determined to earn his pilot's license by soloing on his sixteenth birthday, just as his father had.

Fred, however, was not there to see his son's triumph.

Dear Craig—Well, here I am again, right in the middle of the action! The Khyber Pass is probably the most famous spot on the Indian sub-contenent [sic], traditionally the pass used to invade India-Pakistan. This is where most of the refugees go back and forth now, in-out of Afghanistan.

How's the soaring? I'm so proud of your soloing on your birthday. I love and miss you. Dad

—POSTCARD FROM PAKISTAN
SEPTEMBER 1983

At some point in the mid-1980s, Fred handwrote another curious little document on a legal pad, a sort of extended calling card listing his achievements and titles. The list was not modest, nor entirely accurate: "Frederick C. Cuny," it began, "pilot, seaman, U.S. Marine; statesman, planner, politician; author, editor, literary critic, professor, consultant, researcher; explorer, navigator, student of human behavior . . ."

By the time he was finished, he had found twenty-three different ways to describe himself. Of all twenty-three, only one was negative: "poor father."

. . .

If Fred had been feeling slightly more expansive during that list-making, he might have added one more description: "bad boyfriend."

Perhaps others in the disaster relief field could manage some kind of balance between their careers and their personal lives, but not Fred. With the kind of obsessiveness that had been evident in him from early on—first in his love for flying, then in his dream of a military career—his commitment to disaster relief work quickly became all-consuming, everything else secondary.

Still, as secondary concerns went, women ranked pretty high for Fred. Charming and funny and obviously not suffering for self-confidence, he was more than willing, when time and work allowed, to turn his intense focus on a woman he was interested in—which often meant whatever woman was standing close by.

"He had this way of making you feel like you were the center of the universe," recalled one woman who briefly dated him in the early 1980s, "that he couldn't take his eyes off you and that everything you said was just the smartest thing he'd ever heard. And, of course, he'd always tell you he was only interested in intelligent, beautiful, independent women, so who was going to argue against that? It was pretty seductive."

Over the course of his twenty years on the road there were to be a string of romances—with fellow relief workers, journalists, nurses, diplomats. Most followed a similar pattern of rise and fall. Many women found themselves initially infatuated with the take-charge Texan swashbuckler and storyteller, a man who, for all his braggadocio, had an incongruously gentle, quiet manner about him. Gradually, though, disillusionment set in as they realized Fred was never going to settle down or leave the field. Several other relationships foundered on the simple exigencies of the humanitarian aid profession, Fred heading off to the latest disaster zone or the woman taking on a long-term assignment halfway around the world.

Mike Huston recalled getting together with him in the early 1990s, at a time when Fred had just begun a new relationship with a woman.

"He was really excited about her," Huston said, "kept talking about how smart and vivacious she was, that he loved her and she loved him back. So finally I asked, 'So is she the one, Fred? Are you gonna get married?' And he just got this kind of sad look and said, 'No, there's no point. It just wouldn't work out.' "

In his North Dallas office, Huston stared out over the city.

"And that's why I say I think Fred was the most passionate man I ever met, passionate enough to make any sacrifice. He wanted to be a happily married dad, a husband and a dad. Even as a boy, he wanted those things. But he was willing to sacrifice them, sacrifice anything, because he believed in something, and no price was too great. And he paid a great price."

. . .

Sitting at a window table in a Washington, D.C., restaurant, Jinx Parker chose the words to describe her gradual drifting away from Intertect and Fred Cuny with careful tact.

"All along we'd been trying to build a company, and one of the things you do to build a company is develop certain kinds of expertise and apply it. But I think somewhere there in the mid-eighties, Fred had gotten away from the idea of really establishing a company and began to focus much more on how he was going to make his reputation. Where did he want to take himself? Well, Fred always wanted to be out on the cutting edge, and by then the cutting edge was complex emergencies."

Or, as Fred himself was more likely to call them, "man-made disasters"—namely, wars.

In 1982, Fred's friend Tex Harris had been named the director of a new branch in the State Department's Bureau for Refugee Programs, the Office of Emergency Operations. Joining him there was Don Krumm.

"The idea was that we were seeing more and more of these refugee crises around the world," Krumm said, "and there really wasn't any one office that was dealing with them at their infancy. Once the crisis was full-blown, sure, there were all kinds of outfits that got involved, but not in the early stages when some kind of intervention might lessen the crisis." In the State Department cafeteria, Krumm smiled. "Well, it sounds good on paper, but the fact was, Tex and I didn't know that much about it. So Tex said, 'Let's bring in someone who does,' and that was Fred."

With his newfound allies in the State Department, Fred began to steer Intertect away from its original niche market—natural disaster preparedness and recovery—and toward the far more complex arena of coping with those disasters brought on by war. This meant Intertect consultants increasingly found themselves in some of the most dangerous and politically sensitive corners of the world. In 1984 the Dallas company was awarded a contract by the U.S. Agency for International Development to assess the aid programs for refugees in the war-torn Central American country of El Salvador. That same year it was hired by the UN High Commissioner for Refugees to help coordinate relief efforts in the war-induced famine plaguing the eastern provinces of Sudan—a posting that quickly led to more famine relief work in the neighboring war-wracked country of Ethiopia. By 1987, Fred was shuttling back and forth between his continuing relief operations in the Horn of Africa nations and a new project in the shattered Batticaloa region of eastern Sri Lanka, trying to relocate thousands of villagers and small farmers displaced by that Asian nation's vicious civil war.

Fred was drawn into the more difficult—and obviously far more perilous—field of "complex emergencies" by a blend of factors. Certainly part of the pull, as Jinx Parker suggested, was a desire to be at the vanguard of his profession, a reflection of both his quest for recognition and his intense restless streak. As he told Jinx on many occasions, he quickly became bored if he ever had to do the same thing twice. After fifteen years of leading disaster preparedness seminars, designing earthquake-resistant homes, overseeing postdisaster housing projects, and railing against the traditional humanitarian aid system, Fred probably figured he had effected as much change and won as many disciples and enemies as he was likely to in the natural disaster realm. Then, of course, there was the certain, adrenaline-kicking excitement that comes with being in a war zone, that oddly addictive sensation shared—if not readily admitted to—by most of those who find themselves voluntarily returning again and again to dangerous places: that life is somehow made richer and fuller by the ease with which it might end.

But probably the greatest lure was that it was in the man-made disaster zones of war that Fred saw the greatest chance to radically transcend the traditional relief worker's role, not merely cleaning up in a disaster's aftermath, but working to limit the effects while it occurred—even, perhaps, improving on what had existed before. This, in fact, was simply a logical extension of a political concept he had adopted very early on in his career, the concept of disaster as opportunity.

Like many of the other Young Turks who had entered the relief field informed by the social upheavals of the 1960s, Fred had quickly come to view the tragedies brought on by so-called natural disasters not as events of nature at all, but rather as symptoms of poverty and social injustice. As he pointed out to anyone who would listen, there was a very good reason why almost everyone who died in the two major Central American earthquakes of the 1970s—Nicaragua in 1973, Guatemala in 1976—had been among the poorest citizens. With wealth and land concentrated in very few hands, the poor had been forced to scratch out an existence on the most unstable ground, living in badly constructed homes that would—and did—collapse around them when calamity struck. What Fred and other reformers had advocated after witnessing the devastation in Central America was seizing on the "opportunity of disaster" to build not only better houses but better societies.

In the aftermath of a disaster, he had pointed out, much of the traditional economic system was severely disrupted, and land prices almost always plummeted. In countries where land and wealth were concentrated in a few hands, what better time to institute agrarian reform or establish new cottage industries? Once the immediate physical crisis had been dealt with, Fred had argued, relief agencies should not be distributing food or medicines or blankets, but rather using their funds to buy up land to redistribute to the poor and landless, and taking advantage of the economic ruptures to help the previously disenfranchised start small businesses.

What Fred had failed to appreciate—or, more likely, had refused to accept—were the profoundly ideological considerations that had driven the American government's humanitarian aid policy since the beginning of the Cold War, and it would be hard to find two more naked examples of this than Nicaragua and Guatemala. In the 1970s, both were among the most economically inequitable nations to be found anywhere in the world, the poor and landless majority kept in place by brutal military dictatorships—but dictatorships that had had the good sense to proclaim themselves as pro-Western anti-communists. Quite simply, the American government didn't much care how unjust these societies were, so long as the political status quo was maintained.

In such an environment, Fred's idea for using disasters as catalysts for social and political reform had hardly found a receptive audience among the aid agencies of the American government; instead, it had helped cement his reputation as a malcontent and provocateur—and, given his dangerous talk of agrarian reform and wealth redistribution, quite possibly a provocateur with Red leanings. At the same time, it seems that Fred, the outsider with liberal ideas, hadn't fully appreciated just how ferociously repressive such dictatorships could be. In Guatemala, for example, as benign an activity as teaching Indians to read and write or digging a water well for peasants could be deemed a subversive act by the right-wing government; in fact, several Guatemalans who had been trained during the Oxfam project in 1976 and gone on to work with the poor were later murdered by the government's death squads.

While such realpolitik Cold War considerations in dispensing humanitarian aid had certainly not changed by the 1980s—if anything, they became even more codified under the Reagan administration—the field of "complex emergencies" appeared to afford a lot more maneuvering room. With a natural disaster like a hurricane, all the emergency preparedness seminars in the world could only have a mitigating effect; hurricanes would still strike and people would either have hurricane straps on their homes or they wouldn't. With man-made disasters, nearly every consequence—whether it was sudden floods of refugees or famines or disease epidemics—had the potential to be averted if the right kind of pressure was brought to bear at the right time. Likewise, the aftermath of war afforded even more opportunity for the sort of bold social and political changes to a society that Fred had long wanted to see undertaken in the aftermath of natural disasters. In essence, Fred's steady steering toward man-made calamities in the 1980s was not a departure from the years he had spent combating natural ones but a logical progression, born of the same impulse that had led him into the field in the first place: the reformer's passion to make bad places better.

SET A RECORD
1. In an unlimited hydroplane.
2. For a flight (speed or distance or precision).
3. For some zany thing.

. . .

But, as others have discovered, changing the world doesn't come easy.

If the humanitarian aid powerbrokers had been timid and un-imaginative in their response to earthquake reconstruction or refugee camp design, they were even more so when it came to assuming an advocacy role in a conflict zone. In war zones, there was not just local intransigence or the corruption of thieving government officials to deal with, but warlords and gangs of soldiers and "freedom fighters" armed with Kalashnikovs. And if political considerations had figured promi-nently in the American government's aid policies in the 1970s, the Reagan administration had raised the ideological litmus test to new heights, and nowhere more so than in zones of conflict: all sorts of money were available to consolidate the "democracy" of El Salvador, for example, while crises in war-torn countries deemed ideologically unreliable, such as those in the Horn of Africa, could continue to fester indefinitely. In the man-made disaster zones of the world where Fred increasingly found himself in the 1980s, he was rarely able to do much more than work at the margins of problems.

Still, he labored to make changes where he could. In war-ravaged Sri Lanka he hammered out a revolutionary cooperative agreement among various relief organizations, getting them to pool their efforts and resources, then pressured both government soldiers and the Tamil Tiger guerrillas to allow refugees to return to their homes with at least a modicum of security. In Ethiopia he initiated a novel "local purchase" grain program that involved buying food from the more prosperous regions of the country and redistributing it in the drought-stricken ones, a strategy that both reduced the need for costly emergency airlifts and helped bolster the local economy. And, as befitting the world's "Master of Disaster," he continued to be called upon—or simply happened to be on the scene—when new calamities struck. Tex Harris, his friend and benefactor in the State Department's refugee office, recalled the day in September 1987 when Fred arrived in Durban, South Africa, shortly after Harris had taken up residence there as the U.S. consul general.

"He was coming back from some work in Sri Lanka, but Fred was always trying to visit places he thought were potential disasters, so he wanted to see South Africa and get a feel for the lay of the land. So I met him at the airport, and I don't think we'd even gotten out of the parking lot before it started to rain. I'm not talking rain, I'm talking a two-hundred-year flood—tens of thousands of people homeless, homes destroyed, rivers out of their banks—just absolute chaos. So I called up OFDA [USAID's Office of Foreign Disaster Assistance] and said, 'We've got an emergency here, we've got a disaster, but I've got Fred Cuny in my guest bedroom and I want a contract for him.' They said, 'Done,' and Fred went down and took over a garbage bag factory and turned it into a manufacturing operation for plastic sheeting, then started giving briefings for all the relief people who were coming in. He rented an airplane, went around, did some surveys, it was just incredible. I mean, here some crisis comes along and you've got Fred

Cuny staying in your guestroom—a huge stroke of luck for everybody."

In 1988, when a massive earthquake devastated the Soviet republic of Armenia, leaving some 25,000 dead and a half million homeless, the head of the Office of Foreign Disaster Assistance, Julia Taft, immediately arranged to have Fred on board the first emergency relief airplane.

"We got there even before the Soviet army had arrived," Taft recalled, "and one of the first things Fred did was organize the Young Pioneers [Communist Party youth group] to act as the distributors of aid. Then he went out into the countryside and saw that the small farmers were camping out in the fields, that they'd put their animals inside whatever houses remained so they wouldn't freeze to death. We'd brought over all this plastic sheeting to build temporary houses, but Fred said, 'The only way they're ever going to recover from this is if they have their animals, so we'll just use the sheeting to build animal shelters.' "

Despite the unorthodoxy of the plan—and initial resistance from bureaucrats back in Washington—the sheeting was diverted to building animal shelters from a construction design that Fred improvised on the spot. Not only were the people able to move back into their homes, but the livestock, the bulwark of the local economy, were saved.

MISC.
1. Ski every major region in the world
2. Sail
   a. on a shrimper
   b. on a clipper or squarerigger
   c. on every ocean
3. Fly (as pilot in command)
   a. a light plane to S. America
   b. around the world
   c. in Alaska
   d. through the sound barrier

. . .

Early on the morning of November 9, 1989, the Berlin Wall began tumbling down. It marked an astonishing high point in one of the most profoundly important years in the twentieth century.

In just twelve months, virtually the entire Soviet bloc of Eastern European nations had broken away from their master of forty-four years. In just two more years even the Soviet Union itself would no longer exist, a colossus collapsed under the weight of both external pressures and rot from within. And just like that, with a speed that few could have possibly imagined, the Cold War that had held the planet in thrall for nearly a half century was coming to a close.

For Fred Cuny, a man who had spent nearly two decades in a profession defined by chaos, the unfolding events in Eastern Europe presented yet another opportunity to try to change the way the world worked. At last freed from the old Cold War ideological constraints, there now could be created a "new world order," a partnership between governments and militaries and private organizations that might finally tackle the true, underlying problems that afflicted the disaster zones of the world. And, as one of the architects of that new order, Fred might finally reach the height he had always dreamed of, a man recognized and listened to by his peers, a player standing at the vortex of great events.

At least initially, it appeared Fred might be proven right.

MISC.
4. Ride
    a. camel
    b. elephant
    c. llama
    d. hovercraft
    e. blimp

5. Drive
    a. across U.S.A.
    b. from U.S. to S.A.
    c. Alaskan Highway
    d. in an auto race
6. Make love to the most beautiful women in the world.

CHAPTER 5

*In the early days of the Kurdish relief operation, there was
an air of mystery about Fred Cuny. . . . He seemed to be
everywhere, this tall man from Dallas with graying hair, blue
jeans, and serious cowboy boots.*

"CIA, gotta be," ventured one journalist.

*"This guy is beyond CIA," responded another. "He actually
knows what he's doing."*
—the Dallas Morning News, July, 1991

OVER THE YEARS, many of those closest to Fred—his parents and
brothers, friends and girlfriends—had wondered what it might take to
get him to settle down in one place for a while. In the 1990s an answer
of sorts would be revealed: military siege. For some twenty months
Fred would make a home for himself in the Bosnian capital of Sarajevo,
and in that desperate, war-shattered city he would enjoy a degree of
permanence, even domesticity, he had not known in half a lifetime.

But it would not be that simple. In the span of less than four years and in three different forsaken corners of the world, Fred would experience both the greatest triumphs and most bitter disappointments of his life. In Iraqi Kurdistan he would be instrumental in devising one of the most spectacularly successful rescue missions in history, one that would save countless thousands of lives. In the famine relief operation in the East African nation of Somalia he would be shunted aside and fiasco would unfold almost precisely as he had predicted. On the battlefield of Bosnia there would be a blending of triumph and defeat, the place where he would finally begin to attain the fame he had always sought, but also the place that would shake his optimism to its core, that would instill in him a bitterness that would never leave. And in the story of Fred in these three disparate places, the victories he achieved and the setbacks he endured, would lie the clues to why he could not stop, why, when the next disaster came along, he would go to it—ultimately why, having survived the hell of Chechnya once, he had to go back.

. . .

When Lt. Colonel Mike Hess first learned that a delegation of experts was flying in to Incirlik air force base in southern Turkey—something out of Washington called the Disaster Assistance Response Team, or DART—he was not at all pleased. It was April 13, 1991, and Mike, a forty-one-year-old American army reservist attached to the U.S.-European command staff, was staring into the face of an unfolding catastrophe of epic proportions. Scattered through the nearby mountains of northern Iraq was a vast and increasingly desperate population of Kurdish refugees—perhaps a quarter-million, perhaps two million, no one really knew.

Their presence there was a direct result of the actions—and then the inaction—of the United States Government, and mass death on those mountains would be a horrendous epilogue to the triumph of the Gulf War against Saddam Hussein. To forestall that, the American military had embarked on a massive rescue effort, and the last thing that

Hess or anyone else involved in the operation needed right then was some group of civilian "experts" getting in their way.

"We all just felt overwhelmed at the time," Hess remembered. "We were trying to do a relief operation where we had no idea how many people were in the mountains, no idea where the camps were, or even what their needs were. All we knew was they were dying at extremely alarming rates and every delay in the operation meant X number more people were going to die. So, no, I don't think any of us were real excited about having these guys come in who were going to take up more of our time."

So hard pressed was the rescue effort operating out of Incirlik that the base commander initially refused permission for the DART plane to land, arguing that all landing time had to be reserved for relief supply flights, only to be overruled by the American Embassy in Ankara.

But for Mike Hess and the others working to save the Kurds in northern Iraq, opinions about the DART advisers would swiftly change. Created by USAID's Office of Foreign Disaster Assistance (OFDA), the Disaster Assistance Response Team was a select group of some of the most accomplished civilian and governmental relief experts to be found, designed to act as a kind of rapid-reaction force in the face of calamity. Heading the DART team that landed at Incirlik on April 13 was Dayton Maxwell; second in command, and officially designated as adviser to the chief of staff, was Fred Cuny.

"Well, it became apparent very quickly that these guys had forgotten more about humanitarian relief operations than most of us ever knew," Hess said. "Dayton was a very quiet guy, very bright and thoughtful, and, of course, Fred was larger than life. He had a very engaging personality—he made it very clear he was a Texan—and I just knew right off he was going to be an incredible asset to the mission. In fact, he and I started working together from the minute the DART team came in."

Within a matter of days Fred Cuny would assume a de facto leadership role in Operation Provide Comfort, the joint civilian and military effort to save the Iraqi Kurds. Over the course of the next three months—through ingenuity, tireless effort, and a fair amount of insubordination—he would achieve what most thought impossible.

. . .

It is one of the most hauntingly beautiful places on earth, a vast expanse of snow-capped peaks and meadowed foothills cut by deep river gorges, a land of ancient stone villages nestled in green valleys. Yet Kurdistan is also a place cursed by history and location, its fiercely independent mountain people seemingly destined always to be pawns of their more powerful neighbors.

While its furthest reaches extend into corners of Syria and Armenia, the heart of Kurdistan is the Zagros Mountains, a massif of rugged peaks spanning the confluence of three countries: Turkey, Iran, and Iraq. Against these three nations the Kurds have waged an almost perpetual series of wars for independence or autonomy, and they have always lost. In turn, each of these nations has alternately viewed the Kurds as enemies to be destroyed or as useful pawns for fomenting trouble in the other two; when the pawns are no longer useful, they are simply abandoned and left to their unhappy fate.

In this vicious cycle of intrigue and betrayal, the United States has played a consistently ugly role. In the mid-1970s, CIA advisers helped the Shah of Iran arm and train Kurdish fighters under the leadership of their legendary chieftain, Mullah Mustafa Barzani, in a war against Iraq, part of a complex gambit by the Shah to force territorial concessions from his neighbor. When the Shah and Iraq's Baath regime made a secret peace, the Kurds were offered up in sacrifice, their supply lines into Iran abruptly cut; Barzani, a man who had fought at least fourteen wars in his lifetime, was spirited out of Kurdistan at the last minute and ended his days in a CIA-provided tract house in Oakton, Virginia. By the 1980s the American government found itself on the other side of the Iraq–Iran divide, quietly supporting Saddam Hussein as he waged an eight-year war against the Islamic fundamentalist regime that had come to power in Iran; once again the Kurds were made to suffer.

When Hussein launched his 1988 Anfal campaign against the Kurds—a brutal pogrom in which hundreds of Kurdish villages were razed and thousands of civilians murdered with poison gas—the Reagan administration offered up only the meekest of protests. And certainly every American administration since that of Harry Truman has found it best to look the other way whenever Turkey, a bulwark in the NATO military alliance, has launched its own often-bloody attacks on the Kurds.

Their sad history notwithstanding, in March 1991 the Kurds of Iraq were emboldened to believe their luck was about to change. They were terribly wrong.

In just six weeks the vast multinational army assembled in the Persian Gulf for Operation Desert Storm had shattered the vaunted war machine of Saddam Hussein. In the euphoria, two groups long persecuted by the Iraqi dictator—the Shi'ite Arabs of the southern marshes, and the Kurds in the northeastern mountains—rose up in revolt, quickly chasing the demoralized Iraqi troops from their territory.

But by then Saddam Hussein had played his last card, finally accepting the cease-fire terms offered by the Bush administration, and the Desert Storm juggernaut closing on Baghdad had stopped in its tracks. Left virtually defenseless as the Iraqi army regrouped were the Kurds and "marsh Arabs." Within days, and as Desert Storm alliance forces stood by, the Iraqi dictator hurled his troops against the rebels, exacting a cruel revenge. For the Shi'ites in the south there was little escape, and for the Kurds in the northern mountains the prospects were only slightly better. By the end of March, hundreds of thousands had fled their homes before Hussein's onslaught, fleeing over snow-packed mountain passes for the Turkish border.

Once again, however, the Kurds were to discover they were a people with few friends. With its own large and very restive Kurdish population, the government of Turkey had little interest in seeing more Kurds on their land; as the refugees reached the frontier, most found their path to sanctuary blocked by Turkish troops. With nowhere to go, the Kurds simply huddled in the mountains along the border, and there they began to die in droves: from the cold, from starvation, then from dysentery. By the beginning of April the Kurds of Iraq, a people who had so recently been celebrating their liberation from a murderous dictator, were dying at the rate of several hundred a day.

Spurred by an international outcry, the American government announced the beginning of Operation Provide Comfort on April 6, and the next day U.S. military cargo planes, along with British and French transports redeployed from the Gulf, made their first air drop of supplies to the Kurdish refugees. Six days later, as the magnitude of the crisis became increasingly evident, Fred Cuny was summoned to the mountains.

. . .

When the call came to head for Kurdistan, the fallout of Saddam Hussein's invasion of Kuwait had already dominated Fred's life for some time. In the buildup to Desert Storm, he had been hired by the USAID's Office of Foreign Disaster Assistance as part of an advance humanitarian aid team that was to go into Kuwait in the invasion's immediate aftermath. For several weeks that assignment had meant waiting in Saudi Arabia largely confined to a military base; when the coalition ground forces finally rolled into Kuwait City in late February, Fred and the rest of the OFDA team were among the first civilians allowed in.

While he would later intimate to friends that his gilded-cage existence in Saudi Arabia—complete with a military escort "shadow" and a top-secret security clearance—was the result of his involvement with planning details of Desert Storm, the actual reason was a bit more complex. In fact, Fred had been selected for one of the most politically sensitive tasks to accompany the "liberation" of Kuwait: to help protect its Palestinian population from bloody reprisals by the reinstated, pro-Western government. In this regard, he had a degree of success. While scores of Palestinians were murdered or arrested in the days following the restoration of the Kuwaiti sheikhs to power, Fred and the other OFDA consultants detailed to the antireprisal mission undoubtedly saved a great many lives.

But very quickly Fred's expertise had been more urgently needed elsewhere. In late March he was dispatched to southeastern Iraq, there to assist the tens of thousands of Shi'ite Arabs and dissidents fleeing the marshlands before the advancing Iraqi army. Then an even worse crisis burst forth—Kurdistan—and his assignment changed yet again.

When Fred and the rest of the Disaster Assistance Response Team arrived at Incirlik air base on April 13, the Allied military units involved in Operation Provide Comfort were pursuing a simple two-phase approach to the crisis: first, launch a massive air-drop of basic relief supplies—food, medicine, and blankets—to stanch the loss of life, then get medical and construction units up to the camps to establish some basic level of coordination and infrastructure.

Almost immediately, however, Fred and others in the DART team saw that, if the goal was not just to contain the crisis but actually end it, a vital third phase was required: to get the Kurds down off the mountains.

"The ultimate problem wasn't food, and it wasn't shelter," Mike Hess said, "it was water. The only water up there was snow, and once that snow pack quit—and here we are in the middle of April, so you know it's going to quit soon—those people were finished. Absolutely done."

Where it got interesting was in trying to imagine just where the refugees might go, because the region posed a truly unique set of problems. If the Kurds couldn't stay where they were, there was also no way that Turkey or another country in the area was going to resettle them on their territory. And even though most of their villages had not been badly damaged in the war and could be returned to those villages were now firmly in Iraqi hands.

What the DART advisers advocated was building on the no-fly zone the Allies had already imposed on Iraq in the region by creating a "security zone" in the Iraqi lowlands just across the Turkish border, a staging area that the Iraqi army would be forced to leave and which would be occupied by American and Allied troops. Then, while maintaining a bare minimum of services at the fetid camps along the frontier, much better "transit camps" would be built in the security zone in order to lure the Kurds down to where they could be better cared for, and then transported back up to their villages. For the operation to work, Fred pointed out, it had to be implemented at once so that the Kurds could get home in time for spring planting; a delay of even a few weeks could mean the loss of an entire harvesting season. If that happened, a whole new relief operation would have to be conducted in the region or, worse, the Kurds would have to remain in temporary camps for another year—and, as Fred knew from long experience, "temporary" refugees have a way of turning into permanent ones very quickly.

The plan wasn't greeted with a lot of enthusiasm at the Pentagon. Already worried about "mission creep," the creation of a security zone within Iraq raised the specter of a whole new round of fighting with Saddam Hussein's soldiers just as Desert Storm was winding down. While the DART advisers won over the senior military officers on the scene—most significantly, the overall ground commander, Army Major General Jay Garner—there was considerable resistance higher up the chain of command—and the crucial days were ticking by. Finally Fred took the plan straight to the U.S. ambassador to Turkey, Morton Abramowitz, one of the most respected and influential diplomats in the Bush administration. Now the president of the Carnegie Endowment for International Peace, Abramowitz remembered the day Fred cornered him at a coffee shop on the Incirlik air base.

"I was down there meeting with some of the [military] commanders when Fred came in. I didn't really know him—I'd maybe met him once or twice before—but I certainly knew his reputation, and he just sat down across from me and said, 'I've got a plan that'll get all the Kurds back home in two months.' And I said, 'Well, that's great, Fred, but you're full of crap. That'll never happen.' But then he just started talking—which was something Fred liked to do—and after about two hours he even had me convinced that it might work."

One reason it could work was that Fred's plan neatly dovetailed with a much greater foreign policy concern of the Bush administration. Turkey, a vital cornerstone in the NATO military alliance, was growing more resentful of the Kurdish refugees massed on its border by the day, fearful they would add to its own "Kurdish problem"; if Turkey began launching punitive strikes against the refugees, as some of its senior military commanders were darkly suggesting, it could cause devastating rifts within NATO. After their meeting at the Incirlik coffee shop, Ambassador Abramowitz quickly got in touch with the White House and State Department. On April 19, just one week after the DART team had arrived to take stock of the situation, Operation Provide Comfort was dramatically expanded to include a militarized security zone in northern Iraq. It represented Fred's first crucial victory over the advocates of caution.

· · ·

Just after two o'clock on the afternoon of April 19 an eight-man advance unit of Provide Comfort operatives, including Fred Cuny and Mike Hess, was choppered across the Turkish border and dropped into the newly declared security zone of northern Iraq. They quickly discovered a couple of problems. Not only had they been left in the wrong place, but a wrong place that was right next to an Iraqi fort whose troops had apparently not received word to pull out of the area. As the advance unit walked through wheat fields toward their rendezvous point with a Marine detachment, the wary and heavily armed Iraqi soldiers began coming out of the fort to watch them.

"One of our guys was a little nervous," Hess recalled, "so I said, 'Don't worry, the A-10s [ground support planes] are only an hour away.' Well, Fred just started laughing his ass off. He loved that. As a matter of fact, later on he got us all T-shirts made, and that was the slogan on it."

Finally linking up with the Marine detachment, the group set up camp that first night in a field just below a hill dominated by another Iraqi unit that hadn't pulled back, a dug-in mortar battery. It was not an optimum site. As darkness fell, the Iraqis began exchanging fire with Kurdish guerrillas on the far side of the valley, and those in the advance camp soon found themselves pinned down as 50-caliber machine gun bullets and mortar shells flew over their heads. When Hess asked Fred what they should do, the Intertect director shrugged.

"We should sleep. Ain't nothing we can do."

For the next forty-five days Fred and Mike Hess would be tentmates as their lives became an exhausting swirl of activity: overseeing the building of the transit camps, choppering back and forth to Incirlik to consult with senior Provide Comfort planners, endless visits to the border camps to try and convince the Kurdish refugee leaders that it was now safe to leave their tenuous sanctuary. A steady trickle of refugees began to come down out of the mountains and, once word got back that there was indeed a safety zone in the lowlands, that trickle became a flood.

Fred accelerated the exodus by waging his own hearts-and-minds campaign. Identifying the Kurdish elders and rebel leaders who seemed to have the most sway over the refugees, he began shuttling them through the region in army helicopters so that they could judge the security situation for themselves, then watched as whole camps of refugees quickly packed up and headed for the valley. It wasn't long before Ambassador Abramowitz in Ankara started receiving complaints about Fred from some of the military commanders in the field.

"They'd call up and say, 'Do you know what that goddamned Fred Cuny is doing? He's taking army choppers and using them to haul these guerrilla leaders back and forth. If the Iraqis find out about this, all hell's gonna break loose.' So I'd get hold of Fred. 'For Christ's sake, Fred, what're you doing? You can't do that.' And Fred would say, 'You're right, Mort, I'm sorry, I got carried away.' " In his office at the Carnegie Endowment for International Peace, Morton Abramowitz chuckled. "Like Fred gave a damn. The next day he'd go out and do it again."

Quite soon, though, Fred discovered they had made a small, but potentially calamitous, error.

In drawing the parameters of the security zone in Iraq, planners had only extended the boundary as far south as the city of Zakho. What they didn't realize, because none of their maps showed it, was that just twenty kilometers below Zakho was the far larger and more strategically important town of Dahuk, one of the "model" towns erected by Saddam Hussein in the wake of his murderous 1988 Anfal campaign against the Kurds. Not only was Dahuk home to a huge percentage of the Kurds who had fled, but the gateway to much of the rest of Iraqi Kurdistan—and at the end of April 1991 that gateway was still controlled by Hussein's soldiers.

To Fred and others, the solution was obvious—simply expand the boundary to include Dahuk—but this was hardly music to the ears of the many senior policymakers who had been leery of the security zone concept from the outset. Among those already uncomfortable with Provide Comfort's "mission creep" was Lt. General John Shalikashvili, the deputy commander in chief of the U.S. Army in Europe—and soon to become chairman of the Joint Chiefs of Staff—who had assumed overall command of the operation. After meeting with Iraqi commanders in mid-May and finding them unresponsive to the idea of vacating Dahuk, Shalikashvili appeared to be in no hurry to use the military to make them change their minds.

"It is not the preferred solution that we spread Allied forces all over the place," he told William Branigin of the *Washington Post.* "Ultimately, the solution is not to precede the Kurds into every town and village."

For Fred Cuny and the Allied commanders on the ground, however, the bottleneck at Dahuk was dire. They had succeeded in coaxing hundreds of thousands of Kurds out of the mountains, but the refugees were now overwhelming the transit camps in the security zone and refusing to venture farther; by mid-May these camps, too, were suffering outbreaks of infectious disease.

With Fred's counsel, the Provide Comfort commanders saw a potential way around the impasse; if the mayor of Dahuk could be persuaded to "invite" the Allies in, say to conduct assessments on rebuilding the town's infrastructure, then "advisers" could be sent down as a humanitarian gesture.

"So the commanders on the ground just basically did it on their own," said Kurt Schork, a Reuters correspondent who was in Kurdistan at the time. "Without any approval from up above, they got a bunch of Marines and a few [civilian] relief types together and went down to Dahuk and told the Iraqis to get the hell out—and the Iraqis did. Once that was achieved and Dahuk was in the safe area, it made Fred's whole idea a functioning thing."

When word of the renegade operation reached top commanders in Europe and the Pentagon, it reportedly caused an uproar.

"I was told that Shali [General Shalikashvili] was just incensed," Schork said, "because the military guys on the ground had not just gone off on their own but had disobeyed explicit orders not to go to Dahuk. But the story at the time was that Fred took the steam out of it by orchestrating all these calls from the other multinational brigades that were there—the French and Italians and British. So they're calling up Shali and saying, 'Well done, a brilliant stroke, you really saved the program,' and it made it very difficult for Shali or anyone else to order them back."

Even more difficult when it became clear that grabbing Dahuk was the turning point in the entire repatriation mission. Within days the transit camps in the security zone began to empty as the Kurds trekked back en masse to their homes in Dahuk and the surrounding villages.

At their first meeting at the Incirlik coffee shop, Fred had told Ambassador Abramowitz that he could have the Kurdish refugee crisis solved in two months. He wasn't off by much. On the morning of July 15, 1991, there was a brief ceremony at the international bridge between Turkey and Iraq to mark the end of Operation Provide Comfort. In less than a hundred days the Kurds who had fled to the mountains— finally determined to number around 400,000—had not only been saved from near certain death but were enabled to return to their homes and escape the grim limbo of lives as permanent refugees. As a military band played, all the top commanders of the mission marched past. There was one civilian in the front row: Fred Cuny. When he received a photograph from the Pentagon that captured the moment,

Fred had it framed and mounted directly above his desk at the Intertect office in Dallas.

. . .

If ever Fred Cuny had been given to fantasize about the perfect disaster relief mission, it probably would have looked a lot like Operation Provide Comfort. For the first time a well-coordinated and committed military team had worked in concert with the international humanitarian aid community, and together they had pulled off one of the most successful relief operations in history—not just stemming the loss of life or cleaning up the mess, but actually putting things back together again.

And, of course, Fred being Fred, any such fantasy would have had a strong personal component. In Kurdistan he had been able to bend others to his vision. He had been listened to. He had been in charge. Perhaps most of all, he had won the respect and admiration of some of the seniormost commanders of the American military.

Certainly the mission's success was partly a matter of luck, of good timing and location. As grim as the situation was for the Kurds in their mountain camps, the U.S. air base at Incirlik had been only an hour away. With Operation Desert Storm just shutting down in the nearby Persian Gulf, a virtually unlimited pool of idle manpower could be drawn on for auxiliary support, building camps or clearing roads or distributing food. Finally, with a military infrastructure in place, it had been much easier to coordinate the activities of the civilian relief groups once they began arriving on the scene.

But if Fred realized that Provide Comfort had been made possible by a unique set of circumstances, he was still enough of an optimist to believe the experience could be emulated in future disaster zones. What's more, even as he walked off the Zakho bridge on the afternoon of July 15, 1991, the rapid course of world events was creating both the need and ideal conditions for that to happen.

Since the fall of the Berlin Wall in late 1989, the shattering of the

Cold War status quo had only accelerated. By July 1991 all six of the former Warsaw Pact nations of Eastern Europe had broken free from the Soviet Union's thrall, and the dissolution had now spread into the fifteen republics that comprised the Soviet Union. Even more profound changes were soon to follow. In August, just one month after the conclusion of Provide Comfort, a failed coup against Mikhail Gorbachev would reveal the final bankruptcy of the Soviet Communist system and lead to its rapid dismantling. Before the end of 1991 the Soviet Union itself would no longer exist, fractured into its component parts.

As this new post-Cold War landscape emerged, many foresaw a new era of peace and cooperation—"a new world order" as President Bush crowed. In the realm of man-made disasters, it was possible to imagine a dramatic reduction in armed conflicts, a time when the Third World "proxy wars" which the superpowers had stoked for decades might finally be brought to an end.

Such a sanguine view was not shared by Fred Cuny. Rather than eliminating "complex emergencies," he predicted the end of the Cold War was going to spawn more. A whole lot more.

He had been eyewitness to enough of the East-West proxy wars in Africa and Asia to discern that their ideological veneer had always been just that: political labels slapped on by the rival sides to gain support from the Americans or Russians. The vaunted "end of ideology" simply meant these wars were finally going to be revealed for what they had always essentially been: ethnic conflicts, turf battles between rival governments or warlords, in some cases little more than a falling out of well-armed crime bosses. And without the chastening—or at least, paralyzing—effect of superpower involvement, these conflicts were only going to get uglier, more indiscriminate, more vicious.

Likewise, the end of the Cold War did not address what had become one of the leading causes of new wars around the globe, the rise of religious extremism. Whether it was Islamic guerrilla forces seeking to topple the secular governments of Algeria or Egypt, or Hindu extremists razing Islamic shrines in India, or Jewish settlers seeking to forcibly expand their concept of a Greater Israel into the occupied West Bank, the world was studded with religion-based flashpoints that could ignite at any moment. To this mix could now be added the virulent nationalism sweeping much of Eastern Europe and the former Soviet Union. Already, by the end of 1991, competing nationalist visions had led to open warfare in the Armenian enclave of Nagorno-Karabakh in Azerbaijan and among the federated states of Yugoslavia.

In contemplating this evolving post-Cold War landscape, Fred embraced the same activist's philosophy that he had tried to put into practice in a variety of ways over the previous two decades: that crisis represented opportunity, that it was precisely at the moment of deepest chaos and ruin that radical change could most easily be had. In the chaos accompanying the end of the Cold War, Fred saw opportunity almost beyond imagining.

In this new era, he argued, all kinds of institutions involved in disaster response—militaries, government agencies, private organizations—were going to have the chance, even the need, to reinvent themselves. Priorities had shifted, mandates had become obsolete. Without the U.S.-Soviet stalemate on the Security Council, the United Nations might finally be able to expand past its feeble charter, and the various UN agencies that dealt with disaster given new latitude. Freed from staring across the Iron Curtain, units of both the American military and its NATO allies could be retrofitted to act in disaster zones. No longer driven by the need to parry with the Soviet Union, those agencies in the American government that oversaw foreign development and assistance projects could redirect their attention, away from the alleged "bulwarks of anti-communism" and toward those Third World nations that needed support far more desperately. What Fred envisioned, then, was just the sort of civilian-military-political alliance that had proved so effective in Kurdistan, a force that could provide a coordinated response to crises and perhaps even head off disasters in the making.

Of course, such an alliance would mean huge changes within the private relief community as well. The most obvious casualty would be the relief workers' traditional stance of neutrality in war zones, especially if they worked in tandem with a Western military; just as they had in Kurdistan, relief workers would now be drawn into the very vortex of conflict and forced to pick sides.

So, a kind of trade-off. If Fred Cuny's bold concept came to pass, relief work was about to become a lot more effective, a lot more rewarding, but also a lot more dangerous. It was a trade-off Fred was willing to make; after all, he had been trying to tear down the old system for two decades.

"We've got to get beyond this idea of strict neutrality," he would tell author Christopher Merrill. "We've got to say, 'If people are in harm's way, we've got to get them out of there. The first and most important thing is saving lives. Whatever it takes to save lives, you do it, and the hell with national sovereignty.' "

But all of this was not to say that Fred was the kind of send-in-the-Marines cowboy that some of his detractors in the humanitarian aid fraternity liked to portray. In fact, just a little more than a year after walking across the Zakho bridge, he would emerge as one of the leading voices of restraint as the United States military prepared to involve itself in another foreign disaster zone: Somalia. In the process he would suffer perhaps the cruelest irony of his life.

. . .

One morning in August 1992, Fred and his son Craig were flying low over the scrublands of West Texas in Fred's four-seater Piper Comanche, bound for the tiny town of Valentine. Fred, briefly back home, had caught wind of a 320-acre ranch parcel for sale outside Valentine and wanted to look it over.

"He was always checking around to buy some piece of land," Craig said, "and that's something we'd do whenever he came back through Texas—just hop in the plane and head off to wherever he was interested in at the moment."

Just over a year earlier Fred had slipped away from the Kurdish refugee crisis for a few days and flown back to attend Craig's wedding in Austin; now, as they flew in the Piper Comanche, Craig told his father that the marriage was over. After hearing out his son, Fred was quiet for a few minutes, then asked:

"So, what do you want to do?"

Ever since Craig was a teenager, Fred had encouraged him to take an interest in the disaster relief business. It was an idea Craig had usually resisted, figuring that wherever he went he would only be seen as "Fred's son." Instead, after graduating from Southwest Texas State University, Craig had veered into broadcast journalism, becoming the weather forecaster for a local television station in Corpus Christi. Now, at twenty-five and with his marriage ending, he was looking to broaden his horizons, and one, plan he'd come up with was buying a video camera to document relief projects around the world; he would be around his father more, but he'd also be making his own way. During the flight to Valentine, Craig outlined the idea to his father.

"Well, it sounds like you should come to Somalia then," Fred said. "You can't find a bigger disaster than that right now."

By that summer of 1992 the Horn of Africa nations—Somalia, Ethiopia, and the Sudan—had been a recurring preoccupation of Fred's for over a decade. In that time he had overseen a vast array of development and relief projects in the region designed to cope with a whole host of disasters—famines, wars, droughts—and the huge refugee populations that were their by-product. Earlier that year he had signed on with USAID's Office of Foreign Disaster Assistance and had spent much of the summer on the ground in Somalia, trying to coordinate relief efforts as a new round of famine there steadily worsened. One program he was trying to initiate, "monetization," involved actually selling relief aid at discounted prices, to local merchants, who would then have an economic incentive to get it to the distressed areas. It was a controversial idea, and one that might well make an interesting video documentary. A few days after that plane trip to West Texas, Fred made his way back to the disaster zone; accompanying him this time was his son Craig.

An impoverished desert nation stretching along the coastline of northeastern Africa, Somalia has always been one of the Third World's worst "basket cases," as well as one of its most disaster-prone. A patchwork quilt of dynastic clans, it was the scene of a brutal, seemingly random cycle of war throughout the 1980s as rival warlords sliced away at each other and at the rule of longtime dictator Siad Barre. When Barre was finally forced out in January 1991 the last shred of a central government left too, and as the clan fighting intensified, famine spread over the land. By early 1992, Somalis were starving to death by the tens of thousands.

Yet the relief workers who rushed to this latest calamity in the Horn of Africa found a very different situation from any they had previously encountered. With no central government, Somalia was a bewildering assortment of mini-states ruled over by rival tribal chieftains and warlords, and for many of these men the emergency food supplies pouring in from the outside world were both an easy way to make money and a powerful new weapon of war. Before long, an estimated 80 percent of all food shipments were being hijacked—diverted away from the starving and into the warlords' storehouses—while relief workers were made to pay protection money to the gunmen in order to perform their mission or even to just stay alive. When it became clear that the relief agencies were either going to have to abandon the starving Somalis to their fate or get outside protection, the United Nations sent in a small peacekeeping force in July 1992. It was hardly enough, and international sentiment continued to build for sending a much larger force—one that would include a major contingent of American troops—to restore order.

Interestingly, some of those most skeptical of the idea were disaster relief workers actually on the ground in Somalia, and one of the most vocal was Fred Cuny.

"I think he felt they were just going to go about it all the wrong way," said Vic Tanner, an Intertect consultant who worked alongside Fred in Somalia. "Fred had spent a tremendous amount of time in the Horn, he understood how complex and treacherous the clan politics were, and he worried that the Americans would just come in and try to impose their will on the militias. That was guaranteed to back-fire."

Fred also had a range of concerns about how the military's relief effort was likely to impact the local economy. As he had long pointed out, famines were rarely the result of actual food shortages, but of breakdowns in food distribution that pushed the costs beyond people's means. This was certainly the case in Somalia. Fred's idea was to make the Somalians responsible for the distribution of food by giving them an economic stake in the mission. Not only could this reinvigorate the shattered local market, but it would greatly lessen the security need. Such a clever and sophisticated approach was unlikely if the relief operation was taken over by an international military coalition; instead, they could be expected to flood the distressed areas with massive amounts of outside food, thereby undermining the markets in the un-affected areas, and they were certainly unlikely to embrace any program that might make the clan militias even stronger.

Two more likely features of a large-scale military relief effort worried Fred. Militaries the world over were enamored with "air drops," often measuring the success or failure of an operation simply by how many tons of relief supplies they kicked out of transport planes. Not only were air drops extremely imprecise and dependent on favor-able weather, they were also incredibly expensive; for the cost of one flight of a Hercules C-130, Fred often pointed out, a transport truck with twice the carrying capacity could be bought, used countless times, then donated to local authorities once the crisis passed. Beyond that, the military would, no doubt, follow standard operating procedure and establish more fixed feeding centers in the major towns instead of moving the aid through the countryside, thereby setting in motion one of the most destructive phenomena of most famine relief operations: as those in the countryside learned of the free food to be had at the feeding centers, they abandoned their farms and fields for the towns, which guaranteed not only more refugees but another shortage of food the following year. While Fred supported the air drops and feeding stations that had already been established—the situation in Somalia was simply too dire for any alternative—he also saw the need to phase them out as quickly as possible so that the farmers would return to their villages and fields.

"Fred was really very eloquent about all this," Tanner said. "He, like everyone else, recognized there had to be some kind of security set up for the aid shipments and the relief workers, but he thought bringing in the Marines was a recipe for even more disaster."

But then, with a suddenness that stunned his colleagues, Fred completely reversed himself; by late October 1992 he decided American military intervention was the only solution to Somalia's woes after all.

As he told Vic Tanner, the epiphany had come during a tense standoff at the United Nations compound in Mogadishu when the UN's own guards, members of one of the local warlord militias, staged a mini-revolt over a pay raise, and specifically when one of the guards had trained his Kalashnikov on his son Craig. It was an explanation Fred later repeated in a letter to Veronica O'Sullivan.

"At one point, the guards pointed a gun at Craig and something in me snapped," he wrote. "The next day I called some friends in Washington and learned they were trying to influence the White House to send troops. I immediately volunteered to help, drafted the initial plan and then returned to Washington to help promote it. . . . The Pentagon increased the number of troops [for the operation] far beyond anything I thought they would ever support, but all for the better."

Curiously, Craig had a rather different memory of the incident at the UN compound. "It was kind of tense," he said, "because they were trying to 'impound' all my video gear, and there was no way I was going to let them have it. There was a lot of arguing back and forth, and at one point one of the militias kind of raised his gun up to motion me back, but it certainly wasn't an imminent life-and-death thing. Actually, it was not much different than the sort of encounters you had with these guys almost every day in Somalia."

In fact, it appears Fred had his "epiphany" quite a bit sooner than he let on; while his detailed position paper, "How the U.S. Military Could Assist Relief Operations in Somalia," began to circulate in Washington in November, he had actually written the first draft of it back in August, a full month before Craig arrived in Somalia, and two months before the incident at the UN compound.

"Frankly, I think it was probably a case of him reading which way the wind was blowing," Vic Tanner said. "Once it became clear that the Marines were coming, I think Fred wanted to be a member of the team. Part of it, I'm sure, was the hope that he could steer the military away from making stupid mistakes—and he couldn't do that if he remained in opposition—but I think he also hoped, that by coming on board he could play the same kind of leadership role he had played in Kurdistan."

Indeed, with Bill Clinton sailing toward the presidency that autumn, it appeared Fred was suddenly harboring grander ambitions. On a number of occasions he told Craig that he thought the new administration would tap him as the next ambassador to Somalia. To Veronica O'Sullivan, he set his sights a bit higher.

"I think they are going to offer me the job of Director of the Office of U.S. Foreign Disaster Assistance," he wrote. "I am hoping to be offered Deputy Assistant Secretary of Defense for Peacekeeping, but I think that is rather a long shot."

Whatever combination of factors had inspired it, Fred's position paper on Somalia revealed his extraordinary talent for looking at a problem in all its complexity and devising a strategy against it that might work. It also revealed an understanding of what could go wrong in Somalia that would prove almost eerie in its prescience.

Expanding far beyond the issue of which relief strategies might work best and least, Fred turned to matters military. Above all else, he counseled, the American military should stay out of Mogadishu, the Somalia capital and the stronghold of an overtly antagonistic warlord, Mohammed Farah Aidid.

"The most troublesome element is the likelihood of sniping," he wrote. "The most likely place for sniping will be Mogadishu since it alone offers concealment and escape possibilities."

The expeditionary force should also make every effort to inform the various factions of their movements, Fred pointed out, so as to avoid confrontations that might draw it into the fighting. "The purpose of the intervention is to save lives, not increase the level of violence or direct it to the outside [American] forces. Thus, all military activities in support of humanitarian operations should be planned to avoid contact with armed elements, operate only in relatively secure areas, and not conduct activities that surprise the warring factions."

Fred had written the paper at the behest of his most important advocate in the American political power structure, Morton Abramowitz, who had left the ambassadorship in Turkey to become president of the Carnegie Endowment for Peace. In mid-November, just as the American military expedition to Somalia was reaching its final planning stages, Abramowitz began circulating Fred's paper among senior policy planners at State and the Pentagon, and arranged for a somewhat modified version to reach the desks of the National Security Council. Soon after, Fred's comprehensive list of suggestions—dubbed the Cuny plan—was the object of favorable editorials in several American newspapers.

Yet, to an almost uncanny degree, nearly every recommendation Fred made would be roundly ignored, as if military planners had carefully pored over his report and then elected to do the precise opposite. No doubt Fred felt a twinge of foreboding upon hearing General Colin Powell, the chairman of the Joint Chiefs of Staff, describe the upcoming operation to reporters in early December.

"It's sort of like the cavalry coming to the rescue," Powell said, "straightening things out for a while and then letting the marshals come back in to take things under control."

On the evening of December 9, U.S. Marines stormed ashore in Mogadishu—the one place Fred had urged they avoid at all costs—and made Farah Aidid's stronghold their own headquarters. Moving into the interior, they took control of feeding stations in the major towns; that made relief operations and the feeding stations much safer, but also made refugees far more reluctant to return to their villages and start spring planting. Refusing to countenance either Farah Aidid's authority or that of other warlords, the coalition forces soon found themselves the targets of sniper attacks and hit-and-run raids by gunmen in "technicals," or machine-gun-mounted pickup trucks. Through 1993 the tension and violence steadily escalated, culminating in the ambush and killing of two dozen Pakistani peacekeeping troops by Farah Aidid's militiamen in June. With the UN issuing an arrest warrant for Aidid, the Marines launched a series of unsuccessful sorties to capture him that summer and autumn. What had started as a mercy mission had now become a cat-and-mouse guerrilla war, the American-led coalition forces not only enmeshing themselves in the byzantine clan politics of Somalia but turning most of the residents in Mogadishu against them.

In this regard, the military planners had not only ignored Fred's advice of the previous year, but an essential tenet he had been espousing since the very first days of the post-Cold War era.

"Under no circumstances," he had warned a conference of UN peacekeeping commanders in November 1989, "should foreign military commanders allow their forces to become identified with one side or the other when they are in a peacekeeping or [relief] delivery role. . . . To do so will destroy their credibility and draw them into a conflict which they cannot win."

In Somalia, the ugly denouement came on October 3, 1993, when an elite Army Rangers and Delta Force raiding party sent to seize a group of Aidid's lieutenants was ambushed in the streets of Mogadishu. By early the next morning, 18 American servicemen were dead, and another 72 wounded. Eager to escape the morass he had inherited from the Bush administration, President Clinton would quietly pull the last American soldiers out of Mogadishu five months later. Over the life of the operation, 29 American soldiers had been killed and over 150 wounded.

For Fred Cuny, the fiasco in Somalia was a tremendous professional blow. In Kurdistan in 1991 the American military had been instrumental in one of the greatest relief triumphs of the century, and

Fred had entertained hopes that it might lead to a new alliance in dealing with disasters. Now, with the American military suffering a humiliating defeat while performing another relief operation, such hopes dimmed to barely a flicker. It would be a long time before either American government officials or the public would warm to the idea of sending their soldiers on another faraway humanitarian mission.

But the fiasco had been a personal blow to Fred as well. His dramatic about-face on the issue of military intervention had hurt his credibility among many of his relief colleagues and contributed to his growing—and clearly not totally warranted—reputation as a "hawk." If part of the motive for that about-face had been to secure a policymaking position in the Clinton administration, that had not happened; no offers of ambassadorships or high-level desk jobs in Washington were forthcoming. Most unfairly of all, considering how thoroughly Fred's advice had been ignored, by emerging as an advocate for the military operation, the taint of its failure now attached to him. In the opinion of his colleague Vic Tanner, Fred had managed to get the worst of all possible deals in Somalia.

But Fred had not been there to see it. Frozen out by the American military in its decision-making and seeing that he would be reduced to one more little fish in the big relief worker pond, he had left Somalia in disgust even before the American Marines had come ashore in Mogadishu in late 1992. Instead, he now turned his energies to the latest crisis to capture the world's attention: Bosnia. There, he would begin to attain the authority and freedom of action he had always sought, not as the head of some vast civilian-military alliance but as the emissary of a powerful sharer of his ideas, a soft-spoken, somewhat eccentric Hungarian émigré who had extrapolated the teachings of an Austrian philosopher to make billions in the world's financial markets.

. . .

He was an arriviste in the field of international philanthropy, a slight, rather owlish-looking man in his early sixties named George Soros. In just a few short years he had gone from obscurity to world prominence for his vast—and increasingly controversial—displays of largesse. With his donated millions, Soros meant not merely to address society's ills, but to fundamentally change the course of society, and he found a kindred spirit in Fred Cuny.

Having fled his native Hungary following the Communist takeover at the end of World War II, Soros had graduated from the prestigious London School of Economics, then emigrated to the United States in the mid-1950s to found his own international investment fund, Quantum. Over the next quarter century he had steadily amassed a huge fortune on the international stock and currency market, and Quantum became known as one of the most daring and successful investment funds in the world.

But there had always been something about George Soros that set him apart from the typical financier. Intellectually driven and strongly influenced by the works of the Austrian science philosopher, Karl Popper, Soros had developed a personal theory, "reflexivity," that rejected the historical determinism of classic economic theory, which held that human beliefs had little effect on the course of events and that economies naturally tended toward equilibrium. Rather, Soros argued, there were occasions when the perceptions of individuals could actually dictate events, creating a disequilibrium, and triggering further events to match those beliefs. When he tried to explain the idea in a rather dense 1987 book, *The Alchemy of Finance*, no one took much notice. Much closer attention was paid after 1992 when, putting his theory into practice in a very high-stakes game of brinkmanship, he triggered the devaluation of the English pound and walked off with over a billion dollars virtually overnight.

Beyond merely using "reflexivity" to build an ever greater fortune, Soros saw it as a tool to bring about social change, to build what he called "open societies." While he had established his first philanthropic organization, the Open Society Fund, in the late 1970s, it was in the sudden collapse of the Soviet bloc nations of Eastern Europe—and then the collapse of the Soviet Union itself—that he saw the opportunity to effect events in a massive way. Although clearly grander in scale,

Soros's concept bore a striking resemblance to Fred Cuny's own chaos-as-opportunity philosophy.

In Soros's opinion, the end of the Cold War had ushered in just such a period of disequilibrium on the global political stage that he had often observed in the financial sphere—and just as he had capitalized on those economic periods to make money, so now was the time for the West to boldly seize the moment and reshape the East, specifically, to help establish free-market economies and fully functioning democracies. When he saw the moment slipping away under the laissez-faire administration of George Bush, Soros decided to do it on his own. By 1992 he had established Open Society institutes in every country of Eastern Europe and seven of the newly independent republics of the former Soviet Union, including Russia. These were not little storefront operations. Financed to the tune of some $200 million a year—in many countries, far exceeding the foreign aid offered by the American government—the Soros organization almost instantly became one of the largest and most influential agencies working for social reform throughout the former Communist world.

When it came to the bloody war in Bosnia, however, Soros was propelled into uncharted waters. Rather than funding development schemes to foster democracy or free enterprise, he was for the first time prepared to inject his money into a raging war zone in pursuit of both a humanitarian and political agenda. In December 1992 he convened a meeting of some of the world's leading humanitarian aid experts to announce he would donate $50 million over the coming year on programs to save the Bosnian nation.

By that point, it appeared to many that the outside powers capable of stopping the nine-month-old war between the Bosnian government and its Serb minority—the United Nations, the United States, the Western European governments of Britain, France, and Germany—were doing little more than standing on the sidelines and wringing their hands. In fact, the outside powers had done much worse than that; they had involved themselves just enough to ensure the war's continued savagery and stalemate, which in turn ensured their own continued timidity.

With the Serbs laying siege to the capital of Sarajevo and conducting "ethnic cleansing" pogroms in the territory they controlled, a
UN protection force had been dispatched to Bosnia, but with the nar-
rowest of mandates; they were not there to engage the combatants or
even act as peacekeepers, only to provide security for relief operations.
What no one seemed to realize right away—except, perhaps, the Serbs—
was that the UN Protection Force (UNPROFOR) also played perfectly to
the aggressor's advantage. With neither the mandate nor the weaponry
to fight, the 7,000 soldiers now on the ground in Bosnia—primarily
from Britain and France—represented nothing so much as 7,000 potential hostages should anyone else think of intervening militarily. As
the Serbs continued both the indiscriminate shelling of Sarajevo and
their massacres in the countryside, the UN troops were placed in the
bizarre position of serving as little more than chroniclers of the ongoing slaughter.

If such impotence was an embarrassing spectacle, it was not sufficiently so to spur anyone to find a remedy. Like modern-day Neville
Chamberlains, foreign diplomats and UN envoys would come away
from meetings with Serb leaders to announce that assurances had been
given and progress toward peace made, only to be immediately undercut by the Serbs' next offensive or massacre of civilians. In Washington
and the capitals of Western Europe there was a steady outpouring of
stern talk and parliamentary debate, but little by way of initiative. By
the end of 1992, Bosnian hopes were increasingly pinned on the United
States and the incoming administration of Bill Clinton who, as a candidate, had repeatedly pledged to take decisive action in ending the war.
But even before assuming office Clinton had begun to back away from
this pledge once UN and European leaders warned that such action
might endanger the UN Protection Forces already on the ground. So,
while the rest of the world dithered and debated, the bleeding of Bosnia continued. By the end of that year, with the shelling of Sarajevo
intensifying, it appeared the city—and with it, the Bosnian nation—was
on the brink of collapse.

To George Soros, the West's paralysis in the face of the Serbs'

continued aggression could only give encouragement to other ultranationalists throughout Eastern Europe and the former Soviet Union—
and, as a Jew who had lost family members in the Holocaust, he was
perhaps especially determined to see that the Serbs' ethnic cleansing
atrocities not be rewarded. In convening his panel of humanitarian aid
experts that December, he was adding his name to those trying to save
Bosnia and, with a $50 million kitty, doing it in a big way.

Among those who served on Soros's five-man advisory committee
were Lionel Rosenblatt, the president of the nonprofit group, Refugees
International, and the president of the Carnegie Endowment for Peace,
Morton Abramowitz. Very quickly they and other committee members
suggested that Soros seek out the recommendations of a man who had
been working in disaster zones for over twenty years: Fred Cuny. In
January 1993, Fred flew into Sarajevo for the first time at the behest of
Soros, and he returned with a list of recommendations that neatly fit
into the billionaire's vision.

"Up until then," Lionel Rosenblatt said, "I think we were all
basically thinking, 'How do we use this money to sustain people?' Well,
obviously, the easiest way is to spread it around to the different agencies that are already bringing in relief—the Red Cross, the aid groups—
but Fred had a very different idea. To him, the whole goal was to make
Sarajevo work again, to make it a viable city—not a city of helpless
victims, but a city of survivors, and to do that, you had to involve the
locals. Well, that's exactly the kind of thing George Soros wanted to
hear."

In early March 1993, Fred and a small team of Intertect consultants moved to Sarajevo and set to work on a range of projects designed
to bring the city back to life.

. . .

When designing the 1984 Winter Olympics site in Sarajevo, planners took advantage of an escarpment near the main stadium to build a
peculiar honeycomb-shaped complex of apartments for the visiting
athletes. At one end of this complex stood an incongruous two-story

white house. From March 1993 to October 1994 this house was dubbed the "Embassy of Texas to Bosnia and Herzegovina."

From his office window on the second floor of the "Embassy," Fred Cuny had a view directly onto one of the old Olympic practice fields. After 1984 the fields had been transformed into a park, and after 1992 the park had been transformed into a graveyard.

Even before the latest bloody conflict that returned it to world consciousness, Sarajevo had been a city imbued with two seemingly contradictory auras: one of sanctuary, the other of death.

The feel of sanctuary was both physical and man-made. Hemmed in on all sides by steeply rising mountains, settlement had always been relegated to the valley lowlands along the winding Miljacka River, the terrain dictating the modern city's awkward, tentacle-like sprawl. Situated in the very heart of the Balkans, that great shifting battleground of empires and religions and races, Sarajevo had also served as a kind of eddy amid the swirl, a backwater where disparate cultures met and intermingled. In the narrow stone streets of the old city center the domes and minarets of mosques rose alongside the towers and vaults of Catholic and Orthodox churches. In the carved pillars and cupolas of the national library, a grand red sandstone structure on the banks of the Miljacka, was the unmistakable influence of Ottoman Turkey, while the stolid, imposing edifice of the state opera house a short distance away looked as if transported from Vienna or Berlin. Until 1992 most Sarajevans were quite proud of this polyglot nature of their city, a blending of East and West tucked away in the mountainous folds of Central Europe.

Yet Sarajevo had also always been a place where the reminders of death lay, quite literally, all around. Amid its parks and in the shadows of its oldest buildings were ancient gravestones—sometimes solitary, sometimes in small clusters—the city and parkland having simply been built up around them. These graves were also strewn without apparent pattern over the steep hills that surrounded the old city center, in the ribbon of green pastureland between where the last houses ended and the pine forests began. Most were of Turkish design—high round pillars rather than flat headstones—and over the centuries many had slipped loose from their moorings to lean at precarious angles. As Fred had commented to several friends, it was possible to be almost anywhere in the old city and look up past the surrounding buildings and see the odd tilting gravestones on the hills.

Fred loved Sarajevo, but it also brought him a special sorrow, for during his time there its dueling auras of sanctuary and death were joined as never before. With the Serb attackers commanding the surrounding heights, its defenders pinned on the valley floor, those physical characteristics that had made Sarajevo a refuge had now made it a trap, and those man-made features that had made it a cultural sanctuary—its mosques and marketplaces, its library and National Theater—became special targets for destruction. During the twenty months he would spend coming and going from Sarajevo, thousands more residents would die, and the haphazard sprinkling of graves would become even more ubiquitous, filling not just the view from his office window but highway median strips, vacant lots, and neighborhood parks. The sight of those graves would haunt him, a constant reminder of both Bosnia's ongoing agony and the rest of the world's abject failure to end it.

"There was something about Sarajevo that really captured Fred," his son, Craig said, "and I think it went way beyond just the importance of the work he was doing. He felt a deep kinship with the people. He really liked the Bosnians, admired a lot about their culture, their way of life, and I think they saw that in him and it was reciprocated."

Beyond mere affection for the place, Fred would quickly become one of the most determined advocates of the Bosnian cause. To Rick Hill, Fred's deputy at Intertect, the reason was simple. "Fred always tended to see things a little black and white—good guys here, bad guys over there—and Bosnia pretty well fit that worldview of his. There was very little moral ambiguity there as far as he was concerned. It was very clear who were the aggressors and who were the victims, and he was on the side of the victims. To him, it was like the 1930s in Europe all over again, and the Serbs were the Nazis."

With Intertect operating under the official aegis of the International Rescue Committee (IRC), one of the more activist-oriented and creative nonprofit relief agencies operating in Bosnia, Fred found a lot of ways to spend George Soros's money. With nearly all food supplies being either airlifted or trucked into the city—and thus always vulnerable to the Serb blockade—he and the IRC started a seed distribution program that enabled the increasingly desperate residents to grow fruits and vegetables in their backyards or apartment terraces. Intertect engineers designed a portable gas-powered stove that doubled as a heater, a vital improvement in the cold Sarajevan winters when fuel supplies were scarce. Noticing the array of homemade—and dangerous—devices the residents had used to hook onto the city's functioning gas lines, Fred brought in planeloads of reinforced plastic piping—some 15 miles worth—and linked thousands of homes to the lines.

"That was an unbelievable project," said Aryeh Neier, the president of Soros's Open Society Institute. "Fred managed to enlist 15,000 Sarajevans to dig trenches through the streets to put in the gas lines—and this was while the shelling was taking place."

Of course, surviving a siege means enduring not merely physical deprivations but psychological ones as well. One plaintive cry that Fred often heard from Sarajevans was that their city had once been a cosmopolitan place of culture, and that their intellectual isolation from the rest of the world was almost as hard to bear as their political abandonment. In response, Intertect consultants arranged for pallets of donated literature of all kinds—novels, scientific journals, textbooks—to find their way onto the incoming relief flights, to be distributed through the Soros Foundation library.

But as might have been predicted, no matter how meaningful these small-scale projects might be to the people of Sarajevo, they weren't likely to satisfy Fred's epic sense of scale. Since the beginning of the siege, the city's main supply of well water had been cut, forcing the residents to brave sniper fire and even artillery bombardments to draw water from the river or common outdoor wells; by early 1993 hundreds of Sarajevans had already been killed in this simple pursuit.

To Fred, the shortage of water represented the city's greatest Achilles' heel, and he set about to fix it.

His remedy was not modest. What Fred envisioned was making use of the waters of the Miljacka River by bringing in three enormous water filtration modules and assembling them in relatively safe corners of the city. One site that particularly caught his eye was a road tunnel just east of the city center, half carved from a cliff face above the Miljacka. By Fred's estimation, one of the modules could be assembled inside the tunnel, then water pumped up from the river, purified, and sent on to the city's main reservoir nearby. In short order, Sarajevo would have a major new source of water, enough to reach some 250,000 residents, and the killings at the water wells could be radically reduced.

When he first proposed the idea, there were a lot of skeptics. As the pessimists pointed out, it seemed highly doubtful that the Serbs, enjoying joint control of the airport and the authority to turn back any relief shipment, would ever permit the water modules—each consisting of three separate units, and each unit the size of a semitruck—off the tarmac. Then there was the small matter of getting the module units from the airport to the city center down the long, exposed boulevard that had become known as "Sniper Alley." With Serb gunners picking off drivers going sixty or seventy miles an hour down Sniper Alley, it hardly seemed a test of their skill to hit a lumbering object the size of a house. There was also a problem with the tunnel above the river that Fred so coveted. Serb gunners controlled the heights on the other side of the narrow ravine, at most a quarter mile away, and would enjoy a completely unobstructed view of the site.

To all these concerns, expressed by many people on many occasions, Fred's trademark response was a shrug. "Well, we'll just figure it out."

．　．　．

Damir Lulo is a soft-spoken Bosnian of thirty-eight. Today he is an engineer with the Dallas-based firm of Freeman-Millican, but in

1993 he was another desperate Sarajevan simply trying to survive the brutal siege of his city. It was there that he met Fred Cuny.

"I remember it was March 17," Lulo said. "At the time I was on medical disability from the military, and so applied for a job with the International Rescue Committee. Fred was the one who interviewed me—this huge Texan guy in cowboy boots, maybe the biggest man I had ever seen—and he started talking about this big water filtration system he is going to build. I thought he was joking at first—it was like someone saying we'll build a China Wall in Sarajevo. I was also quite suspicious. I think all of us in Sarajevo had become very cynical by then of all these relief workers; they would fly in, say how sorry they were for us, make all these promises, and then leave. But Fred wasn't like that. He stayed. He did make a lot of big promises but, unlike the others, he actually kept them."

Signing on to the water project, Lulo was immediately amazed by Fred's ceaseless energy and determination. "He was this middle-aged man, almost like a father to all us young guys, but he was working sixteen, eighteen hours a day right along with us—not just supervising, but doing the work with us. I think we were all very impressed by that, and it made us work harder. And, of course, he was living as we did, facing the same dangers, going without the normal things of life."

Even in a city preoccupied with war and aswarm with the sorts of foreigners drawn to such places, Fred Cuny cut a wide swath in Sarajevo. Although his house on the escarpment above the old Olympic stadium had neither electricity nor running water, it quickly became a sort of meeting hall, a place where relief workers gathered to compare notes, and where journalists came to get the alleged inside scoop on the latest political or military developments from the "Master of Disaster." Energetically working his contacts in the American military, Fred occasionally managed to get a crate of Mexican beer and chili-making supplies aboard one of the incoming relief planes, and that night's gathering at the "embassy" would become a low-key party.

"There would always be a half dozen people hanging around the house," said Craig, who joined his father in Sarajevo in late 1993.

"Journalists, engineers, military officers, relief workers—you name it. Any time you went by, you'd have no idea of who you would find there."

At the same time, Fred could display a coolly dispassionate side, as Hazim Kasic, an official at the Sarajevo branch of the Soros Foundation, discovered.

One constant preoccupation of Sarajevans who stayed through the siege was the safety of their families, and at various times a number of people approached Fred to ask if there might be some way he could arrange to get various family members on a flight out of the city. In late 1994, Kasic was trying to get his two young daughters out of Sarajevo and to friends in the United States, but was having problems getting American visas.

"So of course, being close to Fred and knowing he had close ties to the U.S. administration," Kasic recounted, "I expected him to help me. We invited him to a dinner, carefully planned—I remember my wife cooked his favorite meal—and we had a big meal and a good time, and after a while I asked him, 'Fred, can you do anything about this?' and he just very quickly said, 'No.' That was really startling, but that's also what I appreciated about him. Instead of promising this and that and wasting my time, he just said no, and that was it, end of story."

For Fred, the rationale was simple. In coaxing favors from those overseeing the Bosnia relief operation—the American and NATO military advisers in Croatia and Germany, the UN commanders who oversaw the airlift into the city, the officials back in Washington who had a hand in formulating policy—he had a finite number of chits, and he didn't want to waste them.

Yet, on at least one occasion, Fred made an exception to this policy, a result of the last great love affair of his life.

. . .

"I remember it was one of those huge military transport planes," Sonja Vukotic said, sitting in a reception room at the Bosnian Embassy in the Croatian capital of Zagreb. "It came up to the edge of the airfield and then the back flap came down and here comes my mother and

Fred, this huge American man in cowboy boots and . . . well, it's a
very complicated thing. Here I hadn't seen my mother in a very long
time, didn't know if I would ever see her alive again, and then Fred
brings her to me. I think I probably fell in love with him right at that
moment."

The chief of staff for the Bosnian Embassy in Croatia, Sonja
Vukotic is a strikingly attractive woman in her mid-thirties, who speaks
in the carefully composed words of a seasoned diplomat. Shortly after
the war in Bosnia began she had been transferred from her Foreign
Ministry post in Sarajevo to the embassy in Zagreb—a promotion, but
one that had meant leaving behind her elderly mother. Once the siege
intensified, there had been no way to get her mother out to safety.

By lucky coincidence Sonja's brother Jesenko was a doctor hired
on to the Intertect/IRC water project, and one day he approached Fred
about trying to get his mother out of the city and to Sonja in Zagreb.
Taking pity—or, perhaps more likely, figuring that being owed a favor
by a prominent Bosnian diplomat might come in handy—Fred arranged
for the elderly woman to accompany him during his next trip to the
Croatian capital. Waiting for them at the other end was Sonja.

For the next year and a half Fred and Sonja carried on a secret
love affair—secret because a liaison between such a high-ranking Bosnian diplomat and a high-profile relief expert was bound to raise eyebrows in both their professional circles. Instead, the relationship was
carried on somewhat furtively, lent an intensity both by the war and by
the sense that they might be under scrutiny. Often going many weeks
without seeing each other, their communication was reduced to cryptic
letters and telephone calls.

But Sonja was hardly some starry-eyed ingenue who had fallen
under the Fred Cuny spell. Rather, she saw him as an extremely complex man, one driven by both compassion and his own unslaked thirst
for recognition.

"In a way," she said, "he was a romantic, very generous guy, and
he did things out of love for people—but for himself, too, to be the big
Fred. He wanted to be loved and appreciated, and the way he saw to

accomplish that was through the people who were in the zones of war and catastrophe. That way, Fred could help them, and then they would love him. But he needed to have this love from many people. One person, that wasn't enough for him. And when he did something, he wanted it to be finished—'That is enough for this country'—and then he wanted to go on and on to other war zones."

One aspect of Fred's personality that Sonja found particularly entrancing was his extraordinary bravery.

"I don't mean this in the Hollywood way of bravery, and I think maybe I felt it more because there was so much cowardice at the time; everywhere, in the West, in all the Balkans, in Sarajevo, you saw so much cowardice. But with Fred this bravery was something else, almost like a kind of illness. I would be speaking with my brother or mother by telephone in Sarajevo, and they would tell me about Fred walking through the streets in the middle of shelling, when there was not a cat outdoors. He was always smiling, so self-assured that nothing would happen to him. The neighbors would watch him going across the yard to get in his car, and he would be smiling, wave to them, while they were cowering inside."

Certainly one of the reasons why Fred stayed in Bosnia as long as he did—as well as why he managed to find so many excuses to fly up to Zagreb—was his relationship with Sonja. At one point they even discussed marriage. The main obstacle was Sonja's young son.

"My son was six and seven at this time," she said, "and there was absolutely no way I was going to leave my son, and I didn't want to go [into exile] with him to Germany. I wanted to be with my son and have my own career as a diplomat, and Fred and I couldn't find a compromise. Without that son, maybe I would have followed Fred, but with him, there was no way."

Interestingly, for a man many people considered extremely self-centered, Fred never pressed Sonja to choose him over her young son; very much the opposite, in fact.

"There was one thing that could bring tears to Fred's eyes when

he talked," Sonja said, "and that was Craig. He really had this sense
that he was a bad father. He said that he could always remember when
Craig was young and he had to travel, how Craig would say goodbye and
look through the window—'When is Daddy coming back?'—and those
things are difficult for any parent to do for two days, not to talk about
six months. He told me so many times, 'Don't leave your son, don't
make the same mistake I did.' So I didn't."

Ultimately, the relationship with Sonja ended amicably, founder-
ing on the same issues that had followed Fred throughout his life: his
inability to choose a home life over his work, his need to go do battle
against the next catastrophe.

.   .   .

Early one morning in mid-August 1993 a massive C-130 UN
transport plane came in low over Sarajevo to touch down at the airport
in its southern suburbs. Within minutes its rear hatch was opened to
reveal a massive cylindrical object that filled its entire cargo bay. The
mysterious cargo was swiftly loaded onto the bed of a waiting flatbed
semi-trailer, which then headed for the Serb "customs office" at the
airport entrance. Quickly waved through, the truck slowly lumbered
toward Sniper Alley and the city center, then the road tunnel above the
Miljacka River. The first unit of Fred Cuny's three water filtration
modules had arrived, completing a technical and political feat that few
in the besieged capital had ever imagined possible.

Six months earlier, once George Soros had signed off on the water
project, Fred had turned to the Dallas engineering firm of Freeman-
Millican to design a slightly scaled-down version of the standard filtration module, one that could be disassembled and its three main
component units made to fit into the belly of a C-130 transport plane.
After weeks of tinkering, engineers had come up with a model that fit
with barely an inch to spare. Then had begun the long, slow process of
getting the UN—the only organization the Serbs allowed to fly into
Sarajevo—to bring the modules in on their transports.

"This is where we ran into a lot of intransigence, both from UNPROFOR and the UNHCR [UN High Commission for Refugees]," said John Fawcett, the IRC director in Bosnia and the official administrator of the water project. "They were always pointing out all the potential problems—'How the fuck are you going to get them in place?'—telling us that everything had to be worked out ahead of time, but Fred's attitude was, 'If we try to work everything out, we'll end up doing nothing because the situation is always changing and we've got to do what we can now—just go, go, go,' and Fred just ran over them. He had this steamrolling effect, which he was very good at, and if someone got in his way, he'd go to the people at the top, beat 'em up, and get some agreement to push forward. And it worked."

All that, however, was the easy part; Fred still had to deal with the Serbs. Through diplomatic channels he had hammered out an agreement whereby some of the water from the project would flow into a Serb-held neighborhood on the far bank of the Miljacka River, but it was an open question of how many of the Bosnian Serb commanders in the area would adhere to the deal. Of particular concern was the Serb "customs office" at the airport. By UN agreement, all relief shipments coming through the Sarajevo airport had to have prior clearance from both the Bosnians and the Serbs, with manifests submitted in advance to be approved by senior commanders. On most any pretext, the Serbs could turn back shipments at the airport or, for that matter, blast them apart as they came down Sniper Alley.

For the task of winning over the Serb bureaucrats, Fred had turned to an IRC employee, a laconic young Englishman named Brian Steers. Of the time he had spent in Sarajevo, Steers had spent an inordinate amount of it out at the airport, cajoling the Serb customs agents into letting various relief shipments through. In the process, he had become quite friendly with many of the agents.

"The Serbs like to drink," Steers explained, "so I'd bring out some cases of beer and we'd just start negotiating. The way I got a lot of the stuff past was that I was a better drinker than them."

In the summer of 1993, Steers had given his drinking companions a manifest that simply read, "Water filters."

"Well, what's a water filter?" Steers laughed mischievously. "The Serbs didn't have a clue—probably figured it was some little piece of machinery—so they signed off on it. And then the planes come in and they're these enormous fucking tanks that fill a whole plane, and they're going, 'What the hell is that?' But at that point their higher-ups had already approved them and the guys out at the airport weren't going to countermand their superiors, so we just loaded them up and got them into the city before anyone could say anything."

With two of the filtration modules placed in protected corners of the city and the third in the tunnel above the river, Intertect engineers began the task of assembling them. Especially for those working on the completely exposed site above the river, it was a constant source of amazement that the Serb gunners, just three or four hundred yards away and in full view, never opened fire.

"Partly it was a matter of very lucky timing," Rick Hill, the deputy director of Intertect, said. "Earlier that summer, the Serbs had really put the squeeze on Sarajevo, intensified their shelling, until NATO had done some serious saber rattling and the Serbs had backed off; by the time the filters were ready to come in and be assembled they were laying pretty low. Of course, that luck had only come into play because Fred had bitten into this project and refused to let go."

John Pomfret, the *Washington Post* correspondent in Sarajevo at the time, was more blunt. "Basically, the Serbs were cowards. They were very good at killing civilians and very good at thumping their chests, so long as they knew no one was going to retaliate, but the first sign of trouble, they ran for cover. It seems pretty obvious to me that someone somewhere—in the U.S. Government or in NATO—got to them and said, 'You mess with this [water] operation, and we'll come after you.'"

Throughout the autumn and early winter of 1993 the laborers and technicians hired by IRC worked feverishly to bring the water project to fruition. Their obstacles weren't entirely cleared yet, however, and an effort to sabotage the operation would soon come from the most un- likely of sources.

. . .

One of those who spent a lot of time at the "Embassy of Texas" in Sarajevo was Fred's twenty-seven-year-old son Craig. In the summer of 1993, Freeman-Millican, the Dallas engineering firm constructing the water filtration modules for Intertect, had hired Craig and his video camera to document the effort.

"That wasn't all that interesting," Craig said, "but then I con- vinced them that I really should go over to Bosnia and video the whole installation process."

Once in Sarajevo, Craig parlayed that assignment into other cam- era work, before being hired on by IRC to act as a liaison for their various projects in the region.

"Basically, I was a glorified errand boy. A lot of going up to Zagreb and Germany—a few times over to Italy—to make sure supplies were getting on the [relief] flights."

Drawing on the same combination of personality traits possessed in such abundance by his father—charm, resourcefulness, and sheer doggedness—it wasn't long before Craig was one of the most adept supply officers working in the region.

"You soon discover the power of American cigarettes and whiskey over there. I'd fly back into Sarajevo, go up to the Serb customs guards—'Hey, how ya' doin', here's a carton of Marlboros in apprecia- tion for the fine job you're doing around here'—and pretty quick, I was able to bring in anything we needed."

While frequently working to get supplies together for his father's projects, Craig, always conscious of being perceived as "Fred's son," also took pains to stay somewhat autonomous. It was one source of tension between them.

"Fred was always like the papa," Sonja Vukotic said, "and he always wanted Craig to report where he was, while Fred would do the opposite. Fred would leave Bosnia, would go to the States without telling Craig at all, but he wanted to know every day where Craig was, and that was a big problem."

In Craig's own memory, father and son got along fairly well.

"I can only remember really going off on him one time. He was on me about something and I finally just said, 'Who are you? Where have you been the last twenty years?' I think he'd just gotten so used to being out in the field and telling people what to do—'Do this, do that'—that I was just kind of like another one of his projects."

A turning point came when Fred turned to Craig for help with a particularly nettlesome problem. For weeks, a large shipment of steel piping bound for Sarajevo had been sitting on the tarmac at the Zagreb airport, and none of Fred's usual facilitators in the Croatian capital had succeeded in budging it; with its potential conversion for military use, the Serbs at the Sarajevo customs house had already turned the pipe back once. Before heading off for a meeting in Budapest, Fred asked Craig to fly up to Zagreb and see what he could do. Arriving on the scene, Craig quickly loaded the pipe aboard trucks and took it to Split, where he sweet-talked the young woman who coordinated NATO relief flights into hauling it to Sarajevo. It was some serious sweet-talking, for the pipe entirely filled the transport bays of eight C-130s.

When Fred returned from Budapest a few days later, he called Craig.

"So, where's the pipe. Still sitting on the tarmac?"

"Yep," Craig replied, savoring the moment. "On the Sarajevo tarmac. Where do you want it delivered?"

For Craig, it was a rite of passage of sorts; he had faced the sort of impasse his father had confronted his entire life—in fact, an impasse that had stymied Fred—and had found a solution.

"I think it was things like that that made Fred realize I could take care of things on my own," Craig said. "It was in Sarajevo that we really started to become friends, not so much father and son, maybe, but two men who enjoyed each other's company."

. . .

At the same time that he found happiness in the company of his son and Sonja Vukotic, Fred became increasingly embittered at bearing witness to the ongoing slaughter in Bosnia. Never one to camouflage his sympathies, he steadily emerged as one of the most forceful—and angry—defenders of the Bosnian cause among the international relief community in Sarajevo; as for the Serb gunners on the hills, he derisively referred to them as "the Chetniks"—the name of the defeated Serb nationalist army during World War II—or, more frequently, as "the fucking Chetniks." For Fred, this war was about the most fundamental, black and white principles: not about Bosnians and Serbs, or Muslims and Christians, or even about the right to self-determination. Rather, it was a struggle between the forces of civilization and barbarism, and the rest of the world's failure to see it in those terms and act was a failure not just of will or vision but of the most fundamental morality.

Fred had long been a critic of the United Nations, finding its various agencies incompetent and unimaginative and hobbled by weak charters, but in Sarajevo his antipathy reached new heights. With each new European commander of the UN Protection Force proving more timid and appeasing than the last, he began to argue loudly for the force's withdrawal and a lifting of the arms embargo that left the Bosnians crippled. The UN envoy to Bosnia, Yasushi Akashi, had become such a dupe of the Serbs, Fred railed, he should be not only dismissed but brought up on trial for war crimes. "If the UN had been around in the 1930s," he acidly remarked on several occasions, "we'd all be speaking German."

His anger at the Clinton administration and Western Europe was only slightly more tempered—and only because he hoped for direct NATO military intervention. During each trip back to Washington he would have Morton Abramowitz arrange a series of meetings with high-ranking government officials—at the Pentagon, at the State Department, and at the CIA—where he would energetically lobby for action. The government officials would nod sympathetically, comment on how compelling Fred's arguments were, then tiptoe away, and nothing would change.

But Fred wasn't Fred for nothing. If no one else was going to work out a military plan of attack against the Serbs, he was more than willing to take on the task himself. Contacting his old high school buddy, Steve Stevenson, then a colonel in Air Force special operations, he began devising a comprehensive blueprint for air strikes against the Serb forces.

"It became a kind of hobby for him," his son Craig recalled. "He had these detailed maps and he'd get them out, pinpoint the prime targets—he wanted to take out all the bridges going into Serbia—figure out how long the different planes could stay up, where they'd go for refueling, everything. It was kind of funny in a way, because here he was working on this water project, but in his spare time—'Hey, we can win this war, we can take these Chetniks out.' "

The element of bluff notwithstanding, Fred's new "hobby" marked a stunning transformation; here was a man who had made a career out of saving lives, spending his time meticulously drawing up a plan that would cost lives. If there was a contradiction, Fred refused to see it.

On February 5, 1994, he was accompanying the ABC News anchor, Peter Jennings, through downtown Sarajevo when a mortar shell landed in the nearby Markale market, killing sixty-eight shoppers. Rushing to the market, ABC quickly began filming the spectacle, the horrific images being instantly transmitted around the world on a satellite feed. As he stood amid the horror, Fred hoped this might finally be the atrocity that would galvanize world outrage into action against the Serbs—but he also knew very well that the United Nations, and especially the new British commander in Sarajevo, Lt. General Michael Rose, would do everything possible to blunt that outrage if given the chance.

Sure enough, in the tense days following the massacre, with NATO finally threatening to take action, General Rose and other UNPROFOR officials began a whisper campaign to defuse the call to arms, suggesting they had evidence that the deadly mortar shell had actually been fired by the Bosnians themselves. Just as quickly, Fred conducted his own "expert analysis" of the shell's trajectory, then told any journalist who would listen that the mortar had been "definitively confirmed" as coming from the Serb lines. The gambit worked; Rose and his underlings backed away from their assertion—their "evidence" of Bosnian responsibility was eventually proven false—and international support for military action rose. Four days later, NATO gave an ultimatum to the Serbs to pull all their heavy weaponry away from Sarajevo. By the end of the month, NATO warplanes had shot down four Serb planes over central Bosnia, marking the alliance's first use of force in its forty-five-year history.

What Fred had become in Bosnia, then, far transcended the most liberal definition of a disaster relief expert. If he had long ago slipped the bonds of neutrality, he had now also gone past mere advocacy. He had strenuously tried to change both political and military policy toward Bosnia, and when that hadn't worked, he had gone out and created blueprints for action—and, in the case of the Markale bombing, media spin—on his own.

Not surprisingly, such endeavors added to the rumor mill within the disaster relief community, specifically that Fred Cuny was actually an American intelligence agent. Kurt Schork, the Reuters correspondent who had first wondered about Fred's true job after observing him in action in Kurdistan, recalled that the same question was a frequent topic of conversation in Sarajevo.

"People were always wondering if he was CIA," Schork said, "and Fred never discouraged the talk. It was part of the mystique, the image he wanted to put across. My feeling after a while was that it was a kind of strategy for him. It helped him build up this larger-than-life myth about himself, and it also probably helped in getting things done. Of course, the biggest argument against him being CIA—and I started figuring this out back in Kurdistan—was that he actually understood what was going on and got things done."

That assessment was neatly mirrored by the *Washington Post* correspondent John Pomfret, who had also first met Fred in Kurdistan.

"First of all, you have to believe that the CIA would be smart enough to hire a guy like Fred, and I've never seen any indication that they are. You know how you spot the CIA guys in Sarajevo? They're the ones posing as photographers with agency-issued Kodak digital cameras. None of the real photographers here have digital cameras, so that's the level of idiocy you're talking about with the CIA. The fact is, they didn't need to employ Fred because he was already doing whatever they needed—and doing it better than they could, because he cared."

Interestingly, such a nuanced, cynical view was not shared by most Bosnians who worked with Fred; for them, the idea that he was intimately connected to the highest reaches of the American intelligence and military agencies was simply an accepted "fact."

"It was very clear to all of us that Fred was here for a higher purpose," said Kenan Logo, one of the senior Bosnian engineers hired by Intertect. "The gas project, the water project, yes, these were important, but he was also here to do other, bigger things."

* * *

On the afternoon of January 4, 1994, Fred sat in a small government office in downtown Sarajevo, enduring what he would later describe as one of the most frustrating and bizarre meetings of his life. Giving the gathering a somewhat surreal edge was the fact that the day marked the heaviest Serb sniper attacks in several months, with bullets repeatedly cracking off the outer masonry walls of the building.

He had just finished work on his audacious water filtration project, the water was ready to flow, yet for the past several weeks an array of city officials had told him he couldn't turn the system on. Fred had demanded the meeting on January 4 to find out why.

For several hours he politely listened as the authorities offered up a variety of reasons, each more ludicrous than the last. As he subsequently explained to Morton Abramowitz in a long letter:

"They claim one reason the system is not safe is because we do not have a first stage settling tank to clean the water before it enters the system. We have explained repeatedly that in a pressure treatment system, it is not needed. They also claim that because the system is manually operated instead of automatic, it is dangerous, yet they cannot define what the danger is. At one point, they told us they would not allow the system to be turned on until we painted the inside of the tunnel but could not explain what relationship that had to water quality."

Fred soon began to suspect there were other issues at work behind the obstructionism, and that one of them was greed. The trucks then supplying city residents with water were given a daily allowance of extremely precious gasoline, and some of that gasoline was being diverted to the black market and selling for up to $100 a gallon. If Fred's water project came on line, there would be less need for trucks and fewer opportunities for the water authorities to work the black market.

An even more callous explanation was put forward by several UN officials: that the Bosnian government wanted the killing of civilians at the water wells to continue because the images helped maintain international sympathy for Sarajevo. If people could now get water in the comparative safety of their apartment buildings, Bosnia would lose a potent propaganda tool.

Leaving the meeting that day in disgust, Fred spent the next several weeks strenuously lobbying both city and national government officials for the water to be turned on, to little avail. Finally, after several more people had been killed by Serb snipers while standing in a water line, he turned the system on himself, only to have Bosnian authorities come and close it down within minutes. To Fred, the idea that those in power were blocking a project that would save lives—and a project that he and a number of other people had risked their lives to complete—was the most maddening frustration of the many he had suffered in Sarajevo. On a philosophical level, the callous inaction of the Bosnian government—the "victims"—challenged one of Fred's most deeply held assumptions about humanity, one that had guided and compelled him throughout his life: that people were essentially good.

It would not be until August 1994, a full eight months after the system had become operational, that water would finally flow through the Intertect modules and into the city's water supply. The following summer, when the Serbs cut off all other water sources in an attempt to bring the city to its knees, the five new filtration modules—two more had been brought in and assembled in the interim—would be credited with keeping Sarajevo from falling. In time, even those officials who had done their best to sabotage the project would switch sides and claim to have been supporters all along, and Fred's creation would be hailed as a symbol of Sarajevo's refusal to die. For Fred, though, it had undoubtedly come to symbolize something a bit more complex: the indifference of governments to human suffering, the timidity and self-interest that enabled misery to continue. In short, a pretty good symbol for the whole war in Bosnia.

. . .

In late December 1994, Fred stepped out of the Dallas–Fort Worth airport hobbling on a cane, his chest wrapped in a truss.

Two months earlier he had left Sarajevo for the last time. Sonja Vukotic had recently ended their relationship and, with NATO forces finally standing up to the Serbs by carrying out air strikes against their gun emplacements, an uneasy calm had settled on Bosnia. With talk of peace in the air, more humanitarian assistance groups were coming into Sarajevo, and it had been time for the "Master of Disaster" to move on to blacker pastures.

But in early November, while conducting an assessment study on Kurdistan for the Carnegie Endowment for Peace, Fred had been involved in a car accident in southeastern Turkey that had broken several ribs and further damaged his already damaged left leg. It was while still in pain from those injuries that he returned to Dallas. He had just turned fifty.

On this journey home, Fred, a man who had always been obsessed about the passage of time and what he wanted to accomplish, stood at a crucial crossroads. He was getting too old for the brutal rigors of the field, and a part of him had long dreamed of spending more time in Texas with his extended family and beloved airplanes. A few months earlier had seen the publication of his book, *Disasters and Development*, that had been a lifetime in the making. Already hailed as a bible in the disaster relief world, the seminal work could give him entree into any number of senior—and high-paying—policy positions in the governmental or private sphere. Over the past few years he had grown closer to his son, and he now had a grandson, Colton; as he had remarked to several close friends, he wanted to be a better grandfather than he had been a father.

In fact, Fred appeared to have been toying with the idea of leaving the field for some time—certainly his talk back in Somalia of taking a post in the Clinton administration was testament to that—but he was worried about what would happen to Intertect if he wasn't in the fore. The previous summer he had offered Vic Tanner, the Intertect consultant with whom he had worked so closely in Somalia and Bosnia, a permanent position with Intertect.

"Vic was kind of like the son Fred never had," Craig, Fred's real son, said with a laugh. "I think he really was getting kind of tired, he had all these health problems, and he saw in Vic maybe the one guy who could fill his shoes."

Tanner remembered being both surprised and flattered by the offer.

"I'd always looked up to Fred as a mentor, and there's not a lot of permanent posts in the consulting business, so on that level I felt quite honored. On the other hand, it would mean moving to Dallas, where my wife didn't know anyone and wouldn't be able to pursue her career, and I would be out in the field most of the time."

After pondering the matter for several weeks, Tanner decided against the permanent job at Intertect, but wrote Fred a long letter thanking him for the offer. It was then that he discovered something else about the man he had developed such a close bond with. Having been spurned by his protégé, Fred Cuny would never speak to Vic Tanner again.

. . .

If Fred had truly been contemplating a more subdued life, that ended abruptly with a telephone call in late January 1995. It was from Aryeh Neier, the president of George Soros's Open Society Institute in New York, and it was about another man-made disaster in a place that, until a month earlier, few Americans had ever heard of: a tiny Russian province on the northern flanks of the Caucasus Mountains named Chechnya.

But Fred Cuny had heard of Chechnya. For several months in late 1992 he had traveled throughout the former Soviet Union conducting a study of its disaster response capabilities for the U.S. State Department, a mission given urgency by the concern that many of the former Soviet republics might face famine in the coming winter. While that calamity didn't materialize, Fred had seen a whole host of other potential ones looming on the near horizon. Already by 1992 there had been outbreaks of ethnic war in several of the former Soviet republics and, from his vantage point, it appeared many more could erupt at any time; in fact, even while working on the disaster preparedness study that autumn, Fred had suddenly found himself diverted to a refugee crisis when a brutal little war between two Caucasus mini-republics—North Ossetia and Ingushetia—had created 40,000 refugees almost overnight.

For Don Krumm, Fred's old friend at the State Department and one of the officials involved in the 1992 disaster preparedness study, one of Fred's predictions would take on almost clairvoyant resonance in light of later events. It came when Fred spread a large map of the former Soviet Union over a conference table and ran a hand over the Caucasus, the patchwork mosaic of small republics and autonomous regions that nestled at the southern end of Russia.

"By that point, there was already a lot of trouble brewing in the Caucasus," Krumm said, "but I think everyone was kind of focused on the bigger places: Georgia, Armenia, Azerbaijan. But Fred points to this one tiny little spot on the map, and he says, 'Here. If things really explode, this is where it's going to start,' and the place he was pointing to was Chechnya."

Almost immediately after receiving the call from Aryeh Neier in January 1995, Fred began packing his bags. Over the previous four years, he had experienced both the greatest triumphs and greatest defeats of his life. Now he was setting off for a place where there were no rules, no safe havens, where both the perils and possibilities stretched to an endless horizon. He was setting off for his last disaster.

PART THREE

The Scariest Place

CHAPTER 6

Even UN peacekeepers couldn't make that place worse.
—Fred Cuny on Chechnya, March 1995

TO IMAGINE THIS WAR and the way it was fought, it might be easiest first to try to forget what you know about war. Forget the massed formations of the Civil War, or the gruesome stalemate of trench warfare, or the beachheads of World War II, or even the jungle ambushes of Vietnam.

Imagine instead a bright still day, early afternoon. You are standing on a narrow farm road elevated above the surrounding land. To one horizon, the fields stretch away in plots of green and brown, neatly delineated by windbreaks of tall, thin trees. To the other, the fields gradually give over to gold-colored foothills, then pine forests and, in the farthest reaches, a massive wall of rugged, snow-capped peaks. Along the shoulder of the road are wildflowers.

A short distance from where you stand, maybe three miles away, there is a small village over which four helicopters perform an intricate aerial dance. While one of the helicopters hovers directly above the village center to fire rockets down into the houses, the others circle in a tight orbit, providing cover with cannon and machine-gun fire. When the first gunship is done, it slides out to join the circle and another moves in to take its place. They are so close, you feel the concussion of their rockets beneath your feet, smell the burning on the air, but even from this short distance the steady, high rattle of the machine guns sounds benign, rather like dice being shaken in a plastic cup.

Much closer in, not more than two hundred yards from where you stand, is a ruined farmhouse where a small unit of government soldiers are based. Because this is a "tripwire" outpost, tight on the invisible line between government- and rebel-held territory, the farmhouse is ringed with concertina wire and minefields, its soldiers living mostly underground in crude bunkers and trenches cut from the earth.

But on the elevated farm road you stand on the other side of that front, at the outermost limit of the rebels' "liberated zone." Here all is calm. Despite the nearby gunships and the enemy soldiers in full view at the farmhouse, none of the dozen or so rebels manning the position seem anxious to get into the foxhole they've dug beside the road. Instead, they saunter over the pitted asphalt, smoking cigarettes, chatting, admiring one another's weapons, only occasionally looking over at the now burning village.

At first you probably assumed the rebels were government soldiers, for they wear the same uniforms and carry the same weapons as their enemy—but it is those details that provide the essential clue. Where the soldiers are armed with twenty-year-old guns and clad in mere scraps of uniforms—picked out of some army surplus remnant pile or off the bodies of their dead comrades—the rebels' machine guns and grenade launchers are this year's models, many still glistening with original factory grease, their spotless army uniforms still showing the folds and creases of their shipping crate. If you stay at this place until dusk, you will see how this system works. Just at twilight, as the helicopter assault on the village gives over to an artillery barrage, three soldiers at the army tripwire post steal out of the farmhouse and, crouching low, scramble over the open fields to the rebel lines, bringing with them two more grenade launchers to be sold for drugs or food or liquor.

The timing of their visit is fitting, for this is a war waged in eternal twilight. On this eerie, apparitional landscape, nothing is ever quite what it seems, the lines of battle, of who is friend and who is foe, constantly changing in the murk. Yesterday the nearby village was in the "liberated zone," was safe; today it is dying. Perhaps it is because a regimental commander wanted to impress a general, or a gunship navigator made a mistake, or because a business deal went bad. Or perhaps there is no reason at all, simply because the village is there. You'll hear different theories if you ask around, but no one really knows why, and tomorrow it will be another village's turn, or maybe the strip of road you now stand on, or maybe the soldiers in the farmhouse, killed by their own grenade launchers, and tomorrow you won't know the reasons for those deaths either. That's the way it works here, the way it's worked through fifty or seventy or a hundred thousand deaths.

Of all the bad mistakes you can make in this place, this is the first one: to ever imagine there is a pattern, a logic, to any of it. Instead, this is a land and a war where any terrible thing can happen at any moment, where trying to grasp its full range of lies and treacheries and contradictions strains the limits of the human imagination. This is a place, after all, in which the rebel leader has an army bounty on his head and lives as a hunted fugitive, yet this fugitive status does not prevent him from passing through army roadblocks seemingly at will. This is a place in which the army commander in chief lies in a coma, apparently car-bombed by his own junior officers, but what no one can ascertain is which faction of officers tried to kill him: those who wanted him to sue for peace or those who were afraid he would. And this is a war in which the president of a nation stands before international television cameras to proudly proclaim that pacification has been achieved, even while other television cameras capture his army carrying out the most thorough annihilation of a city the world has witnessed in fifty years. Do not ever make the mistake of thinking you have it figured out here.

The second bad mistake you can make is to ever imagine that one side is better—more compassionate, less vicious—than the other. In this war, both sides have committed a stunning array of crimes. They have stormed into villages far away from the war front to take civilians hostage and then murder them. They have used prisoners as slave labor, as human minesweepers, as media ploys, and then killed them too. They have tortured, raped, burned, starved, mutilated, buried alive. For those waging this struggle, both the warriors in the field and the planners behind the lines, terror is now the first weapon of choice, as if they believe the other side might finally be shocked into submission simply by one's own greater capacity for cruelty. In their joint pursuit of this goal, no one is safe: not the aged, not children, not doctors or priests or peace negotiators, and not you.

There is a third mistake you can make in this place, perhaps the deadliest one of all, the one Fred Cuny made. It is the belief that you can change things, bring an end to the madness, the awful mistake of imagining you might somehow save it.

．　．　．

Afterward, no one could quite explain why the attack took place. One popular theory was that it had been intended as a kind of New Year's Eve present to the Russian people and their President, that they might ring in the new year of 1995 with the gladdening news that the troublesome little rebellion on their southern frontier had finally been put to rest. In one bold stroke, the bickering and gloomy self-doubts that had beset the nation in recent weeks would be rendered moot, and all could once again be confident that Russia would endure, its future brighter than just the day before. Another theory, at least as popular, was that the Russian Defense Minister ordered the assault amid a drunken birthday party.

It had been nearly three weeks since some 40,000 Russian troops had crossed into the tiny breakaway republic of Chechnya to disband "criminal formations." The mission had gone awry almost immediately. On one front, a Russian general had found his path blocked by civilian demonstrators and had simply refused to advance further, while other units closing on the capital city of Grozny came under sporadic sniper fire. By the end of December the army was bogged down in the Grozny suburbs, had already taken dozens of casualties, and the flag of independent Chechnya still flew defiantly atop the nine-story Presidential Palace in the heart of downtown. Someone some-where—in the Kremlin, in the Russian military high command—appar-ently came up with a plan to change all that on New Year's Eve.

In the predawn hours the Russian army opened up with a tremen-dous air and artillery bombardment of central Grozny. At midmorning the shelling eased as two massive columns of tanks and armored per-sonnel carriers—some 6,000 troops in all—left the Russian lines and began a slow, methodical advance on the city center from the north and west.

For a time all seemed to go like clockwork, the closing columns encountering little rebel resistance, their steady progress down main boulevards calmly observed by residents from apartment building bal-conies. By early afternoon the 131st Battalion of the Maikop Brigade had taken control of Grozny's main railway station; they parked their tanks and personnel carriers in tight rows in the station square as they awaited orders to move on to the Presidential Palace a quarter-mile away. So successful did the mission appear that the press office at the Russian Defense Ministry got a little ahead of itself, announcing that the palace had been seized and the troublesome separatists who had made it their headquarters sent fleeing for their lives. It was just about then, with the early dusk of winter approaching, that Russian soldiers discovered they had lumbered blindly into a horrific trap.

As the first tanks and APCs of the northern column neared the broad open square before the Presidential Palace, they were blown apart by rebels firing rocket-propelled grenades from the surrounding buildings. As the entire half-mile-long column came under attack, all semblance of order collapsed. Hemmed in by burning vehicles in front and back, whole sections of the column became cut off and exposed to a murderous fire. To escape, tanks and personnel carriers began scattering up side streets, only to discover more RPG-toting rebels waiting for them on balconies and rooftops.

As bad as the situation was for the troops in the northern column, they could at least be thankful they weren't at the railway station. There, the 131st Battalion was completely stranded, and by evening was taking fire from every direction. The battle raged throughout the night, the neatly parked Russian tanks and APCs methodically turned into pyres by rebels firing grenades from the surrounding high-rises. By New Year's Day the stunned survivors were holed up in the railway terminal, being picked off one by one as their commander desperately radioed for reinforcements.

"The whole battalion is wounded and lying in the station," he radioed shortly after 3 P.M. "We are all dying, we need help, do you understand?"

That help would never come, and over the next two days the 1,000-man 131st Battalion would be virtually annihilated.

By nightfall of New Year's Day—and even as the Russian Defense Ministry continued to proclaim the Grozny operation a success—the 6,000-man assault force had completely disintegrated, no longer an army but dozens of isolated bands of disoriented and terrified men, each frantically trying to find some way out of the trap they had stumbled into or waiting for reinforcements that would not come. Their odds for escape were not aided by the fact that the planning of the operation had been incompetent to the point of criminal.

Rather than use their crack Spetsnaz commando units for the assault, Russian commanders had relied almost exclusively on seventeen- and eighteen-year-old conscripts, some of whom had only been in uniform for a month and barely learned how to fire a weapon. Most of the tank and APC drivers couldn't communicate with one another, their radios only linked to headquarters, and few had even been given maps of the city; in the darkness and fire and thick fog, the fleeing units turned in circles and were soon shooting on each other. Most inexplicable of all, no infantry units had been dispatched to cover the advance, affording the rebels in their high perches all the time they needed to train their rocket-propelled grenades on the lightly armored "sweet spot" of the slow-moving vehicles passing below. When the last few survivors managed to fight their way back to Russian lines four days later, fully one third of the attack force had been wiped out, and the streets of downtown Grozny were littered with the bodies of hundreds of young Russian conscripts. In the coming days some of their corpses would be ripped apart by scavenging animals, others mutilated beyond recognition by marauding Chechen rebels with their "avenging knives," but others would remain untouched for weeks, their skin slowly blackening under the gray sky of winter.

Instead of its prowess, then, the New Year's Eve assault would come to symbolize something quite different about the Russian army. In less than four years one of the most powerful militaries ever assembled in world history had so degenerated that it had been soundly routed by a ragtag band of lightly armed rebels, its commanders so callously indifferent to the fate of their own men that they would leave their bodies behind to be eaten by dogs and carrion birds.

After the New Year's Eve fiasco, the Russian commanders apparently decided a change of tactics was in order. Now, having been humiliated in the streets of Grozny, they would "liberate" the city by turning it to ash.

. . .

Chechnya is a remarkably beautiful land, a place of flowers and sweeping vistas. Approached from the north, the country begins where the vast, arid plain of the Volga basin ends, a sudden rise of rolling steppes and pasturelands that gradually climbs to a ridge of barren mountains. From this ridgeline, the great sweep of the Sunzha River valley below is revealed, a fertile arc that is home to the capital city of Grozny and scores of small farming towns. On the far bank of the Sunzha the land starts to slowly rise again, first into grassy, rounded hills, then into pine-covered mountains cut by fast-flowing streams. Finally, in the far southern reaches, the forests end and then there is the jagged line of the Caucasus Mountains, a forbidding, seemingly impenetrable massif of snow-covered 15,000-foot peaks. Somehow the beauty of Chechnya in combination with its tiny size—barely a hundred miles from north to south and some sixty across, it is only slightly larger than the state of Connecticut—makes it difficult to grasp the signal role it has played in Russian history or the tragedies that have befallen it as a result.

It was in the mid-1700s that the Russian Empire, expanding southward into the Caucasus region, first came in contact with the Chechen tribes of the Sunzha Valley. The relationship got off to a bad start and wouldn't show much improvement over the next two hundred and fifty years.

The Muslim Chechens were a fiercely independent people whose primary loyalty was to their faith and their clan. They were also already famous for blood feuds passed down from one generation to the next, and an eye-for-an-eye system of justice that might make modern civil libertarians wince. According to John Colarusso, a Caucasian linguistics expert, one common form of punishment in traditional Chechen society was a particularly unpleasant variation of drawing and quartering; rather than employing the quick dispatch of horses, the four or five strongest men in a village were enlisted to slowly tear the miscreant apart with their bare hands. Clearly, these were not the sort of people to cross lightly—as the Russians would repeatedly discover.

If there was one thing that might unite the feuding Chechen clans, it was the encroachment of outsiders, and the soldiers of tsarist Russia—Slavic, Christian, and empire-building—were most certainly that. In 1818, amid the tsarist campaign to subdue the Caucasian peoples, they built a fort on the plains beside the Sunzha River that they named Grozny—Russian for "terrible" or "fearsome." The name was fitting, but in a way the Russians hadn't intended; where most other Caucasians quickly bowed to the banner of the tsar, the vastly outnumbered Chechens resisted the invaders almost continuously for the next thirty-five years. As Mikhail Lermontov, the so-called "poet of the Caucasus," wrote of the Chechens at the time: "Their god is freedom. Their law is war."

United behind their legendary leader, Imam Shamil, the Chechen warriors repeatedly decimated Russian armies sent to conquer them, while the Russians exacted revenge by razing scores of Chechen villages. The ferocity of the fighting set up a cycle of mutual hatred that would forever endure; when, in 1852, Leo Tolstoy, then a young Russian officer serving in the Caucasus wars, described the attitude of Chechen villagers whose homes had just been destroyed by tsarist soldiers, he could just as easily have been describing 1995:

> No one spoke of hatred for the Russians. The feeling which all Chechens felt, both young and old, was stronger than hatred. It was not hatred but a refusal to recognize these Russian dogs as people and such a revulsion, disgust and bewilderment at the senseless cruelty of these beings, that the desire to destroy them, like a desire to destroy rats, poisonous spiders and wolves, was as natural as the instinct of self-preservation.

In another curious parallel to Russia's later dealings with the Chechens, the finally victorious tsarist army tried to impose a lasting solution on these malcontents by scattering them. In the early 1860s tens of thousands were banished over the Caucasus Mountains into exile in the Ottoman Empire, while many more were herded out of the plains and into the mountain wastelands to starve or scratch out an impoverished existence. It didn't work. Within ten years the Chechens had risen up again.

Certainly no Russian pogrom against the Chechens was as brutal—or so burns on in the collective Chechen consciousness—as Joseph Stalin's purge of early 1944. After charging that many Chechens and their blood cousins in neighboring Ingushetia had aided the German army during its offensive into the Caucasus, Stalin ordered the "deportation to other regions of the USSR of all Chechens and Ingush living on or adjacent to the territory of the Chechen-Ingush ASSR [Autonomous Soviet Socialist Region], and liquidation of the Chechen-Ingush ASSR. . . ."

In the course of a single week in February 1944, Russian security forces rounded up virtually the entire population of Chechnya—some 400,000 people—threw them into cattle cars, and sent them across the wintry steppes to an exile in Soviet Central Asia. Within a year a full third of all Chechens had perished from starvation and disease. In true Stalinist fashion, the name of their homeland was simply erased from Soviet maps.

But the Soviet campaign against the Chechens ultimately proved no more successful than the tsarist ones had been. When they were finally allowed to return from their banishment in the late 1950s as part of Nikita Krushchev's de-Stalinization policy, the Chechens' hatred for their brutal masters had only deepened and made them more determined than ever to resist—and maybe even one day finally win their freedom. They would seize their moment in the early 1990s just as the Soviet Union disintegrated.

Complicating that move would be the fact that hatred flowed both ways in the Chechen–Russian relationship. For their steadfast defiance over more than two centuries, the Chechens had come to occupy a special and dangerous place in the Russian national psyche. If secretly admired for their obduracy and independence, they were more openly reviled and feared for the very same reason, the recalcitrance of these short, swarthy Muslims to accept the "civilizing" influence of Christian or Communist Russia attributed to primitivism, stupidity, and base criminality. So mythic and ingrained had this stereotype become in the Russian mindset that even Alexander Solzhenitsyn, while extolling the Chechens unbroken spirit in exile in *The Gulag Archipelago*, could not help but disparage them at the same time:

> There was one nation that would not give in [to Stalin], would not acquire the mental habits of submission—and not just individual rebels among them, but the whole nation to a man. These were the Chechens. . . . They were capable of rustling cattle, robbing a house, or sometimes simply taking what they wanted by force. As far as they were concerned, the local inhabitants, and those

exiles who submitted too readily, belonged more or less to the
same breed as the bosses. They respected only rebels. And here is
an extraordinary thing—everyone was afraid of them.

By the 1970s, "Chechen" had become synonymous with "mafia"
in the average Russian's mind, a vicious and scheming gypsy-like people never to be trusted. Even today in "democratic" Russia, help-
wanted and rental ads in Moscow newspapers often carry the caveat
"No southerners need apply," while unsolved murders are routinely
attributed to "criminal elements from the south"—a euphemism for
Caucasians in general, and for Chechens in particular.

But, when it comes to waging war, hatred for one's enemy is a
very tricky thing. Throughout history the Slavic Russians, flushed with
their own sense of racial and cultural superiority, have marched confidently into battle against the Caucasian Chechens—those "infidels" or
"barbarians" or "criminals" on their southern frontier—only to meet
with disaster. And, throughout history they have sought to avenge such
disaster by laying waste. In the 1990s history would repeat itself.

In less than two years, between December 1994 and the summer
of 1996, the Russian military would wage a war on Chechnya that, in
the cold calculations of comparative statistics, would place it in the
ranks of the most devastating conflicts of modern times. Out of a
prewar population of some 1,000,000, perhaps as many as 100,000
Chechens would be killed and another quarter million displaced. On
the capital city of Grozny, the Russian military would drop more artillery shells in twenty days than had fallen on the besieged city of Sarajevo in two years, killing as many as 25,000 of the civilians trapped
there. And for those who came in hopes of mitigating the slaughter,
there would be at least one more bad example of comparative statistics:
in Chechnya, the Red Cross would see more of its workers deliberately
murdered than in any other war zone in the international organization's hundred-and-thirty-one-year history.

Arriving just seven weeks after the war began, Fred Cuny would be
able to offer his own grim comparison. Even for this veteran of some

thirty war zones around the world, the conflict in the tiny enclave at Russia's southern frontier was in a class of its own; as he would later tell friends and colleagues, "Chechnya is the scariest place I have ever been."

. . .

Understanding the war in Chechnya can be as simple or as complicated as one might wish. That's because no one has truly determined why it took place at all.

There are a lot of different theories floating around. Some believe it was all about controlling the flow of oil, or that the Russian President was looking for a "victorious little war" to boost his poll standings, or that it was a falling out of organized crime syndicates—even that it was a kind of slow-motion coup by the Russian military against the nominally democratic government in Moscow.

Some theories are so complex as to require graph paper and slide rules to follow: that the Americans secretly goaded the Russians into the war, ostensibly to check Iran's growing influence in the region, but really so that the Americans could then capitalize on Russian "belligerence" to bolster the argument for NATO's expansion into Eastern Europe, or to further undermine the Russian economy, or even to quietly normalize relations with Iran. (The obvious weak link in this theory is that such deviousness would have required keen foresight, a trait rarely evident among American foreign policymakers.) Then there are the innumerable "vodka theories," often quite different in specifics, but all identifying the copious consumption of vodka among Kremlin power-brokers as a chief catalyst.

The fact remains, though, that all of these are only theories. If a real answer is to be found, it undoubtedly rests with the two men—leaders, for want of a better word—most responsible for the carnage. One was a strange mustachioed man named Dzhokhar Dudayev, the self-proclaimed President of independent Chechnya, a former air force general who wore platform shoes to hide his short stature and who, prior to 1991, was best known for his proficiency at high-altitude carpet bombing. The other was Boris Yeltsin, the President of Russia, a blustering buffoon who focused his greatest energies on neutralizing any political rivals even as his nation's economy collapsed, and who had the distinction of showing up drunk in more foreign capitals than probably any statesman in history.

Here, too, though, there are problems in the search for a clear-cut answer. Dzhokhar Dudayev might well have been insane, and now he is dead. Boris Yeltsin, while consistently defying reports of his own demise, might well be insane too. Although Caucasus "experts" and Kremlinologists and historians will no doubt advance their own theories on the cause of the war in Chechnya for decades to come, the most awful explanation may be that tens of thousands died for no discernible reason at all.

· · ·

He was a dapper little man with a broad streak of vanity, his suits always neatly pressed, his pencil-thin mustache precisely trimmed. He took great pains to camouflage his short stature, usually greeting visitors while seated behind a cloth-covered desk so they would not notice his boots' three-inch heels, careful to avoid being photographed standing next to his much taller bodyguards.

What Dzhokhar Dudayev lacked in height, however, he made up for by being a figure of truly towering contradictions. Apparently content with a modest lifestyle, he nevertheless turned his self-styled nation into a playground for gangsters and an international transshipment point for arms traffickers and drug smugglers. Even in the darkest days of the war, while railing about the Russians' three hundred years of "genocide" against his Chechen people and the impossibility of there ever being coexistence between the two, he would turn around and wax nostalgic about his deep affection for Russia, how he hoped that a "special bond" might be created. These about-faces could happen on the same day, even—much to the bewilderment of journalists interviewing him—within the span of five minutes.

To writer Anatol Lieven, observing Dudayev at a press conference on the eve of the war, "The first few minutes sounded rational enough. Then, however, he would rapidly degenerate into hysterical insults and rambling, philosophical, racial, and historical speculations, almost as if possessed by some evil demon. In the course of that press conference, after declaring that a Chechen delegation had left for Moscow for [peace] talks, he three times quoted Harry Truman's alleged words that 'there is no language in which you can talk with Russians,' and four times called Russia a 'satanic power.' "

At other times Dudayev sounded like nothing so much as a frustrated suitor desperately trying to be noticed, suggesting that all problems could be sorted out and peace achieved if only Boris Yeltsin would agree to a personal meeting. Once the war started in earnest, he took to talking about his own life in apocalyptic terms, constantly reminding his followers that Russian assassination squads were closing on him, even while he scrupulously avoided the front lines of battle, scurrying from one mountain village to the next far away from the combat zone.

Until the 1990s there were few signs that Dzhokhar Dudayev was the sort of man who might lead a nation, or had any inclination to try. Like some eighty percent of all Chechens, his family had suffered Stalin's banishment to Soviet Central Asia in February 1944, and it was there that he spent the first thirteen years of his life. If he harbored some deep animosity toward Russia for his people's tortured history, it took a very long time to show; not only did he marry an ethnic Russian woman who bore him three children, but for nearly thirty years he served in the Soviet air force, eventually rising to the rank of major general and winning several medals for his squadron's carpet-bombing sorties during the war in Afghanistan. Ironically, if he was first admired by any Soviet citizens, it was not his fellow Chechens but the Estonians. When that Baltic state began agitating for independence from the Soviet Union in the spring of 1990, Dudayev, then serving as an air wing commander in Estonia, refused a Kremlin order to send his troops out to quash the rebellion. In gratitude, a major street in Tallinn, the Estonian capital, was renamed in his honor.

Perhaps Dudayev showed such restraint with the Estonians because he was already hatching some independence plans of his own. As secessionist fervor spread through the Soviet Union that summer and autumn of 1990, the major general returned to Chechnya to address a newly formed organization called the Chechen National Congress. Composed of a wide spectrum of Chechen elders and politicians hoping to refashion their homeland's status within the now dwindling Soviet Union, the Congress was divided between moderates seeking a measure of autonomy and radicals urging a complete break with Moscow; Dudayev had been invited to speak by the moderates in the belief that, as one of the highest-ranking Chechens in the Soviet military, he would be a voice of caution and compromise.

Instead, the general seized the moment to deliver a speech calling for Chechen sovereignty, instantly becoming the darling of the Congress radicals, who elected him the executive committee chairman. It was all the platform Dudayev needed. Resigning from the Soviet air force, he soon moved back to Chechnya and began to assume power, steadily marginalizing the Congress moderates while escalating his angry rhetoric against Moscow. Before long he was calling for elections to oust the local Communist Party government and for complete Chechen independence.

There was a hitch, though; Dudayev was largely shouting into a void. With the whole Soviet Union coming apart at the seams and Mikhail Gorbachev's power waning by the day, no one in the Kremlin had much time to focus on what some little hothead in Chechnya was proclaiming. For Dudayev, this indifference may have been the greatest insult of all, and in the summer of 1991 he decided to up the ante. Amid the turmoil following the failed Communist coup attempt against Gorbachev in August, Dudayev sent his small band of armed followers to seize the Grozny television station, then announced the formation of a "national guard," largely composed of criminals he had released from prison, to defend the Chechen homeland. After forcing the local Communist Party general secretary to resign at gunpoint and handily winning snap elections—largely viewed as a sham and boycotted by most legitimate political parties—the new President Dudayev proclaimed

Chechnya an independent nation on November 1. If the former major general was trying to get a rise out of Moscow, it finally worked.

By the time of that independence proclamation, both Mikhail Gorbachev and the Soviet Union were rapidly passing into history, and Dudayev's challenge was now directed at Russia and its President, Boris Yeltsin. To Yeltsin, a former Communist Party boss in his home province of Sverdlovsk who had refashioned himself as a democrat, the obstreperous upstart in Chechnya posed a big potential problem.

Although rarely noted by the outside world, the concept of a cohesive Russian nation had always been nearly as shaky as the concept of a cohesive Soviet Union. Instead, the Russian republic was an amalgam consisting of "little Russia"—the homeland of the ethnic Russians that stretched from St. Petersburg to the Volga River—along with some two dozen different ethnic homelands—places like Tatarstan, Chechnya, and Ingushetia—that together comprised "greater Russia." During the tenuous early years of their rule, the Bolsheviks had brokered an array of constitutional agreements that granted these ethnic homelands varying degrees of autonomy depending on their placement on a complex political classification table; one such construction had been the Chechen-Ingushetia Autonomous Region.

Of course, once Communist rule had been solidified, these constitutional guarantees of autonomy had been rendered meaningless, but now, with the Soviet Union collapsing and nationalist fervor spreading like a cancer, there was suddenly the fear that the old agreements would be dusted off and even "greater Russia" might begin to disintegrate into its component parts.

Beyond this there was an added historical complication that made Chechnya's secession even more worrisome to Boris Yeltsin. Along with banishing the Chechens to Soviet Central Asia in 1944, Stalin had also declared the Chechen-Ingushetia Autonomous Region an integral province of Russia by "voluntary union," a decree that had never been rescinded. If Yeltsin let Dudayev's independence proclamation stand, so this reasoning went, it might spur similar bids among those autonomous regions that actually had a far stronger constitutional basis for secession. Five days after Dudayev's declaration of independence, Yeltsin denounced the regime in Grozny as illegal, ordered a state of emergency in Chechnya, and dispatched federal troops to put things in order.

But Dudayev moved just a little bit quicker, racing his "national guard" goon squads out to the airport to greet the arriving federal troops. After a tense daylong standoff, the Russian parliament overruled Yeltsin's state-of-emergency decree and ordered the soldiers home. If the Duma's decision averted a bloody skirmish in 1991, it sowed the seeds for a bloodbath in 1994; Dudayev's independent Chechnya—or Ichikeriya—was now a tacit fact.

In wielding the reins of power, Dudayev quickly proved as capricious and bizarre as the most hard-line of Russian government propagandists had predicted. According to one oft-quoted story, he once told a reporter that, since Chechnya was now an Islamic republic, all Chechen men would be required to pray three times a day. When informed that Muslims actually prayed five times a day, Dudayev shrugged: "Oh well, the more the merrier." On several occasions he talked of the wealth to come by capitalizing on Chechnya's abundant water supply and building a pipeline to Saudi Arabia, nearly a thousand miles away. But it wasn't all just fun and games with Dudayev. After a dispute with the Chechen parliament, he simply declared presidential rule by fiat, then sent his "national guard" gunmen into a pitched battle with the opposition that left more than a hundred dead. As the Chechen economy collapsed and public disenchantment with his rule grew, he took to driving through the streets of Grozny in an armor-plated Volvo, protected by an enormous and heavily armed personal bodyguard largely comprised of the prison convicts he had released in 1991.

Perhaps most noted by the outside, Chechnya rapidly became one of the smuggling capitals of the world under Dudayev's rule, a key transshipment point for narcotics, weapons, and stolen goods flowing between Asia, the Middle East, and Europe. By early 1994, according to one U.S. intelligence report, the small provincial airfield in Grozny had become the second busiest airport in the former Soviet Union, rivaling Moscow's Sheremetyevo, owing to its constant flow of contraband traffic.

Yet it may well have been another feature of Dudayev's rule that finally redrew Boris Yeltsin's ire. Whether driven by some unquenchable desire to humiliate Russia or cannily realizing that his own increasingly shaky hold on power depended on focusing Chechen attention on external enemies, Dudayev could not resist provoking Yeltsin at every opportunity. In 1992 he provided a safe haven for Zviad Gamsakhurdia, the former dictator of neighboring Georgia whom the Russians had toppled for his anti-Moscow rhetoric, then helped him organize his forces for a new bid on power. The next year he announced the formation of the Confederation of Caucasian Peoples, a pipe-dream future republic that would join together all the disparate ethnic homelands of the Caucasus, including—not coincidentally—many that were still legally part of Russia. All the while, his incessant diatribes against Yeltsin and Russia, and his steadily deepening ties with both Islamic fundamentalist groups and leaders of the Chechen mafia were causing thousands of ethnic Russians to pack up and leave Chechnya, further burdening a nation already overwhelmed with ethnic Russian refugees from the former Soviet states.

By the summer of 1994, Yeltsin had had enough. Prodded by a Russian parliament that had grown more nationalistic and right-wing to do something about the long-festering Chechnya problem, he authorized the Federal Counterintelligence Service (FSK)—soon to be renamed the Federal Security Service, or FSB—to launch a covert destabilization campaign against Dudayev by providing weapons and training to several Chechen opposition groups. If not particularly covert, the operation did at least succeed in plunging Chechnya into even greater lawlessness as the rival factions faced off in a series of bloody skirmishes. Of course, it also had the unintended consequence of bolstering Dudayev's standing among the Chechen citizenry by diverting attention from his own disastrous rule.

In late November the Russians tipped their hand in grand fashion

when a well-armed attack force, ostensibly composed of anti-Dudayev
Chechens, was repulsed in the streets of Grozny; among the putschists
captured by Dudayev's men were some two dozen Russian soldiers spe-
cially contracted by the FSK for the mission. For the next three weeks
the two chief protagonists, Dudayev and Yeltsin, engaged in a bizarre
duel of contradictory statements and actions that would finally lead to
disaster.

After first threatening to execute his Russian prisoners as mercenaries, Dudayev suddenly released them and cheerily announced,
"There will not be any war." Almost immediately, however, he began
another round of bellicose, fight-to-the-death speeches in which he
likened Yeltsin to Hitler and Satan. In Moscow, just one day after the
Russian Defense Minister had announced a framework for negotiations
and promised there would be "no military solution" to the Chechen
problem, Yeltsin's Security Council vowed that action would be taken to
"disarm and liquidate" Dudayev's rebels, and Russian warplanes
dropped "warning" bombs on the outskirts of Grozny. It was as if both
governments had somehow fallen into the hands of men suffering from
split-personality disorders.

The crisis only reached new heights of incomprehensibility on
December 11, when 40,000 Russian troops crossed the Chechen frontier from the north, east, and west and began their slow convergence
on Grozny. In some areas the Russian columns found their path
blocked by peaceful civilian demonstrators, while in others they were
met with sniper fire and grenade attacks. The Russian response was
just as varied. The commander of the western army, vowing that he
would not fire on unarmed civilians, halted his advance, while just a
few miles away other Russian units took to machine-gunning demonstrators and fleeing refugees.

"It was absolutely impossible to tell what was going on or who was
in charge," one senior State Department official, speaking on condition
of anonymity, said of those early days. "Here you had a love fest going
on between a Russian general and the Chechens out west, while twenty
miles away the Russians are bombing downtown Grozny. You have

Dudayev saying he's ready to talk peace, then saying the Chechens won't lay down their weapons until every last Russian is gone or dead, you have Yeltsin talking conciliation at the same time that his ministers are vowing total war, and then just when you felt you were starting to make sense of it, they'd all switch places again. You never knew what was going to happen from one day, one hour, to the next."

Perhaps nothing typified the chaos more than Boris Yeltsin's televised address to the nation on December 27. By then, Russian troops had finally closed around Grozny but were meeting stiff resistance, with both military and civilian casualties starting to mount. Faced with growing public opposition to the Chechnya adventure, especially the military's hamfisted reliance on artillery and warplanes, Yeltsin announced an immediate halt to all air strikes on the Chechen capital and again held out the offer of peace talks. Just moments later, however, he was describing Dudayev and his followers as "the most dangerous, powerful, and arrogant forces of the Russian and international criminal and extremist world," gangsters whose power derived from "deceit, money, and threats," and who had to be crushed. It seemed perversely fitting that, within hours of Yeltsin's announcement of a complete stop to air strikes, Russian warplanes blew apart Grozny's largest orphanage.

As the end of the year approached, the Russian President found himself sinking deeper into a morass of his own making. One month earlier his Defense Minister, Pavel Grachev, had promised that the Chechen rebels could be crushed in "two hours with one parachute regiment." Now, after three weeks of steadily escalating fighting, Dudayev and his men still held the Presidential Palace, Yeltsin's government was being assailed both at home and abroad, and hundreds were dead. It was clearly time to either extricate himself from the mess by calling it quits or to strike the crucial blow that might dramatically turn things around. With the New Year's Eve attack on downtown Grozny, Yeltsin apparently chose the latter—apparently, because there is some question as to whether his generals even informed him of the plan ahead of time.

In the wake of that disastrous assault, the Russian military abruptly changed tactics. As the rest of the world watched in disbelief, they proceeded to unleash the greatest artillery bombardment on a population center since the fall of Berlin in World War II. For nearly two weeks the estimated 100,000 civilians still trapped in the city— mostly ethnic Russians who had had nowhere else to go when the conflict started—struggled to survive in a Dantesque landscape of death and perpetual half-darkness, the black fog from burning oil refineries mixing with the dust of collapsing buildings as shells rained down at the rate of one per second. With any venture outside almost a suicidal risk, many residents simply huddled in basements until they slowly starved or froze to death. In a city the Russian soldiers had given a new nickname, "The Coffin," the dead would now not be counted in the hundreds but in the thousands. In fact, it was quite impossible to count them at all, for so intense was the bombardment that many victims were simply obliterated, buried beneath leveled buildings, or consumed by the packs of dogs that roamed the shattered streets.

But even now there would be those touches of the grotesque and surreal that had come to typify the Russian government's conduct in Chechnya. On January 6 a seemingly indignant Boris Yeltsin appeared before television cameras to say he had heard rumors that his air-strike ban on Grozny was being violated, and that he was summoning Defense Minister Grachev to obtain "absolutely clear information" on the situation. On that same day Russian warplanes were flying dozens of bombing sorties over Grozny, complementing heavy artillery units that were dropping thousands of shells on the city every hour—"clear information" available to almost anyone in the world with access to television.

Despite it all, however, the tattered flag of rebel Chechnya still remained atop the Presidential Palace, a taunting symbol of the Chechens' unyielding defiance. And like all such symbols of the past two hundred years, this one obsessed those Russian commanders who had come to crush them.

If the hundreds of artillery shells that had struck the palace had not been sufficient to bring the building down or to dislodge the rebels, the Russians had something in their arsenal that just might do both: a "heavy" bomb designed to cut through ceilings and floors before detonating in a building's core with enough force to possibly collapse the entire structure. Most militaries might have hesitated to use such a weapon on the Presidential Palace since the rebels were holding dozens of captured soldiers inside, but this was hardly likely to be a major concern to Russian commanders; they had, after all, amply illustrated their indifference to their own soldiers' welfare during the New Year's Eve assault.

On the afternoon of January 18 two Russian fighters streaked overhead to drop two "heavy" bombs on the palace roof. Plummeting through the building's nine stories, the bombs detonated in the basement, instantly killing almost everyone there, and shaking the structure to its foundations. That night the last of the Chechen defenders quietly slipped out the back doors of the palace and escaped over the Sunzha River. When Boris Yeltsin heard the long-awaited news he was exultant, announcing that the military campaign in Chechnya was now "practically complete."

This statement, too, would be in error. Far from giving up the war, the rebels hadn't even left Grozny but were simply regrouping in the southern suburbs. Over the next three weeks this area of the city, too, would be reduced to rubble by Russian artillery.

By the end of that terrible month of January, Yeltsin's own Commissioner for Human Rights, Sergei Kovalyov would estimate that between 25,000 and 30,000 people had already been killed in Chechnya and that nearly half of the republic's entire population were now refugees—and the war hadn't even reached the countryside yet. It was just about then that an oversized Texan in cowboy boots arrived in Chechnya hoping to make sure it didn't.

· · ·

On the midmorning of February 10, 1995, Fred Cuny boarded a jet at Moscow's Vnukovo Airport for the three-hour flight to the North Caucasus. Accompanying him were three people: Misha Fishman and

Vyacheslav "Slava" Miklayev, two low-level workers from the Moscow office of the International Science Foundation (ISF), an adjunct of George Soros's Open Society Institute; and Fred's interpreter, a thirty-five-year-old woman named Galina Oleinik.

A single mother with two young children, Galina had first met Fred in 1992 on another Caucasus battlefield—the border conflict between Ingushetia and North Ossetia—and had spent several weeks acting as his interpreter as he toured that devastated region. Afterward, Galina, already displaced by an earlier skirmish between Georgia and her native South Ossetia, had left her war-torn homeland to start a new life in Minsk, the capital of the republic of Belarus. It was there that Fred tracked her down when he took on the Chechnya mission for Soros. The hard-pressed single mother had leaped at the chance to work as his interpreter again, and had been waiting for Fred when he arrived in Moscow.

On that February flight to the North Caucasus, Fred undoubtedly felt conflicting emotions: apprehension, certainly, at what he was likely to face in Chechnya, but probably also a fair degree of high anticipation.

For the first time in his life he was flying into a disaster zone armed with something he had always coveted: a blank check. Although George Soros had earmarked a million dollars for his Chechnya relief mission, Fred knew from past dealings with the philanthropist that this figure could float upward in a hurry if good ways could be found to spend it.

What's more, Fred was about to enter a disaster site unlike any he had ever encountered, a free-fire zone so dangerous and chaotic that few aid organizations dared get anywhere close; even in early February, seven weeks after the Russian encirclement of Grozny had begun, not one blanket or gauze pad from an international relief agency had reached the thousands of civilians still trapped inside. For a man who had always been drawn by the adrenalin lure of danger, but also always frustrated by the bureaucracies and procedures and protocols of the disaster relief system, Chechnya loomed as a kind of ultimate frontier:

a place where, unfettered by others, he might finally attain the profound results he had always sought. Of course, this frontier quality also meant it was a place where it might be very easy to die.

. . .

His first image of Grozny was of burning.

"The entire city seemed to be on fire," Fred would later write to Carl Long's daughter Veronica. "Giant flames were leaping from the burning oil refinery on the north side of the city and hundreds of small fires were burning near the oil field on the south side."

Operating out of Ingushetia, the neutral mini-republic on Chechnya's western border, Fred had spent a frustrating day trying to cross the battlelines and reach the shattered city, until he discovered an astonishing breach in the Russian army's "ring of steel." Standing alongside a road that night, he watched as carloads of rebels drove straight through the Russian lines simply by turning their headlights off; he decided to do the same. Finally reaching the rebel-held enclave in Grozny just before dawn, he was swiftly ushered into a basement. Moments later the Russians' morning artillery bombardment commenced, one that lasted for the next four hours. Fred had never experienced warfare like this—indeed, few men or women have—but already he had begun making lists of where to go and whom to see, devising plans to bring it to an end.

Among those who caught fleeting glimpses of Fred in Grozny that February was Kurt Schork, the same Reuters correspondent who had known Fred in Kurdistan and Bosnia. To the journalist, the sight of the middle-aged Intertect director scrambling amid the madness of Chechnya was nothing short of bizarre.

"It just didn't add up," Schork said. "It seems to me that most of the places Fred went to there was some kind of structure he could fit into. But there was no structure in Grozny or in Chechnya—it was a complete breakdown. There was no aid getting in, there was absolutely no government or institutional structure you could relate to, and in those days just driving from point A to point B was a roll of the dice every time. He was very, very vulnerable, and I just couldn't figure out why he was going at it with such verve."

But of course what had brought Fred was probably the very lack of structure that Schork described. As virtually the only game in town—and it seemed highly unlikely that the UN was going to get there any time soon to screw things up—he could try out anything he liked.

Whatever the impulse, Fred plunged into the Chechen morass with a bravado and energy that both stunned and exhausted his younger companions. In less than two weeks he ranged throughout the war zone, constantly crossing back and forth over the still raging battle lines to talk with as many of the senior commanders on both sides as he could find. In short order he had developed a rapport with both the Chechen rebel commander-in-chief, General Aslan Maskhadov, and his Russian counterpart, General Anatoly Kulikov, as well as with the President and Vice-President of neighboring Ingushetia, "neutrals" who were trying to bring the two sides to the peace table. To gauge for himself the state of Russian army morale he talked to frightened young conscripts in the front lines, then ventured into a Grozny neighborhood in the middle of a bombardment to check on the civilians trapped there. By his own account, he even accompanied a Chechen "rat patrol" through the underground water mains of Grozny as they carried out a series of hit-and-run attacks on isolated Russian positions.

Still, on such a vast landscape of destruction, priorities had to be made, and Fred quickly focused on the most pressing problem that he felt was within his grasp to solve: getting those civilians still trapped in Grozny out to safety.

In mid-February a five-day cease-fire between the two sides enabled many to escape, but an estimated 30,000 residents remained stranded in the city. Of particular concern to Fred were several thousand civilians in the Chernorechiye neighborhood in southern Grozny. The tide of battle had drawn inexorably closer to Chernorechiye in the days before the cease-fire, but after weeks spent huddled in basements many of the residents—mostly elderly ethnic Russians—had been too shellshocked or weak from hunger to take advantage of the respite to get out. On the afternoon of February 19, just as the cease-fire was scheduled to expire, Fred's worst fears appeared about to be realized: Russian tanks and artillery began moving in to seal off the neighborhood, the standard prelude to a saturation shelling operation.

With increasing desperation, Fred spent the next day shuttling between the rival military headquarters, trying to broker another cease-fire that would give him enough time to evacuate the civilians in Chernorechiye and the rest of Grozny. By the evening of February 20 his goal seemed within reach. Maskhadov, the Chechen commander-in-chief, had agreed in principle to the evacuation plan, and so had the on-ground Russian commanders; after all, virtually all the civilians remaining in Grozny were ethnic Russians who had never supported Dudayev's independence bid in the first place. But, of course, logic had never held much sway in Chechnya.

That night Fred hastily composed a memo on his computer laptop and faxed it to Soros headquarters in New York. Even in the frenzied manner in which it was composed, the memo revealed both Fred's penchant for political strategizing—by stretching out the evacuation over ten to fourteen days, he pointed out, it would give time for international pressure to build on Yeltsin to sit down at the peace table—and his talent for using public relations and psychology to achieve his ends.

"The buses chosen should be large (such as the TAM buses built in Yugoslavia) which have enclosed cargo space underneath, because the people will want to bring some of their belongings. (But more important, larger buses are more intimidating than the smaller metro buses and a long line of big buses is much harder to stop than one of small micros when the press is watching). . . . The press should be notified of the action [ahead of time], and then the convoy should set off for Grozny accompanied by the media. Outstanding public figures including members of parliament, retired military officers, human rights groups, soldiers' mothers and others should ride on the buses. . . . Once the convoy is in the vicinity of Grozny, it should be extremely difficult for local commanders to refuse it permission to carry out the evacuation."

His first word was "airplane." Flying was the fulfillment of many things Fred craved: autonomy, control, danger. (Cuny family)

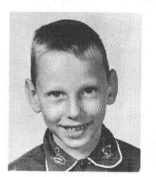 

Left: A shy and awkward boy. Fred at the age of five. (Cuny family)
Right: "Right-wing to the max." Fred enrolled in the officer training corps at Texas A&M to fulfill his lifelong dream of becoming a Marine combat pilot. (Cuny family)

The young relief worker with big dreams. Twenty-six-year-old Fred with his stepdaughter, Shemin, and son, Craig, 1971. His poor skills as a father would be a constant torment. (Cuny family)

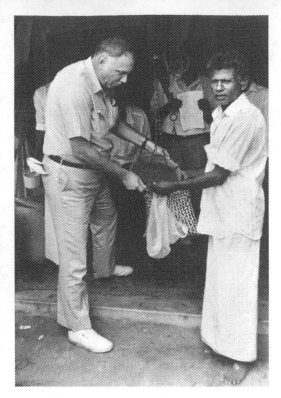

Above: Fred in Bangladesh. Over the span of his career, "The Master of Disaster" would battle against calamity on five continents and in over two dozen war zones. (Cuny family) *Below:* In Somalia, Fred would be shunted aside by the American military—and disaster would unfold precisely as he predicted. (Cuny family)

The Cuny brothers (from left): Chris, Phil, Gene (Butch), and Fred.
(Cuny family)

Above and below: Overseeing the water project in Sarajevo. Fred's project would be credited with saving the besieged city from falling, but he would also come under suspicion as an American spy. (Cuny family)

After being humiliated in the streets of Grozny on New Year's Eve, the Russians tried to "liberate" the city by turning it to ash.
(Stanley Greene/Agence VU)

Above: The path to Bamut. On March 31, 1995, Fred Cuny and four others set off down this road. Only one would return. (Stanley Greene/Agence VU)
Below: Fred beside a captured Russian personnel carrier in rebel-held Grozny, February 1995. He called Chechnya "the scariest place I have ever been"—then began to plan his return. (Cuny family)

Boris Agapov, the Vice President of Ingushetia, took a personal interest in solving the Cuny mystery—but he may have known the truth all along. (Stanley Greene/Agence VU)

The President of Ingushetia, General Ruslan Aushev, played a troubling role in the "body-double" episode. (Stanley Greene/Agence VU)

Omar Hadji (left), with his "avenging knife," and rebel General Ruslan Gilayev. If they knew what happened to the Cuny group, they weren't in a mood to share. (Stanley Greene/Agence VU)

Above: After the Samashki massacre, the doctor kept a photo of Fred on her desk as a reminder that "there are good people out there trying to help us." (Stanley Greene/Agence VU) *Below:* Cannon fodder. Sergei (left), the conscript soldier from Vologda, and a comrade on the "sealed" road in western Chechnya—before things turned ugly. (Stanley Greene/Agence VU)

Ninja warriors answerable to no one. Both sides committed horrific atrocities—and both sides wore the same uniform. (Stanley Greene/Agence VU)

Fred's only son, Craig, would spend four months looking for his father in Chechnya. (Cuny family)

Many reported seeing Cuny in the village of Samashki just hours before the Russian massacre. (Stanley Greene/Agence VU)

But all of Fred's careful planning would be for naught. Unbeknownst to him, Russian Defense Minister Pavel Grachev had already ruled out any further cease-fires with the Chechen "bandits," and the very next morning the heavy artillery arrayed around Chernorechiye opened up. They would continue shelling until the neighborhood was reduced to rubble, and countless more civilians were added to the war's death toll.

Fred's sense of outrage at the act was lent added bitterness by its utter incomprehensibility. In Chernorechiye, the Russian generals had been asked to choose between life and death—not of Chechen rebels, not even of Chechen civilians, but of their own people. For no identifiable reason save indifference, they had chosen death.

Finally convinced that the war could not be stopped and would now spread into the countryside, Fred returned to the republic of Ingushetia and helped lay the framework for establishing a mobile trauma unit at the hospital in Sleptsovskaya, a small town flush on the western border with Chechnya. After that he could do no more. At the end of the month he flew back to Moscow, where he briefed a number of American Embassy officials, including the ambassador, Thomas Pickering, on his experience.

"It was an extremely compelling—and, frankly, horrifying—account," Pickering recalled. "Of course, we'd all seen the images coming out of Grozny, and heard these terrible casualty figures being argued back and forth, but to have a man like Fred Cuny who had actually been there and seen it relating it in this very matter-of-fact way, I think it really brought the awfulness home to us in a way that maybe we hadn't felt before."

Upon his return to the United States, many of those who knew Fred were struck by how he suddenly seemed a slightly different man: more subdued, even haunted. One who noticed it that March in Washington was Paul Goble, a former CIA and State Department official who had known Fred for a number of years.

"I think Chechnya changed him," Goble said. "Up until then, I think Fred had a deeply optimistic outlook on the world and human nature—he must have to have endured all the misery and suffering he'd seen over the years and still keep going. But Chechnya pierced that somehow. He'd always loved people, believed in their intrinsic goodness, but I think in Chechnya he saw the mask of civilization slip. And it scarred him."

. . .

Located on a quiet street named Waterview in the suburbs of eastern Dallas, the small two-bedroom home is neither on the water nor has a view of any. From 1985 on, this was Fred Cuny's home, where he stayed during his infrequent returns to Texas, and where he came back that last time in early March 1995.

For a stranger walking into the house, it would probably be quite difficult to guess what kind of person lived there; a reasonable assumption might be an elderly, well-traveled couple of somewhat modest means. In the living room was a long, rather uncomfortable beige couch and a nondescript coffee table atop a dull yellow rug. Off to one side was a walnut-finish dining table that had seen better days.

Against one wall were a series of shelves, some filled with old hardcover books, others with souvenirs Fred picked up on his travels. In his 23-point "calling card" of the 1970s, Fred had described himself as a "collector of fine art," but it appeared he lacked either the time or the taste for this to be true. Other than a couple of interesting Day of the Dead clay sculptures from southern Mexico, the objects he picked up on his travels tended toward those found at airport gift shops: badly made daggers studded with "jewels," mass-produced figurines, cheap copper tea sets and samovars. The most prominent feature on this wall was a large black and white photograph set in a thin black frame of Company I-3/Sixth Battalion of the Texas A&M class of 1963, some fifty young men posing in uniform on the steps of an administration building. In the back row an eighteen-year-old Fred stood at rigid attention, his chin tucked into his neck, while a few places over to his left was his best friend, Carl E. Long.

From the living room, a short hallway passed the home's single bathroom, its white tiles highlighted with pink trim and wallpaper, before doors on either side let onto the two bedrooms, large but made quite gloomy by small windows and overhanging trees. Leading straight back from the living room was the small kitchen, its appliances dating from the 1970s, a washer and dryer set against one wall. A door from the kitchen opened onto a screened sunroom, about twelve feet long and eight wide, which Fred had turned into a rudimentary den. Along one side of the narrow room was an old fold-out couch, and on the other low shelves held row upon row of books—mostly suspense thrillers or paperbacks on military history. Hung on the faux wood paneling were dozens of framed photographs of airplanes, different craft that Fred owned or piloted over the years. From this room, one door led into the garage—a jumble of boxes and discarded furniture—and another into the small, enclosed backyard. At the far end of this yard a seventeen-foot sailboat, gradually disintegrating, sat on a trailer. In 1995 the house was appraised at $85,000, and it represented the bulk of Fred Cuny's worldly assets.

In early March, after a quick round of meetings with State Department officials in Washington, Fred settled back into the house on Waterview. There he started work on a long article for the *New York Review of Books* about the war in Chechnya.

While harshly criticizing the Russian military for its savage tactics in the war, his main thrust was to warn of what he foresaw as the next stage in the unfolding disaster. Once they had rid Grozny of rebels by laying waste to it, Fred predicted, the Russian army was going to do what the tsarist army had done a hundred and forty years before: push the Chechens out of the lowlands and into the denuded southern mountains. There, those who didn't succumb to starvation or hypothermia in the still strong grip of winter would be easy prey to Russian aerial attacks. By mid-March, Fred had finished the article; it was scheduled to run in the April 6 edition of the *New York Review* under the title, "Killing Chechnya."

Even while writing the article, Fred had maintained his usual hectic pace of other activities. Evenings were often spent visiting his parents or friends, while on several mornings he managed to steal out to the Caddo Mills airfield to soar in his glider. With his old high school friend, Steve Stevenson, a colonel in Air Force special operations, he exchanged a blizzard of faxes. By March 1995 it appeared NATO commanders in Bosnia were finally inching toward taking punitive action against the Bosnian Serbs and, with Stevenson's help, Fred hoped to provide them with a comprehensive battle plan for air strikes.

"He wanted a military consultant because he was exploring different military alternatives to help the people there," Stevenson said. "He'd call up and ask, 'What would it take to run F-4s across to hit such-and-such a target?' and I'd say, 'Okay, let me get one of my weapons officers and we'll see what we can do.' I'd go out and find all the information I could on certain things—a lot of special operations, a lot of details on Allied aircraft, the high-tech stuff that was available, and then we'd fax stuff back and forth."

On a more pacific front, both Fred's career and the financial health of Intertect had never looked brighter. Finally, after years of planning and debate and meetings, a new crisis-fighting organization that he and Mort Abramowitz had long discussed, the International Crisis Group (ICG), was about to become a reality. While Fred had hoped for a more activist mandate, the ICG still represented a revolutionary concept: an advisory group composed of some of the world's most accomplished humanitarian aid experts who would conduct independent assessments in places where disaster loomed, then report back to the American government, the United Nations, and private relief groups to coordinate preventative action. Over the previous four months Mort Abramowitz, the ICG's executive committee chairman, had enlisted a formidable array of international statesmen and business leaders to serve on the ICG steering committee—including Desmond Tutu, Elie Wiesel, and George Soros—and that very month of March the first requests for funding were beginning to circulate through world capitals. Once that funding was realized, Morton Abramowitz hoped to make Fred Cuny the ICG's first executive director.

At the same time George Soros, impressed by Fred's stellar success in Bosnia, had hired Intertect for nearly a dozen other projects throughout Eastern Europe, everything from overseeing the rehabilitation of schools in Albania to coordinating a fuel assistance program in Macedonia. Even the United Nations, despite Fred's stinging criticism of its policies in Bosnia, had recently awarded Intertect a contract to assess disaster assistance programs for Bangladesh.

Fred could also look forward to an excursion in the near future that promised to be both pleasant and professionally important. On April 9 he was scheduled to be one of the main speakers at a landmark conference of civilian and military relief experts at Camp Pendleton, the Marine base just north of San Diego. The event, organized by the State Department and Anthony Zinni, a Marine general with whom Fred had worked closely in northern Iraq, was designed to explore how civilian agencies and the military might work in greater cooperation in future disaster zones, the kind of cooperation that had achieved so much in Kurdistan and been so absent in Somalia. In anticipation of that trip, Fred wrote a letter on March 14 to Veronica O'Sullivan, Carl Long's daughter, who lived in San Diego.

"As [the conference] gets closer, I'll be in touch so we can get together. . . . Would you be able to come and be my guest? If you can get anywhere near the [Pendleton] base, I can send a car to pick you up and bring you to where I'll be making the presentation."

All the while, Fred continued to monitor events in Chechnya, and there the situation was going from bad to worse. Since leaving the war zone in late February, he had continued to work on his plan to evacuate Grozny, but that project had now been overtaken by events; by mid-March, the Russian army had finally pushed the rebels out of the city and overrun their nearby strongholds and was now employing its scorched-earth strategy in the countryside, moving steadily westward toward the frontier with Ingushetia. Even if Fred's immediate worst-case scenario appeared to have been averted—that the Chechens would be pushed into the southern mountains in the dead of winter—an even worse scenario now seemed likely: that the war would spill into the neighboring countries and autonomous regions of the North Caucasus, setting off a chain reaction that would be impossible to contain.

The battlefield was also becoming more dangerous for outsiders. As undisciplined as the Russian army had been in Grozny, the presence of international media and at least the semblance of a military command structure had afforded a certain slim thread of security. With the war now in the countryside, Russian units and checkpoint garrisons were operating with near total autonomy, making up the rules of engagement as they went along. At the same time, the Chechen rebels who had initially welcomed foreigners were becoming increasingly distrustful, steeped in rumors that Russian intelligence agents were infiltrating their areas masquerading as journalists, medics, and relief workers. Within this deepening peril, even the modest mobile trauma unit that Fred had helped establish for Soros in Ingushetia was finding it increasingly difficult to operate.

For most men and women in Fred's position, the decision about whether to return to Chechnya would probably have been an easy one to make; in truth, it seemed to require hardly any decision at all.

Fred had been able to accomplish almost nothing on his first trip to the war zone, and the situation had grown more dire since. On the other hand, he now stood at the threshold of achieving nearly everything he had ever wanted. He had attained the recognition he had always sought in the disaster relief community—and, with it, a financial stability that had been almost a quarter century in coming. He had an enthusiastic supporter in George Soros, a man who shared his bold visions and had the means to bankroll them. His word carried weight. If he felt restless and wanted to take a trip—a perennial condition with Fred Cuny—he could choose from a dozen Intertect project sites around the world, and if he desired an element of danger to that trip, there was always the ongoing mission in Bosnia, now heating up once again.

But against all that was the same pull that had taken Fred to Chechnya in the first place: the lure of the ultimate frontier. In many ways it was a hearkening back to his old philosophy of converting chaos into opportunity. If there was no place in the world more chaotic than Chechnya, then it also meant there was no place that afforded greater opportunity: for autonomy, for creativity, for Fred to fundamentally alter the course of events. And perhaps for something else as well, a need identified by Sonja Vukotic, his former girlfriend in Bosnia.

"Fred needed to be loved," she said. "It was what he was always seeking, and no amount of love was ever enough for him—not one woman, and not one group of people. I think that's why he finally became bored with Sarajevo, because he had gotten all the love and gratitude he was going to get from the people, and now it was time to find it somewhere else."

Shortly after leaving Chechnya the first time, Fred had called Sonja in Zagreb. He told her that Grozny had been a terrifying experience, a thousand times worse than Sarajevo. Sonja recalled that it had been a somewhat awkward conversation, one with a subtle subtext.

"I think he wanted me to say, 'Don't go back, come here and be with me,' " she said, "but I think he knew that wasn't going to happen. And anyway, the way he described Chechnya, how terrible it was, I knew he would go back."

After that conversation Fred never called Sonja again. By the middle of March, just as he was finishing the *New York Review of Books* article, he began making plans to return to the battlefield in the North Caucasus.

.   .   .

Fred seemed to become increasingly preoccupied during those last few days in Texas. For Rick Hill, his deputy at Intertect, the change was quite palpable.

"Fred was always a pretty lighthearted, jovial guy—loved to tell jokes, loved to tell stories—but there wasn't much of that when he came back from Chechnya. He would try to make light of things, but there seemed to be a tiredness about him that I don't think I'd ever seen before."

His son Craig also noticed a difference, although one he'd only ponder in hindsight. "In the past, Fred would always talk about the place he'd just been to—the situation there, who was doing what, how the problem could be solved. But he didn't really do that with Chechnya. He just never wanted to talk about it very much, and when he did it was in this kind of grim, sad way, and then he'd want to change the subject."

One of those most struck by the transformation was Damir Lulo, the Bosnian engineer who had worked with Fred on the Sarajevo water project. A year earlier, Fred had helped Lulo and his wife, Arida, move to Dallas—one of a half dozen emigrating Bosnian families he had sponsored—and Fred arranged to have dinner with the young couple a few nights before he left Texas.

"It was a very strange evening," Lulo remembered. "Always before with Fred, conversation was very easy—he loved to talk—but that night he was very distracted and it made the conversation difficult. That's when he told us he was returning to Chechnya."

As he and his wife drove home that night, Lulo was gripped by a sudden feeling of dread. Turning around, they drove across town to Fred's house on Waterview Drive.

"I knocked on the door and Fred came out, and I said, 'Fred, don't go back to Chechnya. If you need to take a trip, go somewhere else, go to Bangladesh.' "

Clearly touched by his friend's concern, Fred patted Lulo on the shoulder and smiled. "Thank you, Damir," he said softly, "but I'm afraid the Bangladeshes of the world just don't interest me very much anymore."

As they drove away, Arida turned to her husband. "I don't think we're going to see Fred again."

Another who felt a glimmer of foreboding was Fred's mother. On the morning he was to leave, he went by his parents' lakeside house in Rockwall to say goodbye.

"I remember it so clearly," Charlotte said. "He was standing in that doorway there, and it was the first time I'd ever seen him a little reluctant to take off. I said, 'Fred, do you have to go?' And he said, 'It's too important not to go,' and that was it."

Apparently at some point in those last days in Texas, Fred penned a poem to Craig. He placed it in a sealed envelope and taped it behind his office desk. It began:

> Do not mourn for me,
> For I have lived as few men have,
> With honor served
> For those whom God forgot.

The day after Fred left Dallas, a postcard arrived at the Intertect office from Veronica O'Sullivan in San Diego. "I'm so excited about you coming out," she wrote. "I told my mom and dad, and they can't wait to see you also. . . . I'll see you soon. Love—Veronica."

CHAPTER 7

I begged him not to go back, because I was absolutely
certain he would be killed. I said, "Fred, I know the Russians;
they'll kill you and make it look like the Chechens did it."
And he said, "Well, I hope that doesn't prove true."
—Paul Goble, friend of Fred Cuny

THERE WAS ONE great weapon that Fred Cuny carried with him
into virtually every disaster zone of his twenty-four-year career: knowledge.

Before venturing forth, he gathered and read anything that might
prove illuminating about the place: books, newspaper clippings, government position papers, articles in obscure academic journals. He
sought advice from think tank experts, university scholars, journalists,
military officers, U.S. and foreign government officials, other relief
specialists. Once on the ground in a disaster zone, he asked questions
of whoever crossed his path, from presidents to schoolteachers to illit-

erate peasant farmers, as he constantly took pulse and tried to learn more. As a result, in nearly any bad place he happened to find himself, Fred was a virtual encyclopedia of knowledge, a quality he took great pride in and which was constantly remarked upon by his colleagues in the field.

Yet the most striking feature that emerges in charting the path of Fred's return to Chechnya in late March 1995 is his fundamental lack of awareness of what he might face there, the wholly new set of perils he was likely to encounter.

Certainly this was not entirely his fault. When the Russians had finally succeeded in taking Grozny earlier that month and carried their offensive into the countryside, much of the international media that had covered the war simply left. Those journalists who remained could hardly present a coherent picture of the current situation for, with "peace" reigning in some areas, and ferocious combat in others, there was no coherent picture to be had. And, of course, it is in the nature of war that conditions always change, that what held true a month or a week earlier can be rendered obsolete by the march of events. In Chechnya, everything was devolving so rapidly that this time frame for obsolescence could be shortened down to a day or even an hour.

But in other ways Fred's failure to countenance the changes on the battlefield landscape to which he was now returning spoke of a certain willfulness.

Time and again in those last ten days of March he would be confronted with glaring signs of the increased danger he faced in going back; time and again he would choose to ignore them.

A byzantine web of hidden alliances and rivalries had begun to emerge in the war—not just in Moscow and Chechnya, but also in Ingushetia, the officially neutral republic where he would be based; if aware of the extent of this web, Fred would show little finesse in maneuvering through it.

Finally, in those last ten days, an unsettling incident would raise troubling questions about the people who were to accompany him into the war zone, and greatly increase the danger level for all of them; if those questions ever occurred to Fred, they would not arouse him sufficiently to look for answers.

As he set off from Dallas on March 21, catching an American Airlines flight to New York City, it was as if Fred was determined to ignore every warning sign that would be thrown in his path.

. . .

At about 4:30 on the afternoon of March 22, Fred walked through the glass doors of the Soros Foundation headquarters on Seventh Avenue in New York and ascended an elevator to the thirty-first floor. He was there to meet with Aryeh Neier, the president of the Open Society Institute, the umbrella organization for the nearly three dozen Open Society chapters operating throughout the world. It was Neier who, two months earlier, had hired Fred to conduct a needs assessment tour of the Chechen war zone, but that assessment had now been largely overtaken by events.

In recounting the meeting he had with Fred that day, Neier chose his words with an eye toward obliqueness. "I was apprehensive about him going back," he said, "and I think there was apprehension on Fred's part, as well. Part of it was the danger, but for me there were also other factors, internal considerations within the Soros Foundation."

Indeed there were. Almost from the day the Russian chapter of the Foundation opened its Moscow office in 1987, the philanthropic organization had been the target of a persistent smear campaign by Russian ultranationalists, one quietly supported by both the KGB and conservative Kremlin officials. Over the years the right-wing press had accused the Foundation of being a CIA front, an economic Trojan horse for Western capitalists to take over Russia—even, in light of Soros's Jewish heritage, the vanguard of some grand Jewish conspiracy for global domination.

Given this contentious history, the war in Chechnya had placed the Foundation in a very delicate spot. With its whipping-boy role for

Russian xenophobes, any project that was seen as giving aid or comfort to the Chechens was sure to stir a new round of denunciations, a new round of conspiratorial rumors, and possibly jeopardize all the Foundation's other initiatives throughout the nation. The most politically prudent course, then, might have been for George Soros to simply avoid the Chechnya issue altogether, but prudence had never been his strong suit; by earmarking a million dollars for relief efforts in Chechnya and by hiring Fred Cuny as a consultant, the philanthropist had made clear he was not going to be bullied into silence. Sure enough, Soros's pledge and outspoken comments about Chechnya had sparked a new cycle of anti-Foundation grumblings by Russian nationalists.

Fred had certainly not helped matters. The public criticisms he had leveled at the Russian military since his first trip to the war zone had added more fuel to the nationalists' ire. It had also spurred a deepening resentment among many in the Soros office in Moscow, especially at the International Science Foundation (ISF), a separate entity from the Open Society Institute whose director was Alex Goldfarb. The two men had never gotten along, and Goldfarb felt Fred's outspokenness was undermining the ISF's own initiative in the region. In early March, the ISF had begun funding a Russian Red Cross mobile trauma unit in Ingushetia—some twelve doctors sent down from Moscow—and the ISF director feared that project was being tarred by Fred's brush.

The final straw came when Goldfarb read an advance copy of Fred's upcoming *New York Review of Books* article, "Killing Chechnya." While less defamatory than its title suggested, the article presented a scathing critique of the Russians' tactics in Grozny and went on to assert that the Kremlin was engaged in "fruitless combat for an objective that is ultimately meaningless." Incensed, Goldfarb fired off a memo to Neier urging that Fred be immediately removed from the Chechnya project. That memo arrived in New York just as Fred did, and part of his time there was spent lobbying Neier to disregard Goldfarb's angry missive.

So preoccupying was the contretemps with Goldfarb that a disturbing report from the war zone apparently received little notice. On the afternoon of March 21, three of those doing relief work in the Caucasus under Soros sponsorship, Fred's interpreter Galina Oleinik, and two of the Russian Red Cross doctors from the mobile trauma unit, had been stopped at a Russian army checkpoint outside the village of Assinovskaya in western Chechnya. While details were sketchy, their driver had reportedly been roughed up by the soldiers and all had been accused of being rebel collaborators before being released.

It was not at all clear whether the incident was born of the general animosity among the Russian army for the Soros Foundation, or simply a random act by one of the increasingly lawless checkpoint garrisons that dotted the Chechen countryside, but the report out of Assinovskaya suggested to some at the Foundation's Moscow office that it might be time to end the Chechnya mission altogether before someone got killed.

Evidently, no such concerns registered in New York. By his recollections, Aryeh Neier didn't even learn of the incident until much later when it was the subject of a Russian television investigative report. While Fred apparently heard about it while in New York, it seemed to make very little impression on him, either. Elisabeth Socolow, the Soros employee in Moscow who was acting as Fred's liaison on the Chechnya project and who had flown over to New York to join him, recalled his making only one passing reference to Assinovskaya.

"He said something like, 'Yeah, they got stopped at a checkpoint,' " Elisabeth said, "like it was no big deal. Over the next week we were together, he never mentioned it again."

Of course, one reason Fred may not have mentioned it again was that, in light of the ongoing spat with Goldfarb, he didn't want to provide Neier or anyone else at Soros with another reason to question the Chechnya mission. If so, it was a bad mistake; as would eventually be learned, the incident at Assinovskaya had been a far closer call than anyone appreciated at the time, and one that greatly increased the danger to Galina Oleinik and the two doctors should they stay on in the region. They would stay on; in fact, they would be Fred's companions into the war zone.

. . .

Beyond conferring with Aryeh Neier at the Soros Foundation headquarters, Fred's three days in New York were a hectic rush. Along with Elisabeth Socolow, he met with officials at several disaster relief organizations and at the United Nations, most notably with Kofi Annan, then the High Commissioner for Human Rights and soon to become the UN Secretary General. On his last night he met up with Samantha Power, a young disaster relief worker whom he had mentored in Sarajevo. Power had been good friends with Sonja Vukotic, Fred's girlfriend at the Bosnian Embassy in Croatia, and during their get-together at a Manhattan bar, it was to Sonja that Fred's conversation kept returning.

"I think he really missed her," Power said, "and felt that he'd made a mistake in letting her get away."

But Fred's interest went beyond wistful reminiscing. He'd heard a rumor that Sonja had been dating someone in the Bosnian Foreign Ministry and his suspicions centered on the former Foreign Minister himself, an extremely handsome diplomat in his late forties named Haris Siladjic. Knowing that Power and Sonja were still in close touch, Fred conducted a persistent interrogation at the Manhattan bar.

"He kept saying, 'I know it's Siladijic, just tell me,'" Power recalled with a laugh, "but I wouldn't. And actually, it wasn't Siladjic—it was a much lower-level guy in the Foreign Ministry—but that was so typical of Fred. Nobody could break up with Fred Cuny just to break up with him, there had to be somebody else, and whoever he was, he had to be at least a government minister."

On her way to meet Fred that night, Power had remembered a photograph she had taken in Sarajevo of Fred with his son, posing by the gate of the "Texas Embassy," their arms around each other's shoulders. She had brought the photo along to show him.

"Fred seemed very touched by it. He just kept staring at it, and he finally said, 'Can I have it?' and put it in his breast pocket. It's funny because, by all accounts, he was as bad as you can get as a father, but all that night, he'd take out the photo and just stare at it for a while."

On March 23, Fred and Elisabeth Socolow left New York on an overnight flight to Vienna. There they met with a Hungarian diplomat who was about to lead a high-level European delegation to Chechnya in hopes of brokering a cease-fire. The next morning, March 25, they flew on to Moscow's Sheremetyevo airport, arriving in early afternoon. It was a drab, overcast day.

In the opinion of many, it was probably at the very moment that Fred passed through Sheremetyevo customs that he came under the watchful eye of Russian intelligence agents.

. . .

"Each man, in his own way, loses his mind," Major General Alexander Mikhailov said with a smile. "That is a proverb we have in Russia, and that is what explains these different stories about Fred Cuny that have appeared in the newspapers. Journalists in our country today are free and each one, in his own way, loses his mind."

The major general was a trim, lithe man in his mid-forties, his olive-drab uniform crisply pressed. With intense, glittery blue eyes and a habitual half grin, he had the air of someone perpetually in the midst of telling an off-color story.

He hunched over his uncluttered desk, lazily rolled a cigarette between two fingers. "With that in mind, I would like to say that this story that we knew of Fred Cuny beforehand, that for some reason we were watching him—absurd, ridiculous. Maybe five or ten years ago, but not now." He took a quick, short pull on the cigarette, his grin widening into a smirk. "We are a democracy now."

General Mikhailov's office on Lubyanka Square in central Moscow was a pleasant room, done in rich, brocaded wallpaper and antique furniture, with great quartered windows giving a view onto the northern skyline of the city. In fact the entire massive stone building is an incongruously attractive structure; with its delicate overhead chandeliers and parquet wood floors buffed to a high gloss, it would seem more likely to be the site of a national museum or an opera house than of one of the most notorious torture centers of the twentieth century.

As headquarters of Stalin's NKVD—later the KGB—the building on Lubyanka Square was where untold thousands of perceived enemies of the Soviet state were brought, there to be tortured into confession and dispatched either to the gulags or the grave. Today, as the headquarters of the Federal Security Service (FSB)—the domestic offshoot of the old KGB—the building still serves as the nerve center of the Russian intelligence apparatus. Except, in the telling of General Mikhailov, the FSB's press spokesman, it wasn't much of a nerve center at all.

By the time he arrived in Moscow Fred Cuny had emerged as one of the most outspoken—and certainly one of the best-connected—American critics of the Russian military campaign in Chechnya. He had spent much of the previous month lobbying senior officials in the Clinton administration for a change in its Chechen policy. He had testified before a House subcommittee on Capitol Hill. By late March the newest issue of the *New York Review of Books* was already on newsstands, and billed on the cover was Fred's article, "Killing Chechnya." Yet, by General Mikhailov's account, absolutely none of this was known to the FSB.

"Who was Fred Cuny?" he asked rhetorically. "I certainly had never heard of him before. Maybe some other branches of the government knew of him, but the FSB had no reason."

It was a slightly humorous statement—perhaps even intentionally so—because by March 1995 it was becoming increasingly difficult to determine just what the Russian government consisted of or who might be in charge of it.

For years Boris Yeltsin, seemingly only interested in maintaining his own hold on power, had pitted one government minister against another, creating a chaos in which the policies and programs of one ministry were routinely undercut by those of another. An increasing number of Kremlinologists around the world, men and women who made their living by trying to interpret the deeper meaning behind Russia's latest cabinet reshuffle or sudden reversal in economic policy, were coming to the disquieting conclusion that it often meant nothing more than that Yeltsin had perceived a rival. The result was governance by caprice, with each minister or adviser scheming to win Yeltsin's approval, to return to his good graces if they had fallen out—or, in many cases, simply pursuing their own agendas without his knowledge. Nothing had so nakedly exposed this state of affairs as the war in Chechnya. From the outset Yeltsin and his various ministers had put forth a mind-bending array of contradictory statements—peace overtures one day, vows of total war the next—and on many occasions Yeltsin had seemed genuinely oblivious to what was actually taking place in the field. As the war ground on, the chaos had multiplied, with individual government ministries, even individual army units, appearing to pursue their own Chechnya policies. Within all this, the intelligence apparatus—and most specifically, the FSB—represented an especially formidable and autonomous power bloc.

"This is the one branch of the old [Soviet] government that was never truly reformed," a U. S. State Department official explained. "All the old guys are still there, and they do what they want to an astonishing degree. Is it possible that the FSB, or some subbranch of the FSB, was watching Fred Cuny on its own initiative, that it decided to move against him without any approval from above? It's absolutely possible."

One small clue to the enduring power of the intelligence apparatus in Russia is the physical condition of the building at Lubyanka Square. In an economically devastated country, and in a city filled with buildings that are quite literally crumbling from decades of neglect, the FSB headquarters is nothing short of resplendent, its exterior walls cleaned of grime, its wood moldings freshly painted. Another clue lay in the words of Major General Mikhailov as he opined about the war in Chechnya.

"From an objective viewpoint," he said, "I think you can see that we made a mistake there starting in 1992, and we have continued to make that mistake worse ever since. We should have finished up there, the earlier the better, and with any means. Instead we engaged in dialogue with bandits. The very moment that we began to speak with the bandits, we perhaps became bandits ourselves because then we stood on the same level with them. Personally, I think we need to take care of this problem once and for all."

It was a remarkable statement, roughly the equivalent of the FBI press spokesman calling the American government illegitimate, but the major general clearly felt secure enough to elaborate. When asked how he proposed to "take care of" the Chechnya problem—and this at a time when Yeltsin was once again talking of peace—Mikhailov lit another cigarette and thoughtfully scanned the ornate plasterwork of his office ceiling.

"Strangle," he offered at last. "Purge. Smother."

. . .

From Sheremetycvo airport on the afternoon of Saturday, March 25, Fred and Elisabeth Socolow boarded a taxi for the drive to downtown Moscow.

Once, this drive had been a pleasant forty-five-minute affair through countryside and suburbs. By 1995 it had become a grinding two- to three-hour ordeal even on weekends, the road falling apart from lack of maintenance and overwhelmed by a volume of traffic that had doubled, then tripled, in recent years. Now the countryside soon gave over to the dreary outskirts of the ever expanding city, a pell-mell sprawl of high-rise apartments, office towers, and construction sites. It seemed the entire landscape of Moscow was being transformed that spring, construction cranes dominating the skyline, everywhere buildings being erected, renovated, or demolished.

They reached the city center shortly before five o'clock, Elisabeth returning to her apartment in the Arbat shopping district, Fred checking into the Radisson Slavjanskaya Hotel a few miles away. That evening they met with two of the people who had accompanied Fred on his first trip to the war zone and who were scheduled to accompany him again: his interpreter, Galina Oleinik, and the International Science Foundation worker, Vyacheslav "Slava" Miklayev. After Fred outlined what he hoped to accomplish on the upcoming trip, it was decided they would leave for the Caucasus on Wednesday, March 29.

. . .

Svetlana Yashina is an attractive woman of thirty-one, but her face bears the worry lines of someone who has lived a hard life. Meeting in a small, stuffy apartment in central Moscow, the only time Svetlana managed a smile was in describing her older sister, Galina Oleinik.

"She is quite a woman," she said, "very dynamic and smart, and always a very good mother to her boy and girl. Sometimes maybe she annoys some men because she is so decisive."

Decisive might have been one way to describe the thirty-five-year-old single mother from Ossetia; domineering might have been another.

After accompanying Fred on his first trip to the North Caucasus in February, Galina had stayed on in Ingushetia and begun working with some of the Russian Red Cross doctors who had arrived to operate the Soros-sponsored mobile trauma unit. Two doctors in particular, Andrei Sereda and Sergei Makarov, seemed to fall under Galina's sway, and by all accounts, it wasn't long before the feisty interpreter from Ossetia had virtually taken over their mission, accompanying them in their UAZ ambulance as she directed them into some of the worst battle zones in Chechnya.

"She seemed to have this idea that relief work meant you just went wherever something bad was happening," Elisabeth Socolow said, "and I think the doctors were totally intimidated by her. They'd complain, but they'd still do what she said."

On March 24, Galina had flown up from Ingushetia to meet Fred upon his arrival in Moscow. Checking into a small hotel in the Arbat district, she called her sister Svetlana—then living in Minsk—that same evening.

"Right away, I could tell something was wrong," Svetlana said.

"She seemed nervous, very preoccupied. I asked her what was the matter, but she wouldn't tell me."

It was something that other people who knew Galina and had encountered her in recent days had noticed as well. As she waited in Ingushetia to be summoned to Moscow, several observed that the normally gregarious and confident woman seemed agitated, even fearful.

Galina's agitation almost certainly stemmed from her experience on the afternoon of March 21 at the Russian army checkpoint outside the village of Assinovskaya, when she and the two Russian Red Cross doctors, Sereda and Makarov, had been detained and accused of being rebel collaborators. That episode had actually been far more ominous than anyone at the Soros Foundation suspected, or that Galina had let on. In fact, Galina had only managed to save herself and the others from execution through a nearly miraculous sequence of events—and the improbability of those events was now placing her in a whole new kind of danger.

Since the beginning of the war, both Chechens and foreign observers had been made aware of a dramatic difference between the two principal Russian military forces sent into Chechnya, those from the regular army, and those from the Ministry of Interior. The regular army units, composed almost entirely of young and poorly trained conscripts, had little stomach for fighting; most simply wanted to do their time and get out in one piece, and went out of their way to avoid the kinds of confrontations that might impede that. The Interior—or OMON—troops, on the other hand, had quickly earned a reputation for brutality and random killing, and the vast majority of atrocities against civilians had been their handiwork. Within this schema, few OMON troops were more notorious than those operating Outpost 6, a crude series of earthen dugouts and gun batteries perched at a crossroads of the Trans-Caucasus Highway outside the village of Assinovskaya.

In mid-December, at a time when fighting was still sporadic, the soldiers at Outpost 6 had opened up with machine guns on a convoy of refugees fleeing Grozny, killing at least nine civilians, including a family whose car was run over by a tank; when ambulances had rushed to the scene, the soldiers had fired on them as well. In January a reporter for the *Washington Post*, Lee Hockstader, had been stopped at the outpost and appeared to be moments away from execution, forced to lie face down in a ditch beside the road with a gun pointed at his head. As a desperate gambit, it occurred to Hockstader to tell the Rambo-emulating OMON soldiers that he was a personal friend of Sylvester Stallone. The ruse worked; instead of being executed, the reporter had been led into the garrison to spend a night drinking vodka and listening to the half-mad rants of the young outpost commander. In the subsequent months the soldiers at Outpost 6 had added to their reputation for robbing, torturing, and murdering many of those unfortunate enough to pass their way, and on the afternoon of March 21 a similar fate had appeared to be in store for Galina, the two doctors, and their three companions in the UAZ ambulance.

Accused of being rebel collaborators, the group was hustled into an armored personnel carrier and taken to a nearby farmhouse. There the driver was severely beaten for several hours and all six threatened with execution if they didn't confess. Finally, a Russian army helicopter had landed to take Galina and the other two women passengers to an army interrogation center in North Ossetia for more thorough questioning.

It was then, according to an account Galina told to several people in Sleptsovskaya, that events took a somewhat fantastic turn. After landing at a military airfield outside the interrogation center, it was discovered that no authorities were on hand to take the women into custody; on the deserted airstrip, the helicopter commander simply instructed Galina to wait until her captors showed up, then flew off again. The feisty interpreter had a better idea. Hailing a passing army transport truck, the three women said they were cleaning ladies trying to get home and asked for a lift into town. Once out of the military compound, they hopped out of the truck and hitchhiked their way back to Ingushetia. Early the next morning Galina went to the Vice-

President of Ingushetia, who interceded to get the three men still being held at Assinovskaya released.

If she had been incredibly lucky to extricate herself and her companions from Assinovskaya, the incident also underscored the growing danger Galina faced in the region. In recent weeks Russian soldiers at checkpoints throughout Chechnya had become increasingly suspicious of rescue workers and their ambulances, believing they were being used to ferry rebel fighters and weapons—and both Galina and the two doctors she had been traveling with had been spotted all along the war front. What's more, after Assinovskaya, there was at least one lawless unit of OMON troops who felt they had been outsmarted by the woman from Ossetia, and were unlikely to risk a repeat should she ever cross their path again.

But the episode may have ratcheted up the peril she faced on the other side of the front as well. As an Ossete, Galina was a "natural" enemy of the Ingush—and, by extension, the Chechens—and rumors that she might be a Russian spy had been circulating in Chechnya almost since her arrival. There had also been the small matter of her profession. Under the old days of the Soviet Union, all interpreters had to be vetted and approved by the KGB, and the price of such approval, it was universally assumed, was an agreement to double as KGB informants. In 1995 that old stigma against interpreters still existed throughout Russia—and most certainly in Chechnya.

Now, in the wake of her escape from the murderous OMON checkpoint at Assinovskaya, suspicions that she was a spy were certain to take on new vigor among the Chechen rebels, themselves becoming increasingly paranoid as the war dragged on. After all, what was the more plausible reason for her unlikely deliverance, her account of incredible Russian incompetence or the far simpler explanation that the soldiers had finally been convinced she was on their side?

Whether Galina appreciated all these ramifications of Assinovskaya isn't known. What is known is that she consistently downplayed the gravity of the incident, both in its initial reporting and upon her arrival in Moscow to meet up with Fred. Whether fearful of sabotaging the mission and losing a job she desperately needed, or because she had simply become inured to danger, or because she was actually in Chechnya for another purpose, Galina spoke of the episode as little as possible to Soros officials.

"I asked her about it," Elisabeth Socolow said, "and she said, 'Oh yeah, we had some small trouble,' and that was it."

But as to the idea that her sister might have been a spy, Svetlana Yashina was derisive. "That is crazy. If she were a spy, she would have left when she saw there was trouble. She stayed because it was a job and she felt loyal to Fred." She paused to gaze out the window at the crowded streets of Moscow. "But I don't know why she went back. I really can't understand that, because already she was frightened."

· · ·

Over those next three days Fred raced about Moscow, holding a series of meetings with Russian antiwar activists, diplomats, and officials from international aid organizations. He had hoped to meet again with Thomas Pickering, the American ambassador to Russia, but Pickering had just left on a tour of the Baltic republics; instead, Fred talked with several of the senior political affairs officers at the embassy, and tentatively arranged to see the ambassador on the evening of April 4, the same day he planned to return from the Caucasus. By the evening of March 28, Fred's Moscow meetings were over. He was packing his bags at the Radisson Slavjanskaya Hotel for the morning flight to Ingushetia, when a telephone call came from his assistant, Slava Miklayev. A small problem had arisen, Slava explained.

In the five weeks since accompanying Fred on his first trip to the war zone, Slava had been shuttling between Moscow and the North Caucasus, mainly arranging the delivery of supplies to the Russian Red Cross doctors operating the mobile trauma unit in Ingushetia. For the past ten days he had been in Moscow organizing the latest effort, a convoy of relief and medical supplies that was scheduled to leave for

Ingushetia on the morning of March 29; with Slava, Fred, and Galina flying down that same morning, they would be on hand to meet the convoy when it arrived.

That last evening, however, Slava had received a call from the convoy supervisor who explained that, owing to a family emergency, he wouldn't be able to make the journey. After pondering the problem in his hotel room, Fred decided that Slava should now go overland with the convoy, while he and Galina flew on to Ingushetia and waited for him there.

"I told him I would get there on Saturday, the first of April," Slava said, "and Fred said that was fine. He promised to wait for me, to not go into Chechnya until I got there."

On the midmorning of March 29, Fred and Galina boarded a Tupolev jet at Moscow's Vnukovo Airport for the three-hour flight to Ingushetia, arriving there in early afternoon. From the airport they set out on the half-hour drive to the capital city of Nazran, where they met with the President and Vice-President of Ingushetia. They spent that night at the Presidential Guest House in Nazran, just down a pitted dirt road from the Presidential Palace.

Early the next morning Fred and Galina hired a taxi to take them east, back past the airport to the town of Sleptsovskaya, flush on the border with Chechnya. At the Central Republican Hospital in Sleptsovskaya, Fred met a number of the Soros-sponsored mobile trauma unit doctors for the first time. Among them were Andrei Sereda and Sergei Makarov.

At first glance the two appeared to be very different types of men. Sereda, a thirty-two-year-old internist, was rather slight and retiring, his short brown hair rapidly receding. By contrast, the bearded and darker-complected Makarov, a forty-year-old surgeon, was husky and gregarious. Yet the two men did share at least one personality trait: both seemed powerfully drawn to war. In just twenty-four hours they would join Fred Cuny as he set off for the battlefield.

. . .

Central Republican Hospital is a small, decaying two-story building surrounded by leafy trees on a quiet side street of Sleptsovskaya.
On the third floor is the office of the hospital administrator, a compact,
middle-aged man named Mogamed Nakastoyev. It was into this same
office that Andrei Sereda and Sergei Makarov, newly arrived from Moscow, had been ushered on the afternoon of March 3, 1995. As he spoke
of that meeting, and his subsequent dealings with the two doctors, Nakastoyev's tone of irritation gradually descended into naked
anger.

"What were they doing here?" he asked rhetorically. "That I cannot tell you. They never told me anything. They arrived incognito, they
left incognito. They were supposed to receive permission for all matters
from me, but instead they never told me anything."

At first it appeared his anger was that of a petty bureaucrat bris-
tling against those who refused to submit to his authority, but there was
also a none too subtle implication in Nakastoyev's words.

Colleagues at the Moscow Institute of Traumatology, Andrei
Sereda and Sergei Makarov had first volunteered their services to the
Russian Red Cross during the 1992 border war in Moldova, and then in
the 1993 Abkhazian secessionist war in Georgia. In the winter of 1995
they had again volunteered, this time for Chechnya, joining the mobile
trauma unit being dispatched to the region with Soros Foundation
funding. To meet accreditation requirements imposed by the Russian
government, the various doctors had been officially attached to the
Central Republican Hospital in Sleptsovskaya and placed under the
supervision of Mogamed Nakastoyev.

As made clear by the hospital administrator, that arrangement
had begun to fray almost immediately—and largely through the actions
of Andrei Sereda and Sergei Makarov. Usually accompanied by Galina
Oleinik, the two quickly developed the habit of taking their ambulance
across the border into Chechnya and directly into some of the worst
battle zones in the country. They also frequently ventured into mountain villages controlled by the rebels to operate emergency-care clinics
and hand out medical supplies.

All this activity had apparently come to the attention of the Russian military—or at least to the attention of the OMON troops operating Outpost 6 outside Assinovskaya on the afternoon of March 21. Like Galina, Andrei and Sergei had been accused by the OMON troops of aiding the rebels and threatened with execution. In the wake of that incident, the doctors were likely to face a deeper enmity from Russian soldiers throughout the war zone.

But Andrei and Sergei were also being viewed with deepening suspicion by the Chechen rebels in late March. Part of the distrust could perhaps be traced to skepticism over their strange escape from the Assinovskaya checkpoint—at least among those rebels who knew of it—but it also stemmed from an external factor over which the doctors had no control.

The trauma unit mission in the Caucasus operated under the official auspices of the Russian Red Cross, and decals bearing the organization's distinctive red logo and Cyrillic lettering were plastered on each side of medical teams' UAZ ambulances. For all the doctors in Sleptsovskaya, that posed a growing problem.

Throughout history, the Russian Red Cross has been regarded, both within Russian and abroad, as thoroughly infiltrated by Russian intelligence, and that belief had found especially fertile ground among the Chechen separatists. In recent weeks a surge of rumors had been circulating through rebel-held territory that told of Russian and foreign spies posing as medics, journalists, and relief workers; while scrutiny was now being directed at all outsiders, it was particularly intense for anyone affiliated with the Russian Red Cross.

What's more, Andrei and Sergei had become very specific targets of this rumor mill. By the middle of March a whisper campaign had begun spreading through the hospital in Sleptsovskaya, suggesting the two men were actually spies sent from Moscow, using the cover of their UAZ ambulance to get an intimate look at the battlefield.

While he wouldn't directly confirm this belief, Mogamed Nakastoyev, the Sleptsovskaya hospital administrator, came quite close. "I do not know what their real mission was in being here," he said, sitting primly behind his desk. He stared, raised his eyebrows for emphasis. "Do you understand what I am saying? I do not know what their real mission was here."

In a hallway just outside the hospital operating room a burly middle-aged doctor leaned against a wall taking a cigarette break from surgery, the fresh blood spattered over his green smock drawing worried stares from the families of patients gathered nearby. When asked his opinion of Andrei Sereda and Sergei Makarov, the surgeon gave a wan smile.

"That is a difficult question, very difficult." He dropped the cigarette to the floor and crushed it beneath his shoe. "In any event, it's best not to talk badly of the dead."

. . .

After their meeting with the Russian Red Cross doctors on that morning of March 3o, Fred and Galina borrowed one of the unit's UAZ ambulances and drove off. Their first stop was just a few blocks away, at the dilapidated two-story building at the south end of Sleptsovskaya's main square that housed the Russian government's Ministry of States of Emergency and Elimination of Consequences of Natural Disasters— Emergency Situations for short.

Throughout the war in Chechnya, the Emergency Situations office in Sleptsovskaya acted as a kind of guarantor for relief groups operating on the battlefield, providing them with official transit papers, as well as arranging for drivers and guides. Fred had had fairly extensive dealings with the agency on his first trip to the region and knew many of the men and women who worked inside the building.

On that Thursday morning Fred and Galina climbed to the second floor of Emergency Situations to meet with its chief minister, Hamzat Bekov. They were going to Grozny for the day, Fred apparently told Bekov, and they needed a driver. In short order the director arranged for one: a pleasant sandy-haired Chechen in his early thirties named Ruslan Muradov. At about ten-thirty, Ruslan climbed behind the wheel of the UAZ ambulance and the three set out for the frontier.

Until the war, the forty mile drive from Sleptsovskaya to Grozny had been an easy jaunt down the Trans-Caucasus Highway, the main east-west artery that ran the breadth of Chechnya. With that highway now blocked and mined by the Russian army, there were two principal routes from Sleptsovskaya to the Chechen capital.

One was a patchwork link of back-country lanes—some dirt, some heavily pitted asphalt—that led east through the Chechen lowlands and roughly shadowed the Trans-Caucasus Highway. While not appreciably longer than the old highway, this route was slow on account of the series of Russian army checkpoints along its length, and frequently cut altogether when there was combat in the area. The alternative was a dirt road that cut north from Sleptsovskaya, winding over a range of low mountains before connecting up with a fast paved highway that led southeast directly into the capital. Although grueling and much longer than the other route, this path was both free of army checkpoints and well clear of the current battlefields, and it was the route that Fred's group chose that morning.

They reached Grozny shortly after noon. After meeting with several relief officials based in the capital and surveying the further destruction that had taken place since Fred's first visit, the group headed back to Ingushetia, anxious to be out of Chechnya before the dusk curfew took effect.

During that return drive Fred patched a call through to Aryeh Neier in New York on one of the two battery-powered portable radios he had brought down from Moscow.

"It was a fairly short call," Neier recalled, "and mainly dealt preliminarily with some of the recommendations he would be making based on what he'd seen in Grozny. He wanted to set up a small radio station to broadcast information on families' whereabouts because so many families had been scattered by the fighting. He was concerned about a cholera outbreak and wanted to establish a small epidemiological clinic. At that point, quite a few people were coming back into Grozny and finding their homes in shambles, and he thought he could either purchase or design a small kit of tools that they could use to do simple repairs."

In Neier's recollections, Fred gave no indication during that phone call of his plans for the days ahead, but it seems fairly certain he had already made them. At some point on that trip to Grozny, he evidently asked Ruslan to be available the following morning for another journey into Chechnya, one that might last several days. They arranged to meet at 10 A.M. in front of the Emergency Situations building in Sleptsovskaya.

. . .

In more peaceful times, the Caucasus has been described as a land of mystery and intrigue. By March 1995, a visitor might have been more likely to describe it as a snakepit, a place where it was virtually impossible to determine where real loyalties lay. This fog of treachery was not confined to the war zone of Chechnya but extended throughout the region—and nowhere was it thicker than in Ingushetia, the mini-republic from which Fred Cuny was now operating.

With the Chechens, the Ingush had a shared history, ethnicity, language, and religion, and if most were thankful that their tiny homeland had remained a part of the Russian Federation—if only to have escaped the vengeance being inflicted on the secessionists in Chechnya—most Ingush made no secret that their sympathies lay with their Chechen blood cousins. The result was a kind of double-dealing neutrality that made World War II–era Switzerland appear a pillar of moral rectitude by comparison.

By March 1995, Ingushetia, as part of the Russian Federation, was serving as a listening post and supply route for the Russian military in their campaign in Chechnya, but they were also providing much the same services to the Chechen rebels. Both the President of Ingushetia, Ruslan Aushev, and his Vice-President, Boris Agapov, were said to be close friends of Dzhokhar Dudayev—bonds that seemed little affected by the fact that Aushev was still a standing one-star general in the Russian air force, or that Agapov had until recently been a lieutenant general in the KGB.

There were few places where this divided loyalty was more evident—or more bewildering—than in the Emergency Situations office in Sleptsovskaya. While an official agency of the Russian government, the Sleptsovskaya branch was almost wholly manned by natives of Ingushetia. The result was that the Russian government was not only overseeing relief operations in a country that it was waging war against, but doing so through the services of a group of civilian bureaucrats who were tacitly supporting the other side.

Fred Cuny was certainly aware of this nest-of-vipers atmosphere within Emergency Situations and, compounded by the corruption and favor-trading endemic to all Russian government agencies, he probably figured that any bit of interesting news that floated through its doors would very quickly find its way to both warring sides in Chechnya. As a result, it appears he was very careful not to tell anyone at Emergency Situations where he was headed on the morning of March 31.

But even if Fred took great care on that score, it's unlikely he had any idea of the close ties between Emergency Situations and Ruslan Muradov, the local hire who undoubtedly knew precisely what the day's itinerary entailed and may have even had a hand in fashioning it.

From a small mountain village in western Chechnya named Bamut, Ruslan had fled into Ingushetia in early January as the Russian offensive spread west across the lowlands and into the hills. In Sleptsovskaya he had found occasional work as a driver for Emergency Situations and, by his own account, had even driven Fred several times during his earlier visit. But neither Ruslan's choosing to seek refuge in Sleptsovskaya, nor his ability to find such work, was purely coincidental. Since arriving from Bamut, he had been staying with his sister and brother-in-law, both of whom were employees of Emergency situations.

At about nine-thirty on the morning of March 31, the phone rang in Elisabeth Socolow's office at the Soros Foundation in Moscow. It was Fred, calling from the Presidential Guest House in Ingushetia.

Reaching for the notepad she had learned to keep close at hand whenever Fred was likely to call, Elisabeth quickly took down notes on his impressions of Grozny from the day before, as well as his shopping list of tools that would be needed for his home-repair kits. Toward the end of the conversation he said he was going back inside Chechnya that day but would return that evening or by the following day at the latest. Elisabeth, mindful of the lack of security on Russian telephones, did not ask where in Chechnya he was headed, and Fred did not offer the information. Still, she detected a strange tone in his voice as he spoke of the day's plans, a certain hushed quality.

"Are you all right, Fred?" she finally asked.

There was a long pause on the line, before he answered in a very soft voice.

"Just think about me."

. . .

Shortly after eleven o'clock on the morning of March 31 five people emerged from the Emergency Situations building at the south end of Sleptsovskaya's main square. Crossing to the tree-lined curb, they climbed aboard a gray UAZ ambulance with Russian Red Cross decals and pulled away. In the front passenger seat was Fred Cuny, and behind the wheel was Ruslan Muradov. Between them, sitting on a small chair in the passageway leading to the ambulance bay, was Galina Oleinik. Behind her, perched somewhat uncomfortably amid boxes of medical supplies and two bulky battery-powered field radios, were the two doctors, Andrei Sereda and Sergei Makarov.

Once out of Sleptsovskaya, the ambulance headed south, across the Ingush plains for the Caucasus foothills. By noon they had reached the outskirts of the small foothill town of Galashki. There, Ruslan turned left off the paved road, onto a steep, gravel-strewn lane that led down to the Assa River and a low, one-lane metal bridge that forded it.

Within minutes they began climbing again, up a muddy track that led into the Caucasus Mountains. At about 2 P.M. they would cross some unmarked spot on a windswept plateau, and then they would be out of Ingushetia and in the war zone. The first town they would come to upon crossing the frontier was the mountain village of Bamut.

. . .

One of the enduring mysteries is why Fred's group chose to travel the Bamut road. And, as with every other aspect of their disappearance, the theories would range from the simple and innocent, to the darkly byzantine.

About the only certain conclusion that can be drawn from the decision was that they were intent on reaching rebel-held territory and—given the very short timetable Fred had outlined to Elisabeth Socolow—were not planning to venture very far inside. Beyond that, it gets murky.

In recent days Fred had indicated to several people that he was anxious to meet again with the Chechen chief of staff, General Aslan Maskhadov, and through him, gain an audience with President Dudayev. One rumor circulating at the end of March held that both Maskhadov and Dudayev were in a rebel-held village just to the east of Bamut. It's also possible that Galina and the doctors, mindful of their close call at Assinovskaya, convinced Fred to stay well away from any Russian army checkpoints on their dash into rebel territory, and there certainly were no such checkpoints on the Bamut road. Then, of course, Bamut was Ruslan Muradov's hometown; perhaps the guide simply convinced the others that it was the safest route into Chechnya.

Yet none of these possible explanations would prove completely satisfying. The rumor that Dudayev was in the Bamut area was but one of at least a half dozen purported sightings of the President at the time, and all such rumors were widely regarded as rebel disinformation ploys to protect their fugitive leader from Russian assassination squads. From a purely logical standpoint—albeit a dubious vantage point from which to gauge anything in Chechnya—it made far more sense that

Dudayev, a man with an aversion to front-line combat, might be found in his relatively safe "liberated zone" stronghold below Grozny than in the increasingly dangerous environs of Bamut.

Nor would any apprehensions about army checkpoints seem to be a deciding factor. One of the many bizarre aspects of the Russian army's campaign in the countryside was the haphazardness of its checkpoint "system," with some roads studded with garrisons and others left virtually unwatched. As a result, it was quite possible with a little elementary planning to chart a path from Ingushetia to almost anywhere in Chechnya, including rebel-held territory, and to avoid the most troublesome checkpoints altogether. In fact, Fred, Galina, and Ruslan had displayed just such planning the previous day on their trip to Grozny, eschewing the garrison-thick Trans-Caucasus "shadow road" in favor of the northern road that afforded a checkpoint-free passage to the capital. From Grozny, there was then a completely open road down into the rebel's "liberated zone," one that both journalists and relief workers were traveling constantly.

Finally, it's hard to imagine how Ruslan Muradov or anyone else might have convinced the others of Bamut's safety given a detailed report on the latest Russian military offensive that Galina had written for Fred on March 17, just two weeks earlier.

"[The towns of] Shali, Argun, Gudermes and Bamut are currently under intense attack," Galina had written. "For more than a week, Bamut was bombarded by tanks and under constant fire. . . . According to several sources, Russian forces have been given until April 1 when the weather begins to warm up to complete their campaign. . . . Thus, it is possible that combat activity will intensify in the next two weeks."

By the end of March the first three towns Galina had named had all fallen and only Bamut remained in rebel hands—which only meant that the Russians could now direct even more firepower at the village. This they were doing. By March 31 the Russians had cut off Bamut on three sides and were pounding it with artillery and tank fire; the last route into the area from Ingushetia was the narrow dirt track over the mountains that Fred's group traveled. What's more, even if he had chosen to ignore Galina's report, it's quite inconceivable that Fred could have been unaware of the battle raging for the village. Throughout the two days he had spent coming and going from Sleptsovskaya, the Russians' steady shelling of Bamut—only eleven miles away as the crow flies—echoed through the streets of the border town.

Yet, even by the standards of Chechnya, there was something a bit bizarre about the Russians' dogged determination to take Bamut—and one possible answer to that riddle also provides the most intriguing theory of why those in the UAZ chose the path they did.

All the other towns that Galina had cited as targets in the Russians' March offensive were in the valley lowlands, and their seizure fit into the Russian strategy of "pacifying" the plains and pushing the rebels into the mountains. Bamut, on the other hand, was a foothill town with little intrinsic strategic value. Although its location close to the Ingushetia border might make it seem a likely supply route when viewed on a map, the reality was that the rugged and exposed dirt track that linked them was an easy kill-zone for Russian helicopter gunships. What's more, in the steep hills that surrounded Bamut, the Russians' chief advantages over the rebels—planes, tanks, and heavy artillery—were next to useless. From a purely tactical standpoint, it made far more sense for the Russians to simply seal off Bamut and the neighboring villages; with their backs quite literally against the mountains, the rebels would have had little room to maneuver and would have been largely cut off from the bulk of their forces to the east.

But there was at least one more crucial detail about Bamut that set it apart from other mountain villages in Chechnya, a detail that may have explained why the Russians were so intent on capturing it, why the rebels were intent on defending it, and why someone in the UAZ ambulance may have been determined to reach it. Behind a razor-wired fence at one end of the town was a vast underground complex, an old—and officially decommissioned—Russian nuclear missile base.

Of course, "officially" was a very relative term in Boris Yeltsin's Russia. According to some reports, it was to this very area of Chechnya that the CIA had sent a team of agents in 1994, trying to track down rumors that Dzhokhar Dudayev had got his hands on two nuclear warheads.

. . .

In the weeks ahead, as he learned details of Fred's last journey, Damir Lulo, the Bosnian engineer back in Dallas, would be reminded of a personality trait of Fred's that he had first noticed in Sarajevo.

"He trusted people," Damir said. "Sometimes too much. It surprised me, because he was a man who had been in so many bad places, but he had this tendency to believe too much in what people told him. I remember several times in Sarajevo when, after some meeting, we'd be driving away and I'd say to Fred, 'That guy was lying,' and Fred would always be disappointed and surprised. So in Chechnya, I'm afraid that was his mistake, that he believed and trusted in the wrong people."

If so, it still left the question of who and where those "wrong people" were: in the ambulance with him, somewhere on either side of the Chechen battlefield, or back in "neutral" Ingushetia? Or maybe farther back still, in Moscow or even Washington?

Whatever the answer, there would be a peculiar touch of omen about Fred's two journeys into the worst war zone of his life. On his first trip, the place that had held special importance was the city of Grozny. On this second journey, it would be the small mountain town of Bamut. In Russian, Grozny means "fearsome." In ancient Chechnyan, Bamut means "eternal."

CHAPTER 8

If anyone goes missing for four days in Chechnya,
it means they're dead.
—Fred Cuny, March 1995

VYACHESLAV "SLAVA" MIKLAYEV didn't look much like a war
relief worker. In fact, he appeared a bit dangerous himself.

A taciturn man in his late thirties for whom smiling seemed almost a painful act, he still had the powerful build and faintly military
bearing of his years spent in the Soviet air force. There was a sense of
watchfulness in his manner—in his slow, measured gestures, in the
opaque stare of his eyes—and when he spoke it was in a low, unin-
flected monotone, barely above a whisper. As a result, it was hard to
imagine Slava Miklayev as the same man who, by his own account and
those of others, repeatedly risked his life as he combed the battlefields
of Chechnya looking for Fred Cuny and his missing companions. By
way of explanation, Slava gave a slight shrug.

"I liked Fred. He was a good person. He was a pilot. I was a pilot."

Yet, as he spoke of those bewildering days in April and May 1995, there was the suggestion of a more complex reason, a kind of guilt. By an apparently chance turn of events, Slava narrowly missed being in the UAZ ambulance that left Sleptsovskaya that day.

Like tens of millions of his Russian countrymen, Slava Miklayev's life had been turned upside down by the political and economic collapse of the Soviet Union. After a career as a military helicopter pilot, he had been cashiered from the air force following the Soviet Union's disintegration in 1991, then bankrupted by the collapse of the ruble the following year. Considering the staggering unemployment rate in Russia as it made the painful transition to a "free market," the former pilot was extremely lucky to find any job at all. He found one in August 1993 at the Moscow office of the International Science Foundation (ISF), a new initiative by George Soros designed to stem the "brain drain" from the former Soviet Union nations by subsidizing the salaries of scientists and technocrats. For many months Slava worked in the ISF stockroom, mainly boxing up and mailing various Foundation publications to interested parties. In January 1995 he saw a chance to escape the stockroom when Soros launched his humanitarian aid effort for Chechnya; volunteering to assist the mission, Slava accompanied Fred on his first trip to the war zone the following month.

"There I saw that Fred was trying to do very good things," he said. "From that time, I was determined to help him."

Slava faced a major test of that determination shortly after returning from the first trip. Given the broad scope of the mission Fred was envisioning in Chechnya, he was going to need at least one full-time employee to coordinate activities between the North Caucasus and Moscow, and Slava was a logical choice. But Fred had also arranged to remove his projects from ISF control, which meant that to take on the assignment, Slava would have to resign from his position at ISF and become a contract employee of Intertect; in other words, give up a secure, if somewhat menial, job for one that was very controversial, very dangerous, and—not the least consideration for a man with a young family to support in the still devastated Russian economy—ran the risk of ending at any time.

Still, Slava did not hesitate. Shortly after returning to Moscow from that first trip to Chechnya he resigned from the ISF and signed on with Intertect. At the end of February he had set out for the war zone again, accompanying Galina Oleinik and some of the Russian Red Cross doctors who were to operate the mobile trauma unit starting up in Sleptsovskaya. All through March, as he waited for Fred's return, he shuttled between the North Caucasus and Moscow, arranging the delivery of relief supplies from the capital and often traveling with Galina and the doctors, Sereda and Makarov, on their rescue missions over the Chechen battlefield.

If Slava Miklaycv had found in Fred Cuny a man he both respected and trusted, those sentiments were clearly reciprocated. Throughout March, whenever Elisabeth Socolow, newly arrived in Moscow to act as Fred's liaison, called Fred back in the United States with a question, his answer was likely to be the same.

"It was always, 'Ask Slava; Slava knows all about it,' " Elisabeth said.

On the morning of March 25, as Fred and Elisabeth had rushed through the Vienna airport to catch their flight to Moscow, Fred had suddenly ducked into an airport gift shop; he emerged with a small metal lapel pin depicting a Russian attack helicopter. It was a gift for Slava, he told Elisabeth, the same model of helicopter Slava had flown during his days in the Soviet military. At their reunion at the Radisson Slavjanskaya Hotel in Moscow that evening, Fred gave his Russian assistant the pin.

"It was very nice to see him again, and it was a very nice gift," Slava said, still watchful, still unsmiling. "I still have it with me."

. . .

On the evening of Saturday, April 1, Slava Miklayev arrived in the Ingush capital of Nazran. For the past two and a half days he had been on the road, supervising a convoy of Soros-donated medical and relief supplies on the thousand-mile journey from Moscow. In Nazran he drove straight to the Presidential Guest House, a small cluster of two-story buildings set behind a high wall just four blocks from the Presidential Palace, and the closest thing Ingushetia had to a hotel. In talking with the guest-house manager, an elderly, stoop-shouldered man, he learned that Fred and Galina had left the previous morning and had not returned.

Originally, Slava had been slated to fly down to Ingushetia with Fred and Galina on March 29, but a last-minute hitch had altered those plans. On the night of March 28 the designated supervisor of the convoy had suddenly begged off the trip, and it was decided that Slava would take his place. Before parting ways in Moscow that Wednesday morning, Slava had made Fred and Galina promise that they would not go into Chechnya but would wait in Ingushetia until he arrived with the convoy on Saturday evening.

Finding them not at the Nazran guest house, Slava recounted, he figured Fred and Galina were probably in Sleptsovskaya, some forty kilometers to the east. Flush on the border of western Chechnya, Sleptsovskaya was the base of operations for the handful of international relief organizations working in the war zone, as well as for the Soros-sponsored mobile trauma unit attached to Central Republican Hospital. He briefly debated trying to call over to the hospital but decided against it; the phone system in the region, never very good to begin with, had become practically useless since the collapse of the Soviet Union, and getting even a local call through could mean a long wait at the government's telephone exchange office. Instead, and despite his exhaustion from the drive and the considerable danger of traveling in Ingushetia at night—with the war next door, soldiers and police were everywhere and very jumpy—Slava set out for the frontier town. As he approached Sleptsovskaya that Saturday night, the sky over western Chechnya was lit as if by sheet lightning from the flashes of

Russian artillery, the muffled rumble of explosions echoing over the valley like an approaching storm.

At Central Republican Hospital there was no sign of Fred or Galina. Driving the few blocks over to the walled compound where most of the doctors were living, Slava banged on the metal gate until the elderly housekeeper was roused. It was from her that Slava got the first intimation that the promise made to him in Moscow had been broken.

The previous morning, the housekeeper said, Galina Oleinik and a very tall foreign man she had never seen before arrived at the compound. The two doctors who frequently traveled with Galina, Andrei Sereda and Sergei Makarov, had put several boxes of medical supplies in one of the UAZ ambulances and then left with them. With nothing more to be done that night, Slava brought his car into the compound courtyard for safekeeping, then went to sleep.

As he made the rounds of the different relief agencies in Sleptsovskaya the next morning, Slava gradually pieced together a hazy picture of his colleagues' movements, but the more people he talked to, the more confusing that picture became. Evidently the four had set off in the ambulance on Friday morning bound for somewhere in Chechnya, but that was about all the various accounts agreed on. According to some, they had left with a single guide provided by the Emergency Situations office, a young Chechen man named Ruslan Muradov, while others said they had left in the escort of two Emergency Situations officials traveling in a separate car. Likewise, some recalled the group saying they would be returning that same night, while others remembered talk of a two- to three-day trip.

If a little annoyed that Fred and Galina had broken their promise to stay out of Chechnya, Slava was not overly concerned that Sunday. If the reports of a two- to three-day trip were accurate, they might be returning that day. Throughout the afternoon Slava maintained a vigil in the square outside the Emergency Situations building. By dusk there was still no sign of them. At last light, the Russian artillery in western Chechnya started up again.

. . .

Ever since she had detected the hushed tone in Fred's voice on Friday morning, Elisabeth Socolow had been held by a vague sense of unease, one that deepened over the course of the weekend. In that last telephone conversation, Fred had said he would call Elisabeth again when he returned from Chechnya—that night, or Saturday at the latest. By Monday, April 3, there had still been no word.

But, Elisabeth reminded herself, she was twenty-seven years old and had never been to a war zone; Fred Cuny was nearly twice her age, had maneuvered his way over scores of battlefields, and he certainly knew how to take care of himself. In all likelihood, he had gone into some back corner of Chechnya beyond the range of his field radio and had found a good enough reason—a group of refugees in desperate need, perhaps, or a meeting with Dudayev—to stay longer. From what she had heard of Fred's reputation, it wouldn't be the first time he had gone "missing" for a while.

And it wasn't as if Elisabeth didn't have other things to worry about that Monday. As of that morning, she was now the acting co-director of the Open Society Institute for all of Russia, the outgoing director having left for the United States on Friday, and Elisabeth had spent most of the weekend trying to familiarize herself with all the myriad projects going on around the country. Still, she was anxious to talk with Fred, if for no other reason than that his tightly calibrated travel schedule after Chechnya was quickly proving unworkable.

He was planning to return to Moscow on the evening of the fourth, and he had hoped to meet with Ambassador Pickering that same evening. The next day, he would fly on to Budapest for a conference with Katalin Koncz, the executive director of the Open Society Institute in Eastern Europe, then on to New York. Above all other plans, Fred was anxious to be in San Diego no later than the evening of Saturday, April 8, in order to attend the military-civilian disaster relief conference at Camp Pendleton.

In the interim, though, Elisabeth had learned that Ambassador Pickering was going to be out of Moscow until the fifth. If Fred still planned on attending the Camp Pendleton affair, he would probably have to choose between seeing Pickering or Koncz—and Elisabeth couldn't cancel or rearrange anything until she got hold of Fred.

On that Monday morning she wrote two words in her journal as the day's first order of business: "Find Fred."

*　*　*

On that same morning in Sleptsovskaya, Slava recalled, a bit of deductive reasoning made him fairly confident that he knew where Fred and the others had gone.

"They hadn't called on the field radios," Slava explained. "Since those radios only had a range of maybe thirty kilometers, it meant they were somewhere farther away."

On several occasions in Moscow, Fred had mentioned to Slava that he wanted to meet again with General Aslan Maskhadov—the Chechen rebel chief of staff, and a man Fred had developed a good rapport with on his first trip—and, through Maskhadov, hopefully get to the Chechen President, Dzhokhar Dudayev. To that end, the group had probably headed for Maskhadov's headquarters in the town of Vedeno, some seventy kilometers below Grozny in the foothills of southern Chechnya.

If Slava's hunch was right, it shouldn't be very hard to find them. That Monday morning he returned to the Emergency Situations building in Sleptsovskaya and climbed the concrete stairs to the radio dispatcher's room.

At that time, getting to Vedeno from Ingushetia was fairly simple and, while small variations were possible, virtually all routes meant passing through Grozny, then traveling the open road south into the rebel's "liberated zone." Knowing Fred Cuny as he did, Slava was sure the group would have checked in with at least one of the relief agencies working in the capital. From the radio operator's room of Emergency

Situations, he put a call through to the Russian Red Cross office in Grozny and asked them to check around with whatever relief groups were in the city, and with anyone who may have been in Vedeno over the weekend. Slava waited in the corridor outside the operator's room for news.

By early afternoon word came back: no one had seen Fred Cuny or anyone else in the Soros group, not in Grozny and not in Vedeno.

According to Slava, this puzzling news raised a far more worrisome scenario in his mind: perhaps the group had gone into western Chechnya. If so, there was no telling where they might be or how they might be trying to get out, because western Chechnya had now become one of the most chaotic and deadly corners on earth, and was getting more so by the day.

Given the completely haphazard—even arbitrary—manner in which the Russian army was conducting its current offensive in the region, battle was just as likely to suddenly erupt on the road ahead as behind or to either side. What's more, given the perverse mindset common to soldiers in combat situations everywhere, anyone in or near that particular moment's target zone was likely to be viewed as an enemy. The result was that anyone attempting to travel in western Chechnya at that moment was playing a terrifying game of chance.

Added to this was the fact that standard measures of distance had meant very little in western Chechnya even in peacetime. Other than the Trans-Caucasus Highway and a few badly paved secondary arteries, virtually all roads in the region were dirt. In some areas these roads were so badly engineered that even a slight rain created washouts or impassable bogs of mud. In others, the soil was of such an extraordinarily fine, talclike consistency that any rain produced a kind of mud that seemed to share more properties with ice than earth; drivers, even pedestrians, could suddenly find themselves sliding uncontrollably off the surface and into a ditch.

If a hindrance in peacetime, such a mishap could quickly prove fatal in April 1995. Anyone stranded out in the open with a disabled vehicle ran the risk of falling victim to marauding Russian helicopter gunships, especially if it placed them in "violation" of the dusk-to-dawn curfew. On the night of April 2 it had begun to rain in western Chechnya, a steady drizzle that was continuing all that next day.

Even beyond these "normal" dangers, the Cuny group faced an added peril if they were in western Chechnya, for it was here that Galina and the two doctors had escaped their brush with death at the Assinovskaya checkpoint two weeks earlier, details of which Galina had confided to Slava. "I knew that she was a little upset by that," Slava said with his usual understatement, "that she didn't want to meet those soldiers again." By the beginning of April, with the Russians' western offensive expanding and more back roads being "sealed," most any route in or out of the area would now lead the group directly back to the Assinovskaya checkpoint.

With word that no one in Grozny had seen Fred's party, Slava crossed the second-floor hallway of Emergency Situations to the office of the deputy minister, Magomet Dauerbekov. Appreciating the potential seriousness of the situation, Dauerbekov ordered the radio operator to call Russian military units throughout western Chechnya to find out if the group had been detained at any of their checkpoints. The radio operator also called the duty officer at the Russian army's "filtration center" in Mozdok, a prison fifty miles to the northwest where suspected Chechen rebels were taken for torture and interrogation.

As those calls were going out, Slava drove to the Presidential Palace in Nazran, where he asked to meet with the Vice-President of Ingushetia, Major General Boris Agapov. Less than two months earlier Agapov had hosted cease-fire negotiations between the Chechens and senior Russian military officers, and he had frequently sought advice from a highly experienced consultant who had happened to be in the region at the time: Fred Cuny. Now, on the afternoon of April 3, the Ingush Vice-President began calling his own contacts on both sides in Chechnya, asking for any information on the missing group.

When Slava returned to Sleptsovskaya that evening the Emergency

Situations radio operator had more dispiriting news. All Russian units had given the same response: no one had detained the group, no one had seen them.

All the next day, April 4, the fruitless calls continued. It also continued to rain.

Shortly after six that evening, as Slava sat outside the radio operator's office chain-smoking filterless cigarettes, a short, rain-soaked figure appeared in the second-floor hallway. It was Ruslan Muradov, the driver of Fred's group, and he was carrying a note for Slava. Snatching the single sheet of notebook paper from Muradov's hand, Slava quickly read it through. It was in Russian and in Galina Oleinik's handwriting, but it was a message from Fred.

April 4

Dear Slava,

Everything that's happened has of course knocked us off schedule, but everything that's happened doesn't depend on us. We wanted to make it to Atchkoi Martan but we were stopped for several days in Bamut. Shooting on the road, bad weather, mud on the road. We are trying to go by a different road but it's most likely we will still be held up for 2 or 3 days.

From there, Fred turned to the mundane matters of rearranging his itinerary.

Please tell Liz [Elisabeth Socolow] to cancel the meeting with the American Ambassador and all the other meetings. Fred will reschedule them when he returns, and also Kati [Katalin Koncz] in Budapest. Tell Kati that Fred is being held up and will call as soon as he can. Liz knows who that is. Call to the office in Dallas and tell them that Fred will be held up until the beginning of next week.

By Slava's account, the arrival of the note put him in a euphoric mood. "To me, it was very, very good news. I think maybe I even hugged Ruslan Muradov."

Beyond the distinct possibility that the group had been caught in a combat crossfire, Slava explained, his worst fears all along had been that they had run afoul of a Russian checkpoint. In the Bamut region they were in rebel-held territory and, given Fred's friendship with General Maskhadov, were probably being treated as honored guests. And certainly the tone of Fred's note—almost tedious in its concerns—did not suggest a man worried for his safety. Leading Ruslan Muradov into an empty office in the Emergency Situations building, he sat the driver down and pressed him for details. According to Ruslan, Fred and the others had chosen their unusual route into Chechnya after hearing that the two men Fred most wanted to meet—General Maskhadov and President Dudayev—were in the town of Orekhovo, a rebel stronghold just twelve kilometers to the east of Bamut. Rather than execute the circuitous loop through Grozny and then south across the plains, they had evidently decided that the easiest route was to take the back mountain road to Bamut, then follow a forest road that led to Orekhovo. The problem was, the Russians were now escalating their attacks throughout the Bamut-Orekhovo area and it was making the rebels especially nervous about the presence of any outsiders.

By Ruslan's account, the group had first been stopped and questioned about their mission by the rebel commandant in Bamut on the afternoon of March 31. Having satisfied his questions, they had continued on toward Orekhovo the next morning, only to be stopped by another squad of rebels operating along the forest road. This second band of rebels decided that the travelers could not proceed farther until they received authorization; to this end, the identity papers of Fred and the others were collected and sent on to the local head of rebel counterintelligence in the larger valley town of Atchkoi-Martan. For the next two and a half days the group had been shuttled back and forth between the rebels' bunker in the forest and Ruslan's family home in Bamut as they waited to be taken to Atchkoi-Martan to meet with the counterintelligence commander, a meeting repeatedly delayed by both heavy rains and combat in the area.

According to Ruslan, a squad of rebels had finally shown up at his family's home on the morning of April 4 to escort the group to Atchkoi-Martan; it was then that Fred and Galina had hastily written their note and instructed him to deliver it to Slava in Sleptsovskaya. Following the plan worked out with the rebels, Ruslan would now return to Bamut on Friday, April 7, and drive the group back down to Sleptsovskaya. In recounting the story, Ruslan Muradov seemed completely unconcerned—and so was Slava upon hearing it. In fact, so great was his relief that he apparently paid little attention to the last five lines of the note, a hastily scribbled postscript from Galina.

> *Everything above I wrote under Fred's dictation and now I*
> *would like to say something for myself: we as always have*
> *gotten into a mess. The situation doesn't depend on us.*
> *Ruslan will explain in his own words. If we're not back in*
> *3 days, shake everyone up. That's all. . . .*

In closing, Galina had used a somewhat ambiguous Russian phrase; depending on one's translation, it could either mean, "I hope, until we meet," or "I hope we meet again."

.   .   .

On the morning of Wednesday, April 5, Elisabeth Socolow got a call at the Soros office in Moscow from Slava Miklayev. He had excellent news. The driver of Fred's group had returned to Ingushetia the night before, Slava said, and he brought a message from Fred. Instead of reading Elisabeth the short note, Slava simply gave her a very quick rundown of what he had learned from Ruslan Muradov thus far.

Despite Slava's calm assuredness on the telephone, Elisabeth found the report a bit alarming. From everything Fred had told her about his first trip to Chechnya, he had gotten along extremely well with the rebels, and she couldn't understand why the group was encountering such difficulties with them this time, especially given Fred's friendship with General Maskhadov.

To these concerns, Slava was completely dismissive. In front-line combat areas like Bamut, he pointed out, fighters on both sides of the line were liable to be extremely jumpy, and certainly such bureaucratic obstructions as the group was now experiencing had become a fairly common occurrence when dealing with either faction in recent weeks. Slava was sure that once the rebel counterintelligence commander realized the identity of those being delayed—and especially once he learned of Fred's friendship with Maskhadov—he would immediately release the group with profuse apologies. In any event, he told Elisabeth, since the rebels had instructed Ruslan to return to Bamut on Friday morning to retrieve the group, there really didn't appear to be any cause for worry.

If nothing else, Elisabeth now had a set of instructions from Fred on how to revamp his itinerary. That morning she canceled the meetings he had scheduled in Moscow, then called the Open Society office in Budapest and the Intertect office in Dallas to let them know of Fred's delay. She then rebooked his Aeroflot flight out of Ingushetia for the afternoon of Friday, April 7, and reserved him a room for that night at the Penta, the most luxurious hotel in Moscow. At least Fred might get one decent night's sleep before racing off to the symposium at Camp Pendleton.

· · ·

"This was when the confusing days started," Slava Miklayev recalled, "the ones that caused so many problems later."

With Ruslan Muradov's return from Bamut, there was now at least an answer to where the group had gone, but it raised the more baffling question of why they had chosen the route in the first place. Over the past two weeks the Russians had steadily escalated their scorched-earth offensive around Bamut and turned the entire area into an indiscriminate free-fire zone; it was impossible that the group had not known this. Similarly puzzling was Ruslan's explanation that Fred had chosen the route because he had heard Maskhadov and Dudayev might be in Orekhovo. On any given day there were probably a half dozen "sightings" of the rebel leaders across the length of Chechnya, and the Orekhovo "sighting" was likely to be no more authoritative than any other. If Fred was somehow not aware of this new smokescreen ploy by the rebels to protect their leaders, Galina and the doctors certainly were. Yet Slava apparently did not ask himself these questions. After all, the group was about to return, and whatever bad choices had been made were now beside the point.

On Thursday afternoon, April 6, Ruslan went back to Bamut in a friend's car with plans to spend the night at his parents' home, then bring Fred and the others down in the morning. That next day, Slava recounted, he waited eagerly in Sleptsovskaya for the group's return, but when there was still no sign of them by afternoon his expectation began to turn to mild anxiety. Elisabeth had booked Fred on the early evening flight from Ingushetia to Moscow, but then that hour came and went. By dusk, Slava finally accepted that they weren't coming down that day, that there had been another delay.

"So at this point I began to worry some," Slava said, "but then I heard of the radio message."

According to Slava, it was that very evening of April 7 that a worker at the Russian Red Cross compound in Sleptsovskaya reported making radio contact with one of the doctors traveling with Fred, Sergei Makarov.

"Everything is going okay," Makarov was reported to have said, calling over one of the field radios the group had with them. "We'll be back tomorrow or the day after tomorrow."

Before the Red Cross worker could learn anything further, the line went dead.

The next day, April 8, Ruslan Muradov returned to Sleptsovskaya. He was alone. He had been told that Fred and the others had been cleared by the counterintelligence commander in Atchkoi-Martan, he informed Slava, but that they wouldn't be back in Bamut until the ninth. To Slava, the news was reassuring—and dovetailed with the radio message from Makarov—but he was growing apprehensive for another reason.

"I could see what the Russians were doing," he recalled, "that things were about to get very bad in the whole southwest front."

Over the previous forty-eight hours the Russians had escalated their shelling of Bamut and the surrounding villages, and had massed thousands of troops around the lowland town of Atchkoi-Martan; to Slava, it appeared obvious they were about to launch a major ground offensive. Now, with Fred's party having been cleared in Atchkoi-Martan, the only path they could take to return to Ingushetia and avoid the advancing Russian army was back through Bamut—and even that route might be cut once the offensive was launched. At first light on the morning of April 9, Slava sent Ruslan back into the mountains once more.

This second search mission would eerily replicate the first. Once again, Ruslan would find no sign of Fred's group in Bamut. Once again, there would be reports of another brief radio message from Sergei Makarov saying that all was fine, that their return was imminent. Then, early on the morning of April 10, the Russian army launched a massive ground assault all along the southwestern front, quickly overwhelming the rebel forces in Atchkoi-Martan and effectively cutting the entire area off from the outside world.

. . .

Despite Slava Miklayev's steady stream of reassurances all that week, Elisabeth Socolow had not been mollified.

"I think the biggest factor for me," Elisabeth said, "was that Fred had talked so much about the [April 9] Camp Pendleton meeting, how important it was that he get there. So when I was getting these calls from Slava, and he'd say, 'Oh, we've heard that everything's okay, they'll be back tomorrow,' I just knew that it couldn't be by Fred's choice."

Immediately after Slava's first call on April 5, she had tracked down Aryeh Neier, the Open Society president, who was traveling in Macedonia.

"Communications were not ideal in Macedonia," Neier said, "but I could tell Elisabeth was concerned, so I became concerned."

By April 7, with still no word from the group in Chechnya, Neier began contacting Fred's friends in Washington, specifically Mort Abramowitz at the Carnegie Endowment and Lionel Rosenblatt of Refugees International, to let them know there might be a problem. At the same time, Elisabeth Socolow began calling relief agencies operating in Chechnya to ask if they'd seen Fred's group.

On Monday morning, April 10, Elisabeth arrived at the Soros headquarters to find a fax waiting for her. It was from the Moscow office of the International Organization for Migration, an international refugee relief agency that was spearheading relief operations in Chechnya and that had an extensive network of contacts on both sides of the battlefront. For the past several days the director of the IOM office in Ingushetia, Carsten Christensen, had been asking around about Fred and he'd received some ominous news.

> Fred Cuny, representing Soros Foundation in Russia for the Chechnya crisis, has been arrested by the Russian authorities and imprisoned, together with his Russian interpreter. The latters [sic] were actually on their way to try to release two doctors (connected to Soros Foundation) who were put in prison approx. 2 weeks ago. Instead of releasing them, Fred Cuny and his Russian interpreter were detained as well. Apparently, this happened last Friday 31 March. The detention location is named Bamut. . . .

In closing, the IOM offered to intercede with Russian authorities in Chechnya to secure the group's release.

For the first time the possibility of Russian involvement in the group's long delay had been raised—and raised by a very credible source. Now thoroughly alarmed—"hysterical" was how she remembered it—Elisabeth put a series of calls through to the Soros Foundation headquarters in New York, then tracked down Slava Miklayev in Slept-sovskaya on April 11. Once more, Slava tried to calm their fears—as well as to discount the IOM account.

"I told her that this report didn't make any sense," Slava recalled. "It was obvious from the details that they were being given wrong information, maybe on purpose."

For one thing, he pointed out, it was the Chechens who controlled Bamut, not the Russians and—as was clear from Ruslan's account—it was the Chechens who had at least initially delayed the group's return. Further proof that the IOM was operating on erroneous information was the business about the two doctors being held prisoner for the past two weeks, obviously a confused reference to the long-resolved Assinovskaya incident of March 21, and clearly contradicted by the two radio messages that had been received from Sergei Makarov saying that all was well. What's more, he told Elisabeth, while he, too, had grown a little apprehensive over the past several days, especially after the Russians had launched their offensive on the tenth, he was now receiving very encouraging reports from the field. It appeared that Fred's group had also taken note of the Russian buildup in the area and, once cleared by the rebel counterintelligence commander in Atchkoi-Martan, decided against attempting a return through Bamut; instead, they had headed east, out of the immediate combat zone and deeper into rebel-held territory. Just that morning, Slava said, a returning Russian ambulance crew reported seeing members of the group in Vedeno, while another had heard they had crossed into Dagestan, the republic on the far eastern border of Chechnya; in fact, Slava had just dispatched Ruslan Muradov—newly returned from his latest sojourn to Bamut—to Vedeno and Dagestan to track down the stories. In light of all this, he told Elisabeth, the involvement of the IOM at such a delicate moment was likely to only create more confusion and more delays.

By now, however, whatever confidence Elisabeth had in Slava was fast ebbing. After their conversation, she called the IOM back and asked them to take up the case with the Russian military in any way they could. Over the next two days the IOM contacted Russian units throughout Chechnya, as well as officials at the "filtration center" in Mozdok. By Thursday, April 13, they had still been unable to find any trace of Fred or the others, and an even more alarming report had come in from Carsten Christensen in the field. There were now indications that Fred's group had not, in fact, left Atchkoi-Martan, and had still been there when the Russians launched their assault on the morning of April 10.

"That possibility is hardly comforting," the IOM wrote Elisabeth, for Christensen was hearing horror stories about the assault from people who had managed to get out of Atchkoi-Martan. "Carsten quoted evacuees as stating that over one hundred and twenty persons were confirmed killed, two hundred and twenty-plus wounded and that all fifteen-to-fifty-year-old men were 'led north' by Russian military."

On that same day Ruslan returned from his trek to Vedeno and Dagestan empty-handed and with no news. Now, even the resident "don't worry" duo of Ruslan and Slava were sounding nervous.

"For me, that was it," Elisabeth said. "Looking back now, I can see that I should have stopped listening to Slava a lot sooner, but when I finally got him to admit he had no idea where Fred was, no idea when they might get out, that's when everything went to full-scale alarm."

. . .

For Soros Foundation officials back in New York, as well as for the few friends and colleagues of Fred who were aware of the problem in Chechnya, reaction to his delay tended to follow a distinct arc: sanguinity at first, mixed in some cases with mild annoyance.

One aspect of Fred's congenital optimism was a habit of cramming meetings and assessment trips and transcontinental flights so close together that any one hitch along the way—and in war zones there were always hitches—knocked everything else out of line and meant he often ran late. As a result, even as Elisabeth's worry deepened into panic at his continuing delay, most of those who knew Fred best—and especially his Intertect colleagues back in Texas—displayed only passing concern. It was not until April 14, with the IOM and other relief agencies in the field still unable to find any sign of the group, that a true search effort got under way. The first to respond was Lionel Rosenblatt at Refugees International. When Aryeh Neier, now back in New York, called with the latest disturbing news, Rosenblatt immediately packed his bags, arranged for an emergency Russian visa, and caught an overnight flight to Moscow.

"I'd seen enough of these kinds of situations over the years," Rosenblatt said, "to know we had to move fast, that each day that went by diminished our chances of getting him back."

The effort to get him back now swung into high gear. All that following week, while Rosenblatt held meetings in Moscow with both American Embassy personnel and Russian government officials, Mort Abramowitz at the Carnegie Endowment was bringing intense pressure to bear on the State Department. On Friday, April 21, Rosenblatt was joined in Moscow by Aryeh Neier; that afternoon they held a hastily organized press conference to announce that Fred Cuny was missing and to publicly appeal for information. By then, Fred's disappearance had gone from being just another lost-American-abroad case to a top State Department priority.

"The escalation was really quite dramatic," Elisabeth Socolow recalled. "The very first time I called the American Embassy [in Moscow] to say there was an American missing, it was like, 'Yeah? Welcome to Chechnya.' Then, once Lionel and Aryeh got here and Mort started calling around Washington, everything changed."

That was especially true, Rosenblatt recounted, once Ambassador Pickering arrived back in Moscow from an extended trip in the Russian hinterlands. Within days Pickering had set up a special task force of embassy personnel—nearly a dozen in all—to keep track of various aspects of the Fred Cuny case and to exert pressure on top officials of every Russian ministry that might have influence on events in Chechnya. In Washington the matter was now being discussed at the cabinet level, and both President Clinton and Vice-President Gore were kept informed of developments.

On April 23, Lionel Rosenblatt, together with two American Embassy officials, flew from Moscow to Ingushetia, there to begin an on-ground search for answers. They would soon be joined by Fred's son Craig and his youngest brother, Chris. In the weeks ahead many more outsiders—CIA and FBI agents, journalists, humanitarian relief experts—would come to the North Caucasus in an attempt to learn what had become of the "Master of Disaster." In doing so, they would enter a world where, in the words of one State Department official, "everything was true, and everything was a lie."

. . .

The condition has undergone a number of name changes over the decades: "battle fatigue," "shell shock," "traumatic stress." From Hollywood movies, most people have a stylized idea of its physical manifestations—a soldier trembling or whimpering uncontrollably, perhaps, or the vacant "thousand-yard stare." More difficult to render but probably far more profound are the emotional and psychological changes that come over someone who stays too long in a war zone.

When first confronted with extreme danger, the normal human reaction is an adrenaline "rush" which, once the peril passes, drains off very quickly. When the peril doesn't pass, however, when it becomes the permanent state of affairs, the mind's danger impulse cannot keep up; reactions tend to first flatten and then become skewed. What's more, when "normal" conventional combat is compounded by an extreme element of randomness—which is another way of saying terror—those caught in its thrall begin to lose their instinctive ability to gauge peril, the mechanisms of fear subsumed by a kind of apathy. This was one possible explanation for why Ruslan Muradov and Slava Miklayev, two men who had spent much of the previous three months in near constant danger on the Chechen battlefield, had so consistently missed the flagrant warning signs as to what might be happening to Fred Cuny and the others in the southwestern mountains.

None of these missed warning signs were even known about until Lionel Rosenblatt reached Ingushetia on April 23. For the first time, someone other than Slava and Ruslan had a chance to see Fred's note of April 4 and, most tellingly, Galina Oleinik's hastily scribbled post-script.

> *Everything above I wrote under Fred's dictation and now I would like to say something for myself: we as always have gotten into a mess. The situation doesn't depend on us. Ruslan will explain in his own words. If we're not back in 3 days, shake everyone up. That's all. . . . I hope we meet again.*

In all his conversations with Elisabeth Socolow over the previous two and a half weeks, Slava had somehow failed to mention that Galina was clearly frightened.

There was more. On April 24, Rosenblatt sat Ruslan and Slava down to get a full written accounting of what had transpired over the past twenty-five days. He was stunned by what he learned.

Although very awkwardly written, Ruslan's account of events in the mountains painted a far more alarming picture than anything indicated previously. Rather than simply "stopped" by the squad of rebels on the forest road between Bamut and Orekhovo, it now turned out that Fred and the others had been made to lie spread-eagled on the road with guns trained at their heads as their hands were tied behind their backs. And while it seemed their situation had improved after that first encounter—the group had apparently been allowed to move about fairly freely over the next few days as they awaited clearance—Ruslan also described moments when it appeared they were treated as captives. Then there was the driver's strange account of Dzhokhar Dudayev coming to Bamut to denounce the group. When he arrived back in Bamut for the third time on the afternoon of April 9, Ruslan now reported, he was told that Dudayev had been there earlier in the day and had congratulated local fighters for capturing the four "spies."

Ruslan had made no mention of any of these details previously—or at least Slava had never conveyed them to Elisabeth in Moscow.

But there were also some rather glaring inconsistencies in

Ruslan's account, ones that would eventually lead Lionel Rosenblatt and others to question his veracity. In his written statement he claimed to have first encountered Fred and Galina on the morning of March 31 at the Emergency Situations building, failing to mention that he had actually driven them to Grozny on the previous day. Ruslan also claimed that Fred announced the purpose of his trip—to see General Maskhadov in Orekhovo—in the presence of the chief minister of Emergency Situations, Hamzat Bekov. If true, it meant that at least one prominent person in Sleptsovskaya had known where the group was headed from the outset, information that Slava had somehow been unable to discover in three days of hanging around the Emergency Situations building.

Yet it would take some time for the American searchers in Ingushetia to uncover these inconsistencies, let alone appreciate their possible significance. By then, Ruslan Muradov would have quietly slipped from sight.

Perhaps the greatest reason why the Americans' suspicions didn't immediately attach to Muradov was because they initially found Slava Miklayev's account far more troubling. In his written statement he appeared to be trying to accomplish two very different—and mutually opposing—goals simultaneously, both attempting to rationalize his blithe manner in those early days by pointing out the host of reassuring reports he had received, while also signposting the various incidents in those same days that suggested Chechen skulduggery. But there was something more. Not only had Slava never read Fred's note to Elisabeth Socolov during their numerous telephone conversations in the early days, but on April 12 he had been summoned to Moscow to meet with Soros officials; inexplicably, he had not brought the note with him, leaving everyone else in the dark about Galina's frightened postscript for eleven more days. On the basis of this, together with a series of odd incidents over the coming weeks, some of the Americans involved in the search would come to a rather different theory than war fatigue to explain Slava Miklayev's actions. It was a theory that might also explain why Slava had been so quick to dismiss the IOM report pointing to

Russian complicity—perhaps even why he had volunteered for the Chechnya mission in the first place.

"They thought that maybe I had arranged the whole thing," Slava said, his tight-set lips finally breaking into the slightest hint of a smile, "that maybe I was a spy."

PART FOUR

The Manhunt

CHAPTER 9

Almost all our information came from either liars or fools.
The problem was we couldn't tell them apart.
—Elisabeth Socolow on the search for Fred Cuny

BEGINNING IN LATE April 1995 and continuing through that summer, a small stretch of land on the northern flanks of the Caucasus Mountains would be the scene for one of the strangest manhunts in modern history. In an attempt to learn what had become of the four relief workers missing in the mountains, there would come to the republics of Chechnya and Ingushetia a number of Fred Cuny's relatives and disaster relief colleagues. Joining them in the war zone would be a range of local drivers, interpreters and guides, as well as—at various times—Chechen rebels, CIA and FBI agents, Ingush government officials, Russian intelligence operatives, foreign journalists, a Cossack detective, a Mormon blues musician, and a self-styled psychic known as Aunt Fatima.

The effort would extend far beyond the field. At the American

Embassy in Moscow a special task force searching for answers would be presided over by the ambassador himself. The Chechen rebels would form a Fred Cuny search committee, as would the governments of Russia and Ingushetia. The case would draw appeals from international humanitarian organizations, Nobel laureates, human rights activists, and foreign parliaments. It would also draw the personal involvement of at least five heads of state, and be pursued by officials at every level of the American foreign policy establishment, from State Department desk officers up to the Secretary of State and the National Security Adviser. And still the mountains of Chechnya would hold fast to their secrets.

In lieu of answers, over the course of that spring and summer there would be scores of rumors and theories and purported sightings. The missing four were "seen" across the breadth of Chechnya, as well as in at least three neighboring countries. They were reported alive and well and delivering babies in a small mountain village. They were alive—but not so well—in the notorious Russian "filtration center" in Mozdok, or in a rebel bunker hidden away in the woods. They were being held as bargaining chips by Dudayev, as hostages at a Russian fire base, for ransom by bandits in the next republic over. They were dead: caught in a battle crossfire, murdered by renegade rebels, gunned down by trigger-happy Russian troops acting without orders—or killed by those same troops acting on orders that came from the highest corridors in the Kremlin. They were dead because they had encountered a Chechen mafia lieutenant, or a secret cell of Iranian mujaheddin, or an elite Russian spetsnaz unit operating behind the lines, because they had witnessed a massacre, because Fred Cuny had written an article hostile to the Russian army, because one of his companions was a Russian spy—or they were still alive for any of those very same reasons.

Throughout it all, those most earnestly searching for answers—especially Fred's son Craig and his brother Chris—would find themselves plagued at every turn by the same set of questions. How to divine logic in a place and a war that constantly defied it? Whom to trust in a land where treachery and deceit had been elevated to an art form? In a society where nothing worked, and had not worked in a very long time, how to tell the difference between conspiracy and incompetence, to separate the liars from the fools?

. . .

In April 1995, Craig Cuny was twenty-eight years old and living in San Antonio, trying to expand his young video production company from its Austin base. His first hint that there might be a problem in Chechnya came on Easter Sunday, when he called his grandmother Charlotte in Rockwall.

"I was mainly calling to wish her a happy Easter," Craig recalled. "We talked for a few minutes, and toward the end she just kind of mentioned that no one had heard from Fred for a while, that the Soros people in Moscow were getting a little worried. To be honest, I didn't think too much about it at the time, because being late and off radar was pretty typical for Fred."

In fact, in those first days few in the Cuny family or at the Intertect office in Dallas seemed to share Elisabeth Socolow's growing concern; Fred's peripatetic lifestyle, combined with his ever-changing itineraries, had led most of them to long ago give up any hope of keeping close tabs on his whereabouts. Even when the Soros Foundation raised the alarm in the middle of the month and Lionel Rosenblatt raced off to Moscow, Craig, for one, felt it was all a bit of an overreaction.

"You know, I'd been with my father in Somalia, in Bosnia, he'd been going into war zones most of his life, so my personal attitude was, he knows how to take care of himself, he doesn't take stupid chances. I kept thinking, 'He's gonna call from someplace and when he hears about everybody running around, he's gonna laugh his head off.' "

But as the days slipped by and there was still no word, worry began to infect the Cuny family as well. When Lionel Rosenblatt called from Moscow to say he was going on to the North Caucasus to conduct a personal search, an effort that might be aided by having family members present, the Cunys were quickly galvanized into action.

Although a rather dubious distinction, if ever there was a family uniquely suited to cope with the crisis then unfolding in the Caucasus, it was probably the Cunys of Dallas, Texas. Fred's parents, Gene and Charlotte, were a strong, practical-minded couple in their mid-seventies who were not given to panic, and the same was certainly true of his three younger brothers: Phil, Butch, and Chris. If not quite to Fred's ostentatious degree, all seemed to share his basic assumptions on life—that people were essentially good, that all problems had solutions—as well as his formidable blend of confidence, tenacity, and charm that tended to make others bend to their will.

What's more, at least three family members had spent time with Fred in the field and knew their way around a disaster zone. Besides Craig, there was Fred's youngest brother, thirty-five-year-old Chris. Having idolized his oldest brother as a boy, Chris had become an engineer largely at Fred's urging, and had taken several extended leaves of absence from his job to work with him in the Horn of Africa in the early 1990s. Then there was forty-year-old Eric Shutler, Fred's cousin and the son of Fred's own childhood idol, his Marine pilot uncle, General Phillip Shutler. Eric had begun working with Fred on the Soros project in Bosnia in 1994 and had taken over the Intertect office there when Fred moved at the end of the year. Together with Rick Hill, the deputy director of Intertect, these three family members would spearhead the grassroots search for Fred that spring and summer; within days of Lionel Rosenblatt's call from Moscow, all began making their way toward the North Caucasus.

"Even at that point, I was sure Fred was going to show up," Craig said, "and I remember on the flight over feeling kind of annoyed and excited at the same time. I'd just started things up with a new girlfriend and it was a bad time to leave, but I also thought, 'Hey, Chechnya, at least it'll be interesting for a few days.' Well, then I got there."

. . .

As Craig and the other searchers from Texas would discover in those last days of April, they were embarking on a mission in which both the rules and the landscape had fundamentally changed in just the previous few days. For good and for ill, that change would forever color their efforts in the region.

At the start of the crisis the Soros Foundation had adopted a cautious, wait-and-see approach. When rumors about the group's disappearance began to circulate in Moscow in the second week of April, a number of journalists had pressed Elisabeth Socolow for details, only to be forestalled by Aryeh Neier in New York; his feeling was that, until it was determined who was holding Fred, media coverage might only complicate matters. Similarly, the Foundation had resisted filing an official missing-person report with the Russian government. Such a report would give the authorities a legal mandate to detain and question anyone they saw fit, and the first people they were likely to go after would be those Russian critics of the Chechnya war—like the now deposed human rights commissioner Sergei Kovalyov—who might be most helpful in getting answers.

While this low-key strategy would soon be abandoned, it was understandable, even prudent at the time. So vast was the void of reliable information coming out of the North Caucasus that, when Aryeh Neier wrote to other Open Society directors on April 18, no one had yet figured out even how many people were missing: "We have been pursuing a variety of leads and exploring all avenues to locate [Fred] and the interpreter who has been traveling with him. We are not sure who else might have been accompanying them."

In such a void, any scenario was possible. Fred and the still unknown others could be prisoners of one side or the other, stranded by battle in one of Chechnya's remote mountain valleys, or ordinary kidnap victims. With each one of these possibilities, a large-scale search effort or flurry of newspaper articles could lead to disaster. Captors might be spooked enough by the sudden attention to decide to be rid of their problem charges in the quickest way available—a firing squad—while kidnappers could be expected to dramatically hike their ransom demands. Even if they were simply trapped by battle, the glare of a media spotlight could lead either side to suddenly regard them as valuable hostages.

With the silence continuing, however, the cautious route was finally discarded in grand fashion, principally through the lobbying efforts of Lionel Rosenblatt in Moscow and of Morton Abramowitz in Washington. On April 21, with it now firmly established that four people were missing, Aryeh Neier held his press conference in Moscow to announce the disappearances and to appeal for information.

In some respects the timing for such an appeal could hardly have been worse; just two days earlier the Federal Building in Oklahoma City had been blown up by a truck bomb, an event that would thoroughly dominate international media attention for weeks. Nevertheless, dozens of journalists from around the world attended Neier's press conference in Moscow. That same evening, and underscoring the urgency now being felt to gather clues, ABC News featured Fred and the story of his disappearance in their regular Friday evening segment, "Person of the Week." "We do so," Peter Jennings explained, "because he has brought honor to this country."

"Although very worried," Aryeh wrote in a letter to Soros Foundation offices that same afternoon, "I do not feel a sense of despair. There are significant indications that Fred, Galena [sic] and the two Russian doctors have been detained. However, there are many questions as to who exactly is detaining them, which greatly complicates the situation. . . . Large sections of both the US and Russian governments have been mobilized, and there have been significant efforts by others to focus the attention of the other [Chechen] side on the issue. . . . We understand and appreciate the concern that many of you have expressed and will let you know of any further developments."

The result was that the American government's involvement in the case had already become well established, with at least two embassy staffers already in the field, by the time Craig Cuny and the other searchers arrived in the Caucasus at the end of April. The high-priority status the Americans were giving to the case was, in turn, having a ripple effect on the governments of Russia and Ingushetia, and on the Chechen rebel high command. In the classic Soviet-era approach to problem solving, a whole range of committees was being formed to search for the lost group.

While undoubtedly helpful in some respects, this multinational governmental involvement was destined to complicate the manhunt in at least three crucial ways. It would set in place a machinery of bureaucracy through which the searchers would now have to negotiate. It would suggest to everyone in the region that great reward awaited the person who might solve the disappearances, along with great punishment for those found responsible—an impression almost guaranteed to spark a flood of false leads and to push the true perpetrators deeper into silence.

Finally, the American government's role would convince a number of leaders on both sides of the war in Chechnya that either Fred Cuny had vanished while performing an American intelligence operation, or that the manhunt for him was a convenient cover for one or both; to many, the presence of the embassy staffers in the North Caucasus—the first American officials to venture into the war theater since the conflict began—seemed highly significant. All this would set into place an entirely new layer of intrigue in a story that already had too much.

· · ·

Thomas Pickering's office was a small corner room bathed in a dull gray sheen, the sunlight from three windows cut by steel louvered shutters and thick lace curtains. It seemed more likely to be the office of a poorly regarded junior executive than that of the most important envoy in the American foreign service, but there was a good reason for the room's dinginess—and something of a lingering embarrassment to the American government.

Back in the early 1980s, the American Embassy in Moscow was scheduled to move from its cramped quarters on Novinsky Boulevard to far more spacious offices being built several miles away. Only when construction was half-completed was it discovered that the un-supervised local building crew, working from KGB blueprints, had laced the structure with so many listening devices and microwave tran-sponders that it represented both a massive security threat and a cancer-causing health hazard. Despite having already cost the Ameri-can government over a hundred million dollars, the "new" embassy was never finished, and the enormous American delegation to Russia remains squeezed into the small building on Novinsky Boulevard. All its windows are laminated with a special film designed to thwart the eavesdropping microwave beams presumed to still be directed at it, but the steel shutters over the ambassador's windows are a more recent addition; in September 1995 a rocket-propelled grenade was fired at the embassy's sixth floor from an archway across the road, destroying a copying room.

Over the thirty-year span of his foreign service career, Thomas Pickering has held some of the most sensitive and prominent positions in the American government: ambassador to El Salvador, Israel, Jor-dan, and India, U.S. representative to the United Nations in the Bush administration, and, from 1993 to 1996, ambassador to Russia; today he is the Undersecretary of State for Political Affairs. During the past several administrations he has frequently been mentioned as a top candidate to become either Secretary of State or director of the Central Intelligence Agency.

It's easy to understand why, for Pickering, a tall, balding man, fairly bristles with intellectual energy. In conversation, that energy shows itself in a kind of polite impatience, a tendency to lean far forward and give quick, sharp nods that suggest he knows what is going to be said or asked long before it is. In the spring of 1995 he was the most important American official to become intimately involved in the hunt for Fred Cuny.

"Fred was a personal acquaintance," Pickering said, "not a close friend, but when he came back from Chechnya on his first trip, I was very impressed by his grasp of the situation there, his analysis of what was happening. And I personally became involved in the search effort, because it was clear to me in talks with people back in Washington that he was a valuable person, someone who had done a tremendous amount of good in his life. If he was alive and we could find him, it was important for us to do so."

The ambassador took on that mission with an almost crusader's zeal, organizing a task force within the embassy that, at its height, involved some dozen staffers. After meeting with Lionel Rosenblatt in mid-April, he personally called Russian ministers to demand their assistance, then took the almost unprecedented step of dispatching two embassy officials into the field to carry out an independent investigation. At weekly status-report meetings at the embassy, the ambassador would ask pointed questions of each staffer assigned to some aspect of the inquiry.

While deeply gratifying to the Cuny family, this unparalleled level of governmental involvement in the search for a missing private American raised a number of eyebrows elsewhere. The idea that Fred had actually been an intelligence agent and been performing a covert mission when he disappeared was even entertained by some of those American Embassy personnel assigned to the Fred Cuny task force.

"I remember thinking to myself," one staffer said, " 'Wow, this guy must have been doing some really heavy stuff down there,' because this was just not the way things work when an ordinary [American] citizen goes missing. I'd been involved in a few of those before and, to be honest, the embassy doesn't do much: you make a few phone calls, get in touch with the local police, try to keep on top of them a little, but that's about it. With Fred, though, it was a huge priority. So I think probably quite a few of us—at least there at the beginning—just assumed he was CIA."

Eventually the staffer became convinced that the effort had come about through the lobbying of Fred's powerful friends back in Washington, but that still did not fully explain the extraordinary intensity of the effort.

In fact, though, in searching for a possible subterranean motive for the American government's involvement, there emerges a simpler explanation than spies or secret missions: a kind of collective guilty conscience. It was a sense of guilt that had permeated much of the upper echelons of the American foreign policy establishment over the previous five months, and it was one that Fred Cuny had helped instill.

. . .

In early March 1995, shortly after his first trip to the Caucasus, Fred and Anthony Richter, the special adviser to the president of the Soros Foundation, had gone to Washington to confer with a number of high-level government officials. The topic was Chechnya. Over the course of two days they met with some of the most influential foreign policymakers in the Clinton administration, including the Undersecretary of Defense for Policy, Walter Slocombe, the President's special assistant for Russian affairs, Chip Blacker, and Deputy Secretary of State Strobe Talbott. They also met with officials of the CIA and the Defense Intelligence Agency, and held round-table briefings at the State Department which were attended by a number of senior officers dealing with Russian affairs.

By all reports, Fred gave an extremely harrowing eyewitness account of the war during these meetings. At the time, he was still working on his plan to evacuate the remaining civilians trapped in Grozny, and he forcefully lobbied the officials to support a temporary cease-fire in order for that to happen. He had quickly discovered, however, that a huge obstacle to that end was his listeners' astounding ignorance of events in Chechnya.

"Like virtually everyone else we saw," Richter wrote in a memo to Soros headquarters, "[Deputy Secretary of State Strobe] Talbott was taken aback at how chaotic the situation actually is on the ground in Grozny. Unfortunately he did not move to resolute action on the ceasefire issue. He seemed stunned at the likely human toll that the conflict is likely to take in coming weeks and simultaneously at a loss as to where to go next."

That response was mirrored by a member of the State Department's Policy Planning Staff who attended one of Fred's briefings on Chechnya, and who would only speak on anonymity.

"I've been to a lot of these briefings over the years," the official said, "and they're usually pretty tedious, but I can tell you that Fred had everybody in that room riveted. No one even asked a question for the first hour, just sat there and listened to him, and I'd never seen that happen before. I think up until that point none of us truly appreciated the complete depravity of what the Russians were doing in Chechnya, and it really shocked us."

More than anything else, such dumbfounded reactions seemed eerily reminiscent of Boris Yeltsin's display of surprise and indignation in early January upon hearing "rumors" that his air-strike ban on Grozny was being violated, his demand for "concrete information." How could it be that in early March, after eleven weeks of the war in Chechnya being splayed across the front page of every major American newspaper and frequently leading the networks' nightly newscasts, the Clinton administration's seniormost Russia policymakers, including the second highest-ranking official at the State Department, could be "stunned" and "shocked" by Fred's account of that war? It begged a fundamental question: were the men and women in charge of formulating American foreign policy thoroughly disingenuous or complete idiots?

Paul Goble, a former CIA and State Department official who now works at Radio Free Europe, suspected it was a combination of the two.

"Certainly, you can never rule out simple idiocy whenever you're talking about the State Department," he said, "and especially in connection with Russia. Most of their so-called Russia experts have never been outside of Moscow, and have no clue that when you get two hundred miles outside of Moscow you're in a different country and a different century. But when it comes to something like Chechnya, even the State Department had to notice. Even making generous allowances for stupidity, you have to conclude that they didn't see it because they didn't want to see it."

After those meetings in Washington in early March, Fred had complained to a number of people that the Clinton administration seemed to be completely at sea in devising a coherent policy toward Chechnya. The reality, however, was that the Administration had a very clear-cut Chechnya policy, but it was one that Fred—like all other humanitarians—stood on the wrong side of. That policy was to support Russia and Boris Yeltsin no matter what.

In ways that the United States was still discovering in the mid-1990s, the end of the Cold War had its downside. The demise of the Soviet Union suddenly meant that the United States had to deal with fifteen different republics, many of which quickly fell under the sway of bellicose generals, old Communist Party hacks, or outright gangsters, others that were hostile to one another or riven by internal ethnic schisms, and at least four of which had nuclear weapons on their soil. By the end of 1993, just two years after the dissolution of the Soviet Union, five different wars had erupted in the former Soviet republics.

With Chechnya's unilateral declaration of independence, then, it appeared to many in the American government that the next wave of chaos was fast approaching: the disintegration of the fractious Russian republic itself. If Chechnya broke loose, so this reasoning went, then all Russia's other restive autonomous regions would begin agitating for independence as well, and before long the former "evil empire" would have mutated into a potentially far more dangerous Russian Balkans. It was no coincidence that this apocalyptic vision was very actively promoted by the Russian government of Boris Yeltsin.

"I think it was a case of us buying into what the Russians were feeding us," the official on the State Department's Policy Planning Staff said. "Frankly, we didn't know too much about the Caucasus or these various autonomous regions, so when the Russians presented this domino theory—'This is going to spread and spread'—we believed them. I don't think we figured out until much later on that Chechnya was, in fact, a rather unique case."

"Much later on" is a relative term, of course, because certainly by the autumn of 1994 the Russian-promoted domino theory would have seemed pretty flimsy to anyone who bothered to look. In the three years since Dudayev's independence proclamation, no other Russian republic or autonomous region had attempted to secede and the Yeltsin government had recently defused the separatist fervor in even its most troublesome region, Tatarstan, by forging a compromise treaty. Yet these positive developments seemed to go completely unnoticed by the American government.

Added to this blithe acceptance of the domino theory was the fact that, however much the Clinton administration did know of Dudayev's rule in Chechnya, they could not have been altogether thrilled. With the end of the Cold War, the basic paradigm that had dictated American foreign policy for a half century—the balance of power between East and West—was suddenly gone, and American policy around the world was now increasingly being decided on economic and "cops and robbers" issues: a nation's support of terrorist groups, its involvement in drug or arms trafficking, its attempts to build or buy nuclear weapons. With this new litmus test, it was hard to imagine any regime that raised more warning flags by 1994 than that of Dzhokhar Dudayev in Chechnya.

By then his tiny self-styled republic was well on its way to becoming a classic "bandit state," a key transshipment point for narcotics going to Europe from Central Asia, and for weapons being moved throughout the world. On several occasions Dudayev had hinted that he possessed nuclear weapons, presumably bought on the Russian black market or left behind when he kicked the Russian army out of Chechnya, and suggested he might just use them if Moscow didn't stop its interference in his nation's "internal affairs." Even if Dudayev himself didn't grasp the fundamentals of Islam, he frequently talked of turning Chechnya into an Islamic state in the Iranian fashion, something sure to send shudders up the spines of Iran-obsessed American policymakers. What's more, Chechnya was not situated in some forgotten backwater of the globe; rather, it bordered on one of the greatest oil ranges in the world, the Caspian Sea, and the pipelines that carried that oil west to the Black Sea ran directly across the length of Chechnya. If the United States had been moved to war against Saddam Hussein's vast army for his threat to the world's oil supply, it seemed unlikely that it would countenance some two-bit despot in Grozny with his cabal of gangster friends who could shut down a major international oil pipeline simply by turning a valve.

In short, by 1994, in virtually every arena that mattered in the new checklist of American foreign policy concerns—drug and arms trafficking, Islamic fundamentalism, nuclear proliferation, threats to the world's oil supply—the little general in Grozny had emerged as just the sort of leader the Americans would most like to be rid of.

But here again, though, one comes up against the same conundrum that attaches to all things Chechen: how to determine where conspiracy ends and incompetence begins. As incredible as it might seem, there are, in fact, few signs that the American government took notice of Dzhokhar Dudayev, or was even aware of him, before the Russians brought him to their attention.

"Chechnya simply wasn't on our radar," the State Department's Policy Planning Staff official said. "You have to take into account what was happening all across Russia at that time. In '92 we'd been worried about a famine in Russia, of people actually starving to death. In '93 there was a coup attempt, a gun battle in downtown Moscow. The Communists and ultranationalists were in the ascendancy, there were constantly rumors that Yeltsin was about to die, so how much attention were we going to pay to some saber-rattling general in Chechnya?"

If the Clinton administration truly took no notice of events in Chechnya, it was at least partially because of its slavish devotion to Russian President Boris Yeltsin. With Russian nationalists and Communists gaining in popularity, Washington clung to the mercurial President as the one man who could be counted on to continue to steer Russia toward a free-market economy and some reasonable facsimile of "democracy." On the more cynical level of realpolitik, Yeltsin was also the one Russian leader most likely to submit to Washington's will on a whole range of issues—the expansion of NATO into Eastern Europe, ratification of the long-delayed SALT II treaty, a unified response to the war in Bosnia—if it helped maintain his own tenuous hold on power. Boris Yeltsin might very well have been deranged—and not a few American policymakers privately thought so—but it was a derangement that was yielding great dividends for Washington.

So determined was the Administration's defense of their golden goose in Moscow that it led, at times, to almost comical excess. In August 1996, when a stiff and obviously very ill or very drunk Yeltsin staggered and slurred his way through a short speech after being re-elected president, the anonymous official from the State Department's Policy Planning Staff stoutly defended his performance. "He wasn't slurring his words," the official maintained. "That's just his regional accent."

Given such a loyal marriage, it was hardly surprising that the Clinton administration was not concerned about Chechnya—at least publicly—so long as Yeltsin wasn't concerned. When that dramatically changed—when Yeltsin sent his troops across the Chechen border on December 11, 1994, authorizing them to use "all means necessary" to crush Dudayev's "criminal formations"—the Americans quickly fell into lockstep.

"It's an internal Russian affair," President Clinton said as the invasion got under way. "We hope that order can be restored with a minimum of violence and bloodshed."

Even more remarkable were Secretary of State Warren Christopher's comments on December 13. "It's best in such matters to leave it to the judgment of President Yeltsin. . . . I'm sure he thought through what he was doing before he did it," Christopher said with a straight face, "and it's best we let him run such things."

As law-and-order operations went, however, the Russian offensive quickly proved a tad excessive, and when the horrific images of the devastation of Grozny began to play on American television screens, even the Clinton administration finally had to speak out against the brutality. But there was a key distinction in this; the Administration's criticisms were solely directed at Russian tactics, not at their ultimate goal to crush Chechen independence or at their use of force to do so. Having given their tacit stamp of approval for the invasion at the outset, the American government could now do little more than express dismay—or, when it suited them, ignorance—as the scale of slaughter grew.

What all this meant to Fred Cuny as he held those high-level meetings in Washington in early March was that he had embarked on a truly quixotic mission, one that, given his occasionally overoptimistic view of human nature, he may not have fully grasped; the "stunned" response and lack of decisive action he encountered upon detailing Russian atrocities in Chechnya was not born of ignorance, but because none of his listeners wanted to hear about them.

"The Administration was in bed with Yeltsin," Paul Goble said, "they had completely accepted his lies about Chechnya, and no one had the courage to stand up and say, 'This is wrong, we've got to change.' When a guy like Fred walks in and forces them to look at what's going on, he's a problem because he's a threat to their own cowardice."

If lacking courage, though, it appears the practitioners of realpolitik in Washington may have at least had their consciences pricked by Fred's disappearance. All he had been looking for in those meetings in March was for someone in the Administration willing to intercede with the Russians so that he could evacuate the tens of thousands of civilians still trapped on the battlefield. He had found no one, he had gone back to the battlefield on his own, and now he was gone.

"I think a lot of people around here felt kind of sullied by that," another State Department official said, also insisting on anonymity. "There was a sense that Fred had come in here with a pretty modest set of requests, he'd been ignored, and a lot more people had died as a result. If we could help find him in Chechnya and get him out, then maybe it would assuage the guilt a bit."

Of course, such an innocent explanation wasn't likely to satisfy all the other players in the drama.

. . .

In his office at the FSB headquarters in Lubyanka Square, Major General Alexander Mikhailov recalled the first time he heard of Fred Cuny. "The Americans came to us and said he was missing in Chechnya," the general offered, "that they needed our help in finding him. And, of course, we provided that help, gladly and at once. To the question of whether we were curious about the [American] government's involvement—perhaps, perhaps we were curious. But if this curiosity existed—and I have no way of knowing if it did—I can state that it did not enter into our actions in any way. We proceeded on the basis that Fred Cuny was a private citizen, because that was the assurance we were given, and we had no reason to doubt that assurance."

In contrast to Mikhailov's easy acceptance of the American government's innocent intentions, many Russian nationalists took a much darker view of the manhunt in Chechnya. To them, the involvement of American Embassy personnel suggested a CIA operation: that either Fred Cuny was a CIA agent, or the CIA was using the search for him as a pretext to gain a firsthand look at the war, or, most ambitious of all, were planning to blame Russian forces for his disappearance so that Yeltsin could be blackmailed into concessions on a larger matter.

But, sitting in his office on Lubyanka Square, General Mikhailov professed not to be terribly interested in the American government's role in the manhunt. Rather, he saw the entire episode as a cautionary tale on the importance of following bureaucratic procedures.

"For some reason," he said, "Fred Cuny failed to register with us before going to Chechnya. Foreigners like him should consider when they go to a place like Chechnya—a place where there are no American national interests—what the possible consequences of their actions might be. When an individual arrives in the framework of an official status for international diplomacy—and I would like to underline official status—we're prepared to answer for his safety. Thank God to this day that individuals who have gone to Chechnya on official status, who have registered with us, none of them have disappeared yet. But Fred Cuny did not do this. We don't know why—and we don't have time to speculate—but this he did not do."

The trim major general lit another of his imported cigarettes, his habitual half grin again sliding into a smirk.

"Instead, he went in an unofficial capacity to meet with bandits, and those bandits dealt with him in the only way they know how."

But those who came to search for Fred that spring and summer would quickly arrive at a decidedly different theory than Mikhailov's. To them, it seemed that, if the lost group were dead, it was the Russians who had the clear motive; after all, Fred had emerged as a vocal critic of the Russian campaign in Chechnya. And if such an execution order had come down from somewhere high up in the Russian government, the most likely suspects were officials at that agency whose job it was to keep track of critics of Russia: namely, the FSB.

The searchers soon found evidence to bolster that suspicion. By early May articles began running in right-wing newspapers in Moscow claiming that Fred Cuny was alive and working as a CIA adviser to Dudayev, information allegedly provided by an unnamed "Russian security official." To a lot of officials in the American government, it appeared the FSB might be trying to cover up their role in Fred's disappearance by launching a smear campaign, a scenario lent greater credence when it was determined that the unnamed "security official" was none other than FSB Major General Mikhailov.

Lending further credence to this scenario was a May 15 report from John Colarusso, a linguistics professor at McMaster University in Ontario, Canada, who had traveled extensively in the Caucasus and who had conducted his own long-distance search for clues by working his contacts in both Chechnya and Moscow. Quoting an unnamed "highly reliable Russian source," Colarusso wrote that:

Mr. Cuny was taken into custody by some low-level [OMON] field commander in the Interior Ministry almost as a precautionary move on or about April 10 and he was brought to the detention center at Mozdok. There it became apparent to the local Interior Ministry commander that Mr. Cuny had collected embarrassing evidence linking high circles in Moscow to some atrocities in Chechnia [sic] . . . and Mr. Cuny was executed. When his fate was revealed to higher levels within the Interior Ministry, further panic ensued and the FSB was enlisted to eliminate all evidence and perhaps some witnesses as well.

If his information was accurate, Colarusso was not confident of a speedy resolution.

My friend concluded by saying that perhaps Mr. Cuny had died by mischance in battle, but he was convinced that we would not know the true outcome of this incident until some time well into the twenty-first century, when someone in retirement would come forward with a confession. He expressed his regrets.

. . .

Sitting in his North Dallas office at the engineering firm of Itex on a brutally hot afternoon in July 1995, Chris Cuny scanned the neat array of papers on his desk—stacks of project reports, rolled tubes of architectural blueprints—as he tried to find the words to describe his experience in Chechnya.

"I'm an engineer," he finally said, in the soft, light drawl shared by all members of the Cuny family. "I'm used to dealing with time frames and schedules and statistics. I'm used to dealing with facts." He turned to point to a high stack of papers and manila folders on a credenza against the wall. "That's what I collected in Chechnya. I've got another stack even bigger at home. But what is it? It's not facts. There are no facts in Chechnya. What it is is rumors, stories, leads. We've chased literally hundreds of leads, and we have never been able to bring any of them to fruition." He stared at the stack of papers for a long moment, then wearily shook his head. "This has been the most unbelievable, frustrating, confusing thing I've ever been associated with in my life."

A few miles away, in the cramped third-floor office of a ramshackle building on North Hall Street that represented the world headquarters of Intertect, Rick Hill mirrored those sentiments. A laconic forty-two-year-old Oklahoman, Rick had worked on a wide variety of Intertect projects around the globe over the previous seven years, and possessed that peculiar blend of vitality and haggardness that is the hallmark of relief workers everywhere: a deep, leathery tan, a wiry frame just this side of gaunt. In July 1995 he, too, had recently returned from the Caucasus.

"I'd been in a lot of conflict situations with Fred," Rick said, "Sri Lanka, Iraq, the Sudan, Somalia—and I felt I'd developed some instincts about how to read people, what information you can trust and what you can't. But when you get to Chechnya those skills just don't work. The disinformation and hidden agendas you encounter in other places, it's all child's play compared to Chechnya."

From virtually the moment they arrived in the North Caucasus, the searchers from Texas discovered they were dealing with a far more bewildering—and ominous—situation than they had imagined. They were also totally dependent, both for information on what had happened thus far and for assistance in proceeding further, on people whose trustworthiness was open to doubt. Those questions started with the two men who, together, had provided the entire narrative of the group's last known movements: Ruslan Muradov and Slava Miklayev. While much of Muradov's account was suspect—and bordering on incoherent—particular derision had been directed at his story that had Dzhokhar Dudayev in Bamut congratulating local rebels for capturing the four "spies."

"Dudayev was in the area of Bamut, but he didn't say the things Ruslan reported," Boris Agapov, the Vice-President of Ingushetia, told a reporter from the *Toronto Star*. "Either he dreamed it up, or somebody else was telling him a story."

By the end of April, however, Ruslan had already slipped from sight—and even greater suspicion was being attached to the account and actions of Slava Miklayev.

"There was just a whole series of incidents," Chris recalled, "that made us begin to think he had a hidden agenda going—things he said he'd done which we then found out he hadn't, meetings we'd set up that he somehow managed to sabotage. It also turned out that he knew a lot more English than he let on, and he had this habit of always wandering into the communications room—needed to change his shirt or something—whenever we were trying to talk on the phone. It finally got to the point where we just told him to take off."

But Ruslan and Slava were merely the beginning. As the searchers soon began to realize, the possibility of ulterior motives extended to all the various factions that had now taken to the field or that were professing a desire to help them.

From the Chechen rebel leadership, extending up to Dzhokhar Dudayev himself, came solemn vows of assistance, along with great displays of outrage at any suggestion that they might have harmed Fred Cuny, "the great friend of the Chechen people." Yet even they conceded that the group had come under suspicion in the Bamut area and had been at least temporarily detained by their fighters. It also became clear very quickly that their Fred Cuny Search Committee barely existed beyond its name.

From the Yeltsin government came repeated claims that FSB agents were energetically scouring the countryside for clues. It was an assertion that the searchers from Texas found scant evidence to support; if anything, the few FSB agents they encountered on the ground appeared far more interested in keeping tabs on them. In his office in Moscow, however, FSB Major General Mikhailov fairly bristled with indignation at any suggestion that his agency wasn't pulling its weight:

"We have done everything we can, in the conditions that are before us, to clarify the situation, to bring to light what has happened to Fred Cuny. These statements about our lack of participation in the search—or, more severely, our conflicting with the search—are baseless, groundless. The sad truth is that it's very difficult for us to work in the current conditions in Chechnya because the Dudayev side has taken a less than constructivist approach."

Perhaps most bewildering of all was the role of the Ingush government in the whole affair. Both President Ruslan Aushev and Vice-President Boris Agapov professed great friendship for Fred and made finding him a top national priority, dispatching a steady stream of their Emergency Situations officers to assist the manhunt and even assigning a Cossack detective, Peter Kozov, to help the Cuny family. At first glance this assistance might have seemed the most trustworthy, since Ingushetia was officially neutral in the conflict—except it was a neutrality with that special Caucasian twist.

As part of the Russian Federation, Ingushetia served as a back base and supply line for the Russian military in their campaign in Chechnya, but it also provided much the same services to their blood cousins, the Chechen rebels, and both President Aushev and Vice-President Agapov were said to be close friends of Dzhokhar Dudayev. At the same time, the Emergency Situations officials' quiet whispers of support for the Chechen cause, along with Peter Kozov's stout proclamations of complete autonomy, became harder to gauge when it was remembered that all were actually on the payroll of the Russian government.

Even the American government's role in the search was open to suspicion. Most of the officials who came to assist the private effort in Ingushetia were drawn from the political and intelligence offices of the embassy in Moscow. Were they sincerely trying to help in the search, or merely using it to get a look at the battlefield? This latter possibility was certainly the suspicion of other players in the field—the Chechens and Ingush, as well as the Russians.

What confronted the searchers, then, was a maze of intrigue, one in which every faction that was ostensibly helping them also had a potential ulterior motive.

This tangle of possible hidden agendas and secret motives was further compounded by the almost surreal—and, to the outsider, completely impenetrable—network of deals and alliances that reigned on the Chechen battlefield.

Beginning in March, the Russians had launched a particularly crude carrot-and-stick campaign in the countryside. Mayors and village elders in communities selected for "pacification" were given a simple choice: either they could avoid any unpleasantries by kicking out the rebels in their midst or they could resist and suffer the same fate as Grozny. Enough communities had accepted the Russian carrot to turn the war "front" into a crazy mosaic, with the Russian army and Chechen rebels coexisting in de facto "peace zones"—and even establishing fledgling free-market economies where weapons were exchanged for food or vodka—often within a mere mile or two of bitterly contested battlefields. If Fred and the others had run into trouble at one of these "coprosperity spheres," it was entirely conceivable that one side would cover for the misdeeds of the other in order to preserve the local peace and commerce. At a higher level, given the sophistication of the Chechen mafia in both Chechnya and Moscow—and their extensive ties with top officials in the Russian government and military—a deal could have been brokered far away from the fighting, an apparatchik in Moscow getting word to his local smuggling partner in Chechnya to do away with the group, for example, or a Chechen mafioso in St. Petersburg—or Istanbul or Vienna—sending word to a reliable Russian colonel at the front to do the same.

"The whole time I was there," Rick Hill said, "I felt like I was in some scene out of *Apocalypse Now*. The Chechens are buying up arms from the Russians, the Russians are being paid off to let the Chechens go through [checkpoints], and you often can't tell them apart because there's no standard uniform. A lot of these different units, they've adopted ninja warrior personalities—headbands, kamikaze insignia—and you start to realize that anything can happen because these guys are basically just looking out for themselves."

Added to this was the paranoia and crude propagandizing that existed in even peaceful parts of the country. As the searchers from

Texas discovered, if they rolled into a Chechen village and started showing around photographs of Fred, they were liable to get radically different answers depending on how they couched their questions.

"If you just showed them the photo—'Have you seen this guy?'—no one would say anything," Craig recalled. "If you said, 'He was an American relief worker and now he's missing,' the Chechens would say, 'Oh yeah, he was here, he left toward the Russian line, so they must have done something to him.' And, of course, if you went to the Russians, they'd say, 'No, never saw him, the Chechens must have killed him.'"

Not least were the questions that attended the missing group itself, of why they had chosen such an improbable and perilous path into Chechnya, if someone in the UAZ ambulance had been pursuing a mission that had nothing at all to do with humanitarian aid. Galina Oleinik had been an interpreter for visiting foreigners for many years, and in the old days of the Soviet Union all interpreters were officially vetted by the KGB and assumed to double as informants. Sergei Makarov and Andrei Sereda were employees of the Russian Red Cross, an institution routinely infiltrated with spies since the time of Stalin. And, while rarely voiced, the searchers from Texas even wondered about Fred.

"I know I thought about it," Craig said, "thought about it quite a bit. Not that he was a full-fledged CIA agent, but it certainly crossed my mind that maybe someone in the American government had asked him to check something out."

In such a climate of conspiracy, some of those conducting the manhunt in the Caucasus soon began to suspect that there might be one entity that knew more than it was telling: the American government. Those suspicions centered on events that were to take place in Moscow on May 9.

On that date the Yeltsin government was planning a gala affair to commemorate the fiftieth anniversary of the end of the Great Patriotic War, or World War II, a celebration that was to be attended by heads of state from around the world, including President Clinton. In the immediate aftermath of Russia's brutal incursion into Chechnya and the leveling of Grozny, Washington and a number of European capitals had considered snubbing Moscow by sending lower-level delegations, but in the end Clinton had not only agreed to attend but allowed Yeltsin to refashion the ceremony as a "summit." To Chris Cuny, for one, the continuing dearth of any hard information in the field raised the specter that the Russians were holding his brother captive—or worse, keeping news of his death under wraps—until after the Moscow summit so that no embarrassing questions would mar the proceedings. Given the Clinton Administration's devotion to Yeltsin, it occurred to Chris that this might be the American government's wish as well.

On the afternoon of May 10, Chris, Craig, and Lionel Rosenblatt flew from Ingushetia to Moscow, there to meet with President Clinton and put some blunt questions to him and his closest foreign policy advisers. Checking in to the Radisson Slavjanskaya Hotel, they enjoyed a moment of gallows humor over a typo on their reservation card; the Soros Foundation had somehow become the "Sorrows Foundation."

. . .

Early on the morning of May 11, Craig Cuny descended to the exercise room in the basement of the Radisson Slavjanskaya Hotel in Moscow, hoping that a little weight lifting might either shake off his fatigue or allow him to finally get a few hours' sleep. Along with Chris and Lionel Rosenblatt, he had flown up from Ingushetia the day before for an audience with the visiting American President and his foreign policy staff but, anxious and restless, had spent much of the night staring out the hotel window at the Russian capital.

At the door to the exercise room he was stopped by two plainclothes security men who, hearing his American accent, quickly waved him through. Inside the small, windowless room, Craig immediately saw the reason for the security: there, red-faced and panting as he pedaled away on a stationary bicycle was President Clinton. Their formal meeting was slated for that afternoon but Craig decided it would seem odd not to introduce himself now. Waiting until the President had finished his regimen, he stepped over to the exercise bike.

"Oh, yeah," Clinton said, while shaking his hand, "I talked to President Yeltsin about your father last night and he seemed genuinely concerned. In fact, he called over the head of the FSB and said, 'Do whatever it takes to find this man.'"

After thanking the President, Craig started to step away, but Clinton wasn't done chatting just yet. "So, where you from?"

"San Antone," Craig replied.

"All right." Clinton smiled. "That's a cool city."

When Craig went back upstairs and told his uncle and Lionel Rosenblatt of the encounter, he was met with amused disbelief; like his father, Craig had a bit of a reputation for telling tall tales.

"I didn't really try that hard to convince them," he said. "I figured, 'Well, let's see what happens at our meeting [with Clinton].'"

Early that afternoon the three were ushered into a small reception room of the American Embassy on Novinsky Boulevard where they were met by virtually the entire foreign policy leadership of the American government: Secretary of State Warren Christopher, National Security Adviser Anthony Lake, Deputy Secretary of State Strobe Talbott, along with Ambassador Thomas Pickering and a half dozen senior embassy officers. After some fifteen or twenty minutes spent in discussion of Fred's case, an advance man came through the door.

"Gentlemen, if you'll please rise, the President of the United States."

Striding into the room, Clinton scanned the faces of the dozen or so men there before stopping at Fred's son. "Hey, Craig," he said with a grin, "how's it going?"

In the moment of stunned silence that followed, Craig stepped forward.

"Mr. President, I guess I oughta do the introductions. I assume you know these guys," he said, waving a hand over the Secretary of

State and National Security Adviser, before turning to introduce Chris and Lionel Rosenblatt.

If somewhat awed by the gathering—as well as by his nephew's almost cheeky chumminess with the President—Chris Cuny also knew that this meeting was going to be short and probably the only chance he would ever have to get answers to some of his questions. He quickly got to the point.

"We've been looking for my brother for two weeks now, and we've gotten nowhere. My biggest concern is that you guys know something you're not telling us, that something has happened but it's being kept quiet so as not to disrupt the summit. Then, once the summit is over, Fred is going to appear, there's going to be a body, and you'll say, 'Well, that's too bad.' I just want to know the truth."

It was a remarkably blunt accusation to make before the President of the United States—the kind of brazen directness that suggested traces of Fred—but if Clinton was offended he didn't let on. Instead, he listened as his advisers politely but emphatically denied having any more information than the family did. They also let slip, however, that they feared the Russians might be employing precisely the stall tactic Chris described.

"And, of course, if the Russians were responsible, it made perfect sense," Chris Cuny said. "Wait for Clinton to get out of town, for the foreign media to pack up and go home, then bring out the bodies. At least after that meeting I was pretty convinced that, if it was going to play out that way, the American government wasn't in on it."

As if by clockwork, that very night, with the summit winding down and Clinton scheduled to soon leave for Washington, Chris got a call at the Radisson hotel from the North Caucasus. It was from Peter Kozov, the Cossack detective contracted by the Ingush government.

"We have a body," Kozov reported, "a foreigner. I'm 98 percent certain that it's your brother."

•   •   •

That night in the hotel room, Chris and Craig Cuny went through the solemn process of composing a news release and obituary for Fred, their feelings of grief at least partially subsumed by seeing to the logistical details of getting his body out of the war zone.

According to Peter Kozov, the body had been found by Chechen rebels in an earthen grave outside the small village of Gutingen in south-central Chechnya, in an area recently vacated by the Russian army. While much of the corpse's face had been destroyed, apparently by two point-blank execution shots to the back of the head, it appeared to be that of a middle-aged foreign man; he had been dead for about a month and was wearing jeans and boots. As much as they didn't want to admit it, both Chris and Craig knew at once that the body almost certainly had to be Fred; its description as well as the time of death simply fitted too neatly to leave much room for doubt. It was Elisabeth Socolow, who had come over to the Radisson to lend support, who first detected an odd detail in the story.

"I wonder how they know it's a foreigner," she said.

"Why not?" Chris replied.

"Well, if the face is missing, what are they judging by? How do you tell the difference between a Russian and an American body? Does Fred have some kind of scar or birthmark or something?"

In fact, Fred had quite a number of scars, as well as a permanent metal sheath in his left leg, but those were features that neither Peter Kozov nor anyone else in Chechnya were likely to know about. In the hotel room, Chris and Craig suddenly felt a lot less certain about just who was buried in the field outside Gutingen.

Those uncertainties grew as they pondered the remarkable specificity of Kozov's account. Just how did the detective know the middle-aged man had been dead for a month? For that matter, a body lying unprotected in an earthen grave for a month was likely to be so severely decomposed that even determining its gender could be difficult to the untrained eye, let alone its approximate age.

"This is the kind of thing we were constantly coming up against," Chris recalled. "Along with these incredibly vague, third-hand ac-

counts—'My cousin says his best friend's uncle gave a foreign man a
ride on his motorcycle'—you'd get these pinpoint-specific reports
that'd make you think you were on to something. 'Geez, with all these
details, it's gotta be true.' Then you start thinking about the details and
you realize, 'Wait a minute, no one can possibly know that.'"

Still, with the body outside Gutingen there was finally at least one
tangible story that could be either verified or discounted. After Kozov's
call, Chris arranged for Rick Hill, who had remained in the North
Caucasus, to try and retrieve the body and take it to a spot where an
autopsy could be performed; in the meantime, Chris would have Fred's
dental records sent over from Dallas. The plan looked simple enough
on paper, but this was Chechnya.

Together with an interpreter, Rick set up operations in a kind of
safehouse in the town of Noviye Atagi, in the rebel-held area just below
Grozny and a mere twenty-five kilometers from the gravesite in Gutingen. There ensued a series of complex negotiations with the Chechen
commanders. Rick wanted the body brought to Noviye Atagi for an
autopsy, but the Chechens had a better idea; after several days of stall-
ing, they suddenly whisked the body off to the mountain town of
Shatoi.

It was a rather incomprehensible decision for several reasons. In
moving the body, the rebels had not only eschewed the relatively safe
route down to Noviye Atagi, but gone in the opposite direction, through
a murderous free-fire zone patrolled by Russian helicopter gunships,
all to deliver the corpse to a town, Shatoi, that had become the Russian
army's latest target for encirclement and destruction. For the next week
Rick and American diplomats wrangled with Russian military commanders for a temporary cease-fire that would allow them to cross the
battlefield to retrieve or at least view the body.

"Finally we got the clearance," Rick said. " 'Okay, it's all arranged, we're going to lay off shelling the road, you guys can go
across.' " Rick gave a thin smile. "Well, that probably should have been
the tip-off right there."

No sooner had the three-car convoy traveling under a diplomatic flag entered the free-fire zone than the Russian artillery opened up again, with one shell landing a mere thirty yards away. Leaping from their vehicles, the convoy members sought refuge in a burnt-out farmhouse, then took advantage of a lull in the bombardment to race back the way they had come.

"It kind of seemed like they wanted us to go back," Rick said, "so we did."

When foreign diplomats finally were able to reach Shatoi and examine the body, several weeks later, they almost instantly determined that it was not Fred. The dead man was probably less than six feet tall—a good two or three inches short—and his "cowboy boots" turned out to be soft hiking shoes. A local dentist examining what was left of the jaw quickly concluded that the teeth didn't match the dental charts from Texas, and an X-ray showed there was no metal brace in the left leg. And there was one more curious detail about the corpse. It appeared that perhaps his face had not actually been obliterated from the gunshot wounds to the back of his head but rather from the liberal application of sulfuric acid.

For the searchers, the strange episode in Shatoi seemed perfectly emblematic of all their frustrations over the previous month, an episode of either such colossal ineptitude or byzantine conspiracy as to be impossible to make sense of. Of all the thousands of unclaimed bodies that lay scattered across Chechnya, what had led the rebels to that one, or caused Peter Kozov to claim with such certainty that it was Fred's? If the rebels had concocted the "body double" as a way to implicate the Russians—and if the face had been deliberately destroyed it surely suggested this—why had they appeared to go out of their way to stymie the investigators and draw suspicion on themselves? And why had the FSB, while still denying any knowledge as to the missing group's whereabouts, so vehemently dismissed any possibility that the corpse was Fred's even before anyone had viewed it—and simultaneously escalated their whispering campaign that Fred was a CIA agent and very much alive? Even the reason for the Russian artillery attack that had delayed the body-recovery team was open to labyrinthine speculation. Maybe it was just another example of miscommunication among the Russian military, or maybe the Russians were truly afraid it was Fred's body—or maybe even some Russian field commander had done it as a favor to the rebels holding the body because more time was needed for sulfuric acid to do its disfiguring work.

"You'd find yourself endlessly debating these kinds of things," Rick Hill recalled, "and coming up with all these absurd scenarios. Except they weren't any more absurd than a lot of the stuff that had already happened."

As with everything else on the battlefield of Chechnya, there would appear to be no answers to the questions surrounding the "body double" in Gutingen. Instead there would be one more mystery suspended in limbo, a faceless body whose name and sad story would remain forever lost in no man's land.

CHAPTER 10

We are not the allies of any particular theory to this story. We are only the allies of facts, and to this moment we do not have any facts. Until then, these different theories are just things that give room for conversation.
—FSB General Alexander Mikhailov
    on Russian disinformation campaign against Fred Cuny

ON THE MORNING of May 15, 1995, a UAZ ambulance left the border town of Sleptsovskaya and headed south across the plains, toward the foothills of the Caucasus Mountains. Inside were Chris Cuny, Magomet Dauerbekov, the deputy minister of Emergency Situations, as well as one of the American consular officers deputized to aid in the search for Fred Cuny. A few days before, the searchers in Ingushetia had been told that the rebel commandant of Bamut, presumably the same man who had briefly detained and questioned Fred's party on the evening of March 31, had information and was willing to share it; now the searchers were rep-

licating the lost group's last journey to meet the commandant.

Crossing the Assa River and wending east through the foothills,
they came to a slight curve in the rugged dirt track, halfway across a
windswept and exposed mountainside, and there they stopped. According to popular rumor, the curve marked where Ingushetia ended and
Chechnya began.

If not the precise spot, it was close enough. Several hundred yards
farther on, Russian artillery shells were pounding a ridgeline, sending
plumes of smoke and dust into the clear sky, while helicopter gunships
trolled the nearby valley depths.

After a few minutes' wait, three heavily armed rebels in Russian
camouflage fatigues emerged from a treeline to approach the group.
The oldest member of the squad, a bearded man in his forties, identified himself as Hamid Shahalov, the commandant of Bamut.

"Your brother is alive," he told Chris Cuny. "He can be released
for two million dollars."

"Where's the proof that he's alive?" Chris asked.

Shahalov seemed to take umbrage at the question. "My word is my
proof. That's all the proof you need."

"Well, actually, it's not," Chris replied. "I need more than that if
you think I'm going to come up with two million dollars."

For the next half hour the two men dickered over the price tag,
their negotiations given odd punctuation by the steadily intensifying
Russian artillery barrage slamming the ridgeline just beyond. Eventually Shahalov scaled his demand down to a half million dollars, and
Chris stopped pushing for proof because the commandant "was getting
kind of belligerent—and he had a gun and I didn't." Telling Shahalov
they would get back in touch, Chris and the others then turned around
and drove back to Sleptsovskaya.

Very soon, however, they learned that Hamid Shahalov was not
the commandant of Bamut, and never had been. Rather, he was a
small-time criminal who had allied himself with the rebels and appar-

ently saw in the ongoing manhunt a chance to make a lot of quick money.

Coming close on the heels of the "body double" episode in Shatoi, the encounter with the "commandant double" on the frontier made the searchers realize they had now stumbled into a classic crime investigation conundrum: the more high profile their efforts, the more they were prone to get false leads—and the more anxious they appeared for those leads, the more vulnerable they were to scams with high price tags.

"I think we'd kind of made a mistake early on," Rick Hill said, "in that we had too many people out there, and some members of the team were fairly eager in trying to make contact with various factions, so that there was a certain frenzy to the activity that probably didn't serve us well. There was the feeling that, if Fred were being held for ransom, maybe we were looking a bit too desperate—and, of course, in that part of the world Americans appear to have pretty deep pockets."

At the end of May the searchers from Texas tried a change of tactics. Operating on the premise that Fred and the others were still alive, they quietly put the word out that their mission in the region would soon come to an end.

"The idea was to turn down the heat some," Rick said, "that if they were being held for ransom, maybe the kidnappers were laying low because of all the different [governmental] agencies involved. But we were also posturing a little to give off the impression, 'Well, we're here now, but we're not gonna be here much longer,' to imply that the window for a deal was closing."

The gambit yielded nothing.

But the episode with Hamid Shahalov on the Bamut road underscored an even more dispiriting point to the searchers: after a month in the region, the Chechen morass remained just as opaque as it had been on the day of their arrival. In April it had taken nearly three weeks to simply determine how many people were missing along with Fred. By late May, after three weeks of scouring the countryside and working with the professed cooperation of a rebel army and three governments, the searchers had still not even firmly established the identity of the real commandant of Bamut. In fact, pinning down that most elemental detail was still several more weeks away.

"Well, let's face it," Craig Cuny said, "we were not professional searchers and when we first got there, we were very glad that all the different components—the Russians and Chechens, and especially the Ingush—seemed to be interested in finding out what had happened. But after a while you start thinking, 'Hey, wait a minute, no one really cares as much about this as we do, we don't seem to be getting any closer to answers, and at least somebody in this whole equation probably has a vested interest in derailing this thing.' For so long there, we kind of sat back and let the official investigators do their work and we were just there kind of as figureheads, doing whatever we could to keep pressure on people. We finally decided we couldn't do that anymore."

In truth, it was not a decision entirely of their own making. By early June the various official agencies involved appeared to be steadily losing interest in the manhunt. The government of Ingushetia had grown impatient with the searchers' incessant demands, and Peter Kozov, the Cossack detective, had left for an ulcer cure shortly after the body-double episode and never returned. Back in late April, with the rebels promising all help and swift action, the Soros Foundation had provided their Fred Cuny Search Committee with a satellite phone linked to the search headquarters in Sleptsovskaya, but no call had ever come. The American Embassy had begun quietly scaling back its involvement, pulling its consular officers and communications specialists back to Moscow; rather than a semipermanent presence in the North Caucasus, its assistance to the searchers would now consist of occasional visits and strategy sessions over a radio linkup. By June, even the obstructionism and clumsy meddling of the Russian FSB agents in the area had become desultory.

That month the private search effort began to scale back as well. Lionel Rosenblatt had long since returned to the United States, and he was now joined by Chris Cuny and Rick Hill. Remaining at the headquarters in Sleptsovskaya—a small house behind a high wall shared with an Ingush family of four—was Eric Shutler and Craig and a new translator, Greg Smith. A thirty-one-year-old lapsed Mormon and accomplished blues guitarist, Greg had spent the previous two years playing in Moscow nightclubs, and had first come to the region in May as the interpreter for two Western journalists tracking the Fred Cuny story. After hitting it off with Craig, Greg had offered to return if the searchers ever needed his help; that call had come in early June.

The manhunt now became a rather homespun operation. With Eric largely handling matters at headquarters, keeping in touch with both the American Embassy in Moscow and the Intertect office back in Dallas, Craig and Greg took to roaming the Chechen countryside in the "Fredbulance," a gray UAZ ambulance identical to the one Fred and the others had disappeared in, distributing leaflets and questioning villagers. While there was a liberating feel to the enterprise—no more sitting around smoke-filled rooms listening to petty bureaucrats talk of protocols and procedures—it also raised the risk level, especially whenever a Russian army checkpoint appeared in the road ahead.

"A couple of times," Craig recalled, "we got into situations where we'd come up to one side of a checkpoint and the first guy would wave us through, so we'd start away. But then someone else would decide they wanted to talk to us, and the way they let us know that was to start shooting over the top of the ambulance. We learned pretty quick that whenever you're waved through you pull out real slow and keep checking the rearview mirror to see if someone's taking aim."

They also learned that the most dangerous driving time was in late afternoon.

"The Russian troops are so undisciplined and have been bribed all day with bottles of vodka, so there's a pretty good chance they're completely fucked up. Also, night is coming on, which is when the rebels usually attack, so they're getting tense. Basically, you're dealing with a seventeen-year-old kid with a bad attitude who's scared and drunk and holding an AK-47. That's not a pleasant ordeal."

Greg Smith recalled one day when fifteen army checkpoints had to be negotiated.

"By the end of it, I was completely wrung out. I didn't smoke, but I remember really wanting a cigarette that night."

It was that same night that Greg was given a stark illustration of just how quirky the war had become. Reaching a small town in eastern Chechnya just at sunset, he and Craig sought refuge in a local hospital when nearby Russian artillery batteries opened up. The bombardment steadily intensified until the local rebel commander picked up his portable phone and called over to the Russian side.

"Keep it up," he told his Russian counterpart, "and we're going to come over there and kick your ass."

Within minutes the shelling stopped.

But what Greg remembered most from that time was Craig's unceasing energy and optimism. "It was really incredible. Here we were in this hellish place, week after week of seeming to get nowhere, and we'd roll into some village and Craig would hop out of the ambulance, a big friendly smile, and start handing out these fliers. If you didn't know the context, you'd think he was handing out leaflets to a store opening or something."

Only once did he recall seeing Craig's spirits falter. It came at the end of a long day of canvassing villages in the central Chechnya foothills, as they drove back toward Sleptsovskaya.

"He was just very quiet, staring out at the road, and then he says, 'You know, I think he's dead. I think my father's dead.' And I remember thinking to myself, 'Well, yeah. I mean, take a look at this place,' but of course I didn't say it. But then it just passed, very quickly, and Craig was back into his joking, upbeat mode, and we just continued on."

.   .   .

One afternoon in mid-June, after another day spent futilely touring the Chechen countryside, Craig and Greg pulled the Fredbulance to the bank of the Sunzha River, just outside a small agricultural town named Samashki. At that point in western Chechnya, the Sunzha ran swiftly and relatively clean, not yet completely deadened by the waste from the oilfields and industrial parks around Grozny. In the surrounding fields were wildflowers and, twenty miles to the south, the snow-capped peaks of the Caucasus shone against a blue sky. It reminded them both of something that was very easy to forget in Chechnya, that this was a place of remarkable beauty, that whatever was ugly about it, both in peacetime and war, had been the handiwork of man. Taking the stretchers from the back of the ambulance, they laid them at the river's edge and whiled away the afternoon, sunbathing and drinking warm Ingush beer while Greg strummed his guitar.

In the six weeks since he had arrived in the Caucasus, Craig had driven thousands of miles in search of his father, not only combing the war zone but venturing into a half dozen neighboring republics and autonomous regions. He had met with President Clinton and lesser officials from three governments. He had spoken with hundreds of civilians, scores of Chechen rebels and Russian soldiers—and if he still did not know what had happened to Fred and the others, he now at least had some pretty strong ideas of what had not.

He no longer believed they might be kidnap victims; simply too much time had passed without a credible ransom demand. He did not believe they were being held in another republic or at the Russian "filtration center" in Mozdok; Fred was such an imposing and out-of-place figure in the region that there would have been a reliable sighting of him somewhere by now. In fact, Craig was now almost thoroughly convinced that the group had never gotten any farther than western Chechnya, and one place that especially aroused his suspicions was the town near where they sunbathed that afternoon: Samashki. Despite the beauty of its surroundings, Samashki had been the site for one of the worst atrocities in an atrocity-filled war, and it had taken place at the precise moment that Fred and the others might have been in the area.

Since the start of the war Samashki had been a key rebel stronghold, and the Russian army had made the agricultural town astride the Sunzha River a primary target for "pacification" during their March western offensive. By April 6 they had "sealed" Samashki, surrounding all approaches with tanks and heavy artillery, and the deputy commander of Russian forces in Chechnya, Lieutenant General Anatoli Antonov, had delivered an ultimatum to the town elders: they had until 7 A.M. of the following day to force out the rebels in their midst, as well as hand over 264 guns. The elders' protestations, that they had no control over the rebels and no such weaponry, fell on deaf ears. In any event, the OMON troops encircling Samashki didn't seem much interested in ultimatums; artillery and tanks opened up on the town that night and continued through the morning.

Shortly after noon on April 7, the elders walked out of the town under a white flag for another meeting with Russian commanders. General Antonov was gone and, ominously, the officers who now appeared to be commanding the operation refused to identify themselves. The elders were given an extension until 4 P.M. to turn over their weapons and evacuate the town. At three-thirty, as civilians were frantically packing to escape before the deadline, the Russian artillery batteries ringing Samashki opened up in full force, followed shortly after by converging columns of tanks and armored personnel carriers.

Over the next thirty-six hours, and despite encountering little resistance, the Russian troops ripped Samashki apart, flamethrowering whole streets, dropping grenades into cellars where families hid, shooting down those who crossed their path. One of their victims was a much-decorated war hero from World War II. To protect his home and family, the old man had put on his old Red Army uniform with its array of medals and ribbons, and sat on a chair outside his front gate as the Russians approached; instead of being spared, he was machine-gunned where he sat, his home then stripped bare by the looting soldiers.

By the time the slaughter was over, at least 150—and perhaps as many as 400—civilians were dead; the precise number would never be determined, for the Russian army then blocked all relief groups from Samashki for the next three days, during which scores of bodies were reportedly burned or thrown into mass graves. Even after their "cleanup" operation, the troops tightly controlled access to the town, turning back all but the most intrepid journalists and relief workers.

Since first learning of the Samashki massacre, Craig and the other searchers had wondered if the town might hold the key to Fred's disappearance, and an intermittent trickle of rumors had bolstered that theory. The strongest had come in late May from none other than Rizvan Elbiev, the rebel counterintelligence commander in Atchkoi-Martan to whom Fred and the others had been taken on April 4. Through an intermediary, Elbiev claimed to have released the group on the morning of April 7; because they were anxious to get back to Ingushetia, they had not tried to retrace their steps west through Bamut, but had instead set out directly north, across the Sunzha Valley plains. The decision was logical enough; once out of Atchkoi-Martan, it would have been only a few miles through the fields before the group reached the Trans-Caucasus Highway "shadow road," and then only a short jaunt back to Sleptsovskaya.

Except that the five-mile drive from Atchkoi-Martan to the Trans-Caucasus shadow road meant driving straight across the war's no man's land and directly through the front lines of the Russian army, then preparing for the April 10 offensive. If the group had managed that hurdle, they would have then run squarely into Outpost 6 outside Assinovskaya, the OMON checkpoint where Galina and the doctors had narrowly escaped execution less than three weeks earlier. And once past the checkpoint, the group would have driven straight into Samashki, arriving there just in time for the massacre. If the account were true, it meant Fred and the others had ventured onto a landscape where death lay waiting all around.

While it was curious that Rizvan Elbiev had chosen to sit on this crucial information for well over a month, the searchers had subsequently heard other reports that lent credibility to his story. Several survivors of the Samashki massacre who had made it to safety in Ingushetia claimed to have seen a large foreign man in the town just before the Russian attack started. A variation on the theme came from a CNN stringer named Yuri Romanov. According to Romanov, a Russian officer had told him that Fred's group had been detained and murdered at the Assinovskaya checkpoint, their bodies buried beside an old bus stop on the Trans-Caucasus Highway just a few meters from the post. One day in mid-June, Craig and Greg Smith finally managed to steer the Fredbulance past the Russian checkpoints encircling Samashki and enter the devastated town.

"You could instantly see that something really brutal had happened there," Craig said. "Whole streets were wiped out, places in rubble, everything riddled with machine-gun bullets. I remember one street in particular where everything on one side was completely burned from about waist level up, like they'd come down the street with a flamethrower and just pointed it in that direction as they drove along. But the biggest sign was that it was such a somber place. The people there, the survivors, had obviously gone through something incredible and you could see it in their eyes. In most Chechen towns people were very friendly and talkative—even if it was just to bitch about the Russians—but in Samashki it wasn't like that. They really didn't want to talk, and they had a kind of shell-shocked manner about them."

Still, even in Samashki, the familiar pattern eventually repeated itself. Over the course of that day Craig and Greg collected the widest possible array of "eyewitness" accounts on the missing group: they had been there just as the artillery bombardment commenced, they had never been there, there had been two of them, there had been six of them, the large American man had been there alone wearing a light blue windbreaker and carrying a video camera. In Samashki, as in the rest of Chechnya, the ghostly shadows of Fred and his companions were everywhere, and then they were gone.

. . .

At about eleven on the morning of June 24 a blue sedan left Bamut and headed west, toward the frontier with Ingushetia. Inside were five men, including Ramzan Ferzuali, the new rebel commandant of Bamut. Waiting to meet them just across the Ingush frontier was an erstwhile Chechen fighter, "Magomet."

A veteran of the siege of Grozny, Magomet had been wounded in battle in western Chechnya in late March and, for the past two months, had worked with the Cuny family search team. If Magomet could be trusted—and most indications were that he could—he was a valuable source. It was he who had unmasked Hamid Shahalov, the Bamut "commandant double" who had demanded a three-million-dollar ransom for Fred. He had also identified most of the senior rebel commanders who had been in the Bamut area at the time of Fred's disappearance.

He had been able to do so, Magomet explained to Craig, because Ramzan Ferzuali, the new Bamut commandant, was a lifelong friend as well as a comrade in arms during the battle for Grozny. After the fall of the capital in early March, Ferzuali had been named deputy commandant of Bamut and had been in that post when Fred's group arrived in the town on March 31. While Ferzuali had already provided his personal recollections of that March 31 encounter to Magomet, he had recently gathered further details and was making the journey in the blue sedan on June 24 to pass those details on to Magomet.

According to the account Ferzuali had provided so far, Fred's group had no sooner arrived in Bamut than they came under the critical gaze of the commandant at the time, a man named Moli Astimirov, and of Shirvani Albakhov, a colonel attached to the chief of staff for the Bamut region. For several hours Astimirov and Albakhov had questioned Fred and the others at the rebel headquarters in Bamut on suspicion that they were spies; it was Ferzuali—at least in the version he gave to Magomet—who had energetically argued on the group's behalf, insisting to his commander that all those in the UAZ ambulance were legitimate relief workers. Astimirov had finally been convinced and released the group.

From there on, Ferzuali's account had largely dovetailed with that of the driver, Ruslan Muradov. After spending that night of March 31 at the Bamut home of Muradov's parents, the party had continued on toward Orekhovo, only to be stopped by another group of rebels on the forest road. The next day, April 2, they were brought back to the Muradov home in Bamut to await clearance from Rizvan Elbiev, the counterintelligence commander in Atchkoi-Martan.

It was at this point, however, that Ferzuali's information got interesting. According to what he had already told Magomet, Ferzuali had seen Fred and the others several times on April 2 and 3 during their wait in Bamut, and noticed that Shirvani Albakhov, the chief of staff colonel, seemed to always be nearby. When the group finally left for Atchkoi-Martan on the morning of April 4 they were in the company of Albakhov.

Then, on April 15, amid the Russians' all-out offensive in the region, Moli Astimirov had been killed, and Ferzuali had taken over as commandant of Bamut. Soon after, he began hearing stories that the party of relief workers had disappeared, but had taken little interest in the matter until he was approached by his old friend Magomet and asked for help. Now, on the morning of June 24, he was making the perilous trip out of the war zone to tell Magomet what else he had learned, and he was bringing Colonel Albakhov along to answer Magomet's questions.

To Magomet, this meeting might finally provide the essential clue to unlocking the mystery. Albakhov was the one man who absolutely knew what had happened after the group left Bamut on April 4, because he had been with them.

At about eleven-forty on that morning Magomet, standing just inside Ingushetia, watched as the approaching blue sedan rounded the last curve of the barren mountain on the Chechen side of the frontier. Suddenly a Russian helicopter gunship that had been lurking in the depths popped over the ridgeline. Before anyone had time to react, the helicopter gunner had trained a sophisticated flamethrower cannon on the sedan and let loose a stream of fire. In an instant, all five occupants, including Ramzan Ferzuali and Shirvani Albakhov, were burned alive. With their deaths, quite possibly some of the most critical clues to the Fred Cuny mystery were eliminated, as well.

. . .

"First of all, I have never heard of this account," Major General Alexander Mikhailov said in his Lubyanka Square office, "and I would caution against putting too much faith in the account of a bandit. I also find it interesting, this pattern among the Chechens, that just when someone is ready to talk about Fred Cuny—'Oh, too bad, they've just been killed.' In some ways, maybe I even feel sorry for them. They know they are trapped by the facts of this case, and the only way out for them is to put the gun in the hands of dead men."

It was an intriguing comment for the FSB major general to make for several reasons. Since at least the time of Lenin, the unrivaled masters of the "post-mortem confession" have been those in the very intelligence apparatus that Mikhailov now represented. What's more, by the summer of 1995 it appeared that it was the FSB, far more than the Chechens, who were employing a variation of that technique in the case of Fred Cuny.

By the end of June the smear campaign in the Russian nationalist press, claiming that Fred was somewhere in the Caucasus Mountains acting as an intelligence adviser to Dudayev, was not only continuing but had taken on fantastic new embroidery. According to one story, he had been the mastermind of the recent outrage in the Russian town of Budyennovsk, in which Chechen rebels had herded thousands of civilian hostages into a hospital and executed at least two dozen before winning safe passage back to Chechnya. According to another, Fred was actually on loan from the CIA to the Turkish government—historical allies of the Chechens—and was directing secret arms shipments to the rebels out of the neighboring republic of Dagestan. In most cases the ultimate source of these stories was found to be the same as most of the earlier ones: the FSB and, most specifically, Major General Mikhailov. But sitting in his office on Lubyanka Square, the general dismissed that assertion with a lazy wave of his hand.

"We are not behind these stories. At no time have we been behind these stories. As far as who is to gain from them, you'd have to ask the journalists who are writing them directly. Of course, it is theoretically possible that Fred Cuny is working for Dudayev—and I stress theoretically—but we have never stated this or moved this opinion forward." The major general lit another cigarette and scanned his office ceiling, a habit that seemed to show itself whenever his thoughts wandered into the creative sphere. "And actually, one could almost see all these stories as a disinformation effort of a very different kind, an attempt to discredit the FSB."

Upon hearing of Mikhailov's novel theory, an American intelligence officer laughed.

"Well, it's funny because it is such an absolute lie," he said. "The fact is, these stories about Fred were coming down to us from the highest ranks of the FSB, not just Mikhailov, but from [FSB director Sergei] Stepashin himself. This was a concerted campaign by the Russian intelligence agencies, and most of the time it wasn't even covert; they were coming to us with the stories."

One American diplomat involved in the search told of a letter Defense Minister Grachev sent to his American counterpart, William Perry, in July in which Grachev claimed they had convincing evidence that Fred was working with Dudayev.

"When the Pentagon wrote back," the diplomat said, "basically asking, 'Are you nuts?' Grachev sent another letter saying, 'Oh, sorry, our mistake; he's actually a prisoner of Dudayev.' "

At all levels of the American government, the Russians' odd and persistent claims about Fred were a source of both puzzlement and alarm, although initially, some had viewed them as a hopeful sign. One long-standing Soviet tradition had been to "unmask" American spies whenever the Kremlin felt world opinion turning against it, and since the Chechnya invasion had hardly been a public relations coup, it seemed possible that Fred Cuny was the latest such "spy" to be found. It had also seemed possible that the Russians were trying to feel their way out of an embarrassing situation; if, for example, Fred had been taken to Mozdok and tortured but was still alive, the price for his freedom might be a spying "confession" that would serve to taint his victim status. As time went on, however, with no such feelers extended by Russian authorities, the Americans took a more ominous view of the media campaign.

"It certainly seems very worrisome to us," a State Department official said that July, once again diffident, once again insisting on anonymity, "because, at least from our end, it raises the possibility that they know more than they are telling. Why maintain this really rather unsupportable line if, in fact, you have nothing to hide? I find the back and forth with the Russians on this, frankly, suspicious. I think that's as far as I can go. There's no proof of anything, but it's not reassuring."

In Moscow, Ambassador Pickering was considerably more forthcoming.

"We've seen a huge increase in these kinds of spurious stories directed at Americans in general in recent years, and this may be one more. As to why that would be, I'd have three basic guesses. First, the FSB might think this kind of thing is a way to protect their own existence. They're not thinking about our reaction but about maintaining their own funding, and a good way to do that is to make it appear there are spies everywhere. Second, they're throwing out these stories to try to gauge our reaction in some way. Or third, they see this as a way to cover themselves for . . . something their own people may have been involved in."

Yet, there was a fourth possibility, and it went to the core of something that had always bedeviled the West in trying to fathom events in Russia.

"They lie," another State Department official said. "It's not second nature to them; it's first nature. I'm not saying Russians are genetically programmed that way, but I do think there's been a kind of historical imprint that tells them that lying protects you and the truth gets you in trouble—and if you look at their history in this century you can certainly understand why. It makes it incredibly difficult to figure out their motives at times because, given a choice between telling a truth that will exonerate them or telling a lie that will cast suspicion on them, their knee-jerk reaction is usually to do the latter."

The official also pointed to another prominent feature of the collective Russian psyche, the inferiority complex they have always displayed toward the West, the constant need to prove they're just as powerful, just as in control as Americans and Western Europeans.

"It might seem completely crazy to us, but what all this stuff the

Russians have put out about Fred Cuny might come down to, is some guy sitting in an office somewhere who just doesn't want to say, 'We don't know what happened.' There's a lot of situations in which Russians would rather look guilty than ignorant."

By July, those still following the Cuny mystery in the North Caucasus were openly comparing his story to that of another humanitarian who had vanished in another war. In 1944, Swedish diplomat Raoul Wallenberg had disappeared in the Hungarian capital of Budapest, just as the advancing Soviet army was entering the city from the east and the German army was retreating to the west. Eventually, it was established that Wallenberg had been sent to a Siberian gulag on Stalin's orders and had died there.

Such comparisons could not have comforted the Cuny family. Fully solving the Wallenberg mystery had taken investigators over forty years.

. . .

There is something distinctly Texan about the Hurst Harbor Marina on the south shore of Lake Travis outside Austin. Along with hundreds of standard power boats and twenty-foot fishing cruisers, cigarette racing boats and jet skis, there is a phalanx of massive floating palaces: sixty-five-foot houseboats of three and four stories bedecked with state-of-the-art sonar and navigational equipment, and capable, in theory at least, of being seaborne for weeks at a time. It's all a little strange on a body of water that is, after all, only twelve miles long and a half mile wide.

At the far southwestern corner of the marina, however, there is an anomaly—and to many of the weekend sailors, an eyesore: a small homemade houseboat of plywood and Styrofoam that appears to be gradually sinking into the warm brown water. In 1993, Craig Cuny bought the houseboat for $7,000 from the eccentric old man who had built it, and it was to this boat that he returned from Chechnya in the middle of July 1995.

The official reason for his return was that his three-month visa for Russia was about to expire and he had to leave the country to have it renewed. Unofficially, the rest of the Cuny family were growing worried about the strain of his protracted stay in the war zone and had imposed a vacation.

"I didn't want to leave when I had to," he said that month, lounging in a plastic deck chair on the houseboat's patio, "but now that I've been back a few days, it's really sunk in that I needed this break. More than anything else, Chechnya is just such a hassle at this point. I mean, you have the emotional stuff you're dealing with, but what's really constant over there is all the bullshit you have to contend with day in and day out. The ambulance isn't the best vehicle, and it's trying to get gas or dealing with the mechanic who's trying to rip you off—just all the everyday ordeals."

Still, after a brief respite, perhaps ten days or two weeks, Craig was planning on going back to the North Caucasus. He had made contact with a wealthy and well-connected Chechen businessman named Shirvani.* A member of the Chechen diaspora in Jordan, Shirvani had recently returned to Chechnya and had offered to use his contacts with the rebel leadership to explore some new avenues in the manhunt. To Craig, the businessman seemed sincere—and at least one person who did not appear to have a hidden agenda or an interest in shaking him down for money. Just before Craig's departure for Texas, Shirvani and his "associates" had begun canvassing various rebel commanders in search of answers.

"So, we'll see what happens," Craig said with a shrug that day on the houseboat. "At this point, we don't really have anything else to go on, so I don't see how it can hurt."

While Craig unwound on Lake Travis, Chris Cuny was still trying to coordinate the dwindling search effort from his office in North Dallas. He had taken a long leave of absence from his engineering firm—from mid-April to mid-June—and had then assumed the frus-

---

* At the Cuny family's request, the businessman's name has been changed.

trating task of coordinating between the Soros Foundation in New York, Craig and Eric Shutler in Ingushetia, and those in Washington—like Mort Abramowitz, Don Krumm, and Lionel Rosenblatt—who were still working the hustings to keep the American government involved.

"At this point, we're kind of down to two theories," he said that July. "The one we most believe—or I suppose it's the one we most want to believe—is that the Chechens captured him and that he's still alive, because they appear to have a motive for keeping him, that they could use him as a political chip at some point in the future, whether for money or to get somebody released by the Russians or whatever. The other theory is that the Russians grabbed him, and if that happened . . ." Chris's voice trailed off. "Well, that's not a very happy scenario."

Giving this latter scenario greater credence, of course, was the FSB's ongoing smear campaign against Fred. As to motive, there was Fred's testimony before Congress lambasting the Russian military's tactics in Grozny, as well as his *New York Review of Books* article.

"It was clear that both those things made a stir in Moscow," Chris said. "I think it's very likely—in fact, I'd give it a very, very high degree of probability—that the group was being watched by the Russians from the moment they got there."

At the same time Chris's long-held suspicions about the United States government had not been fully allayed. "Let me put it this way. I trust [Ambassador] Tom Pickering. He's given me every reason to, because he's worked really hard on this thing. But do I think the FBI or the CIA knows something they're not telling us? Yeah, I do. I really do. I think there's a lot to the puzzle that they know, or that they suspect, but they're not letting on. Somebody somewhere is holding the key, and I think our government, if they know, they've decided they can't tell us at this point for some reason."

More than anything else, though, the Cuny family just wanted it to end. Sitting in his office on that hot July day, the search for his brother still consumed Chris's thoughts and much of his time, but now even his hopes were beginning to falter. An FBI team had recently gone to

Ingushetia to ask around on the case, but they had not been allowed into Chechnya or even to the border town of Sleptsovskaya; after a day in the region, they had flown back to Moscow. At the same time, the Soros Foundation, which had been bankrolling the manhunt to the tune of some $70,000 a month, was gently letting it be known that the money spigot couldn't stay open much longer.

"Obviously, we can't drag this on forever. There is going to come the time when . . . But what I'd like to say—to everybody, the Chechens, the Russians, the American government—is, 'Look, I'll sign any affidavit or any consent you want that says I'm not going to make a big political uproar about this. I just want to know definitively one way or another so that I and my nephew and my entire family can get on with their lives.' At this point, that's it, that's all we want."

Chris pensively scanned his desktop as his voice dropped to a mere whisper.

"Well, I'll tell you what my worst fear is. My worst fear is that this thing is just going to continue forever, that we'll never . . ." He lapsed into silence.

Just a few days later, however, Chris got a call from Eric Shutler in Ingushetia; he'd received a message from Shirvani, the Jordanian businessman.

"He's learned something," Eric reported, "but he wants to tell it to Craig."

On August 2, Craig flew back to Moscow, then caught a flight down to Ingushetia. The next morning he set out for Grozny and a meeting with Shirvani.

. . .

They met in the living room of Shirvani's house on the southern outskirts of the capital. After small glass cups of heavily sugared tea had been poured and sipped, the businessman stared across the wood table at Craig.

"I have found out what happened," Shirvani said. "I'm sorry to have to tell you this, but your father has been executed."

Over the course of that afternoon, the businessman laid out in detail what he had learned. It was a story that cast blame on both sides in the Chechen conflict.

According to Shirvani, a sophisticated FSB "black operation" had been directed against Fred and the others in the UAZ ambulance that day. A document that had circulated among the rebels in the Bamut area at the very end of March alleged that four spies—one foreigner who was an "anti-Islamist" and three FSB agents—would soon appear in the region. A day or two later Fred, Galina, and the two doctors had rolled into Bamut. It was that "spy list," Shirvani explained, that had led to the group's being detained and questioned on the evening of March 31 by the Bamut commandant. After clearing that hurdle, the group had continued on toward Orekhovo, only to be stopped a second time by the fighters in the forest. On April 4 they were sent on to the counterintelligence commander in Atchkoi-Martan, Rizvan Elbiev, their fate in limbo.

So far, Shirvani's information didn't break a lot of new ground, although it did reinforce and lend credibility to the account of "Magomet," the former Chechen fighter who had been working with Craig. Likewise, for some time Craig and other searchers had been hearing whispers—from Magomet and others—about some kind of spy list circulating in the Bamut area just before Fred's arrival. In fact, there had been the suggestion of such a list as far back as April in the testimony of the driver, Ruslan Muradov, and his account that had Dzhokhar Dudayev congratulating the Bamut fighters for capturing the four spies.

While Muradov's particular claim had been widely derided as a fiction, the searchers had also tended to dismiss the entire spy-document story as a post facto rebel concoction. All along there had been two basic facts that the rebels couldn't deny, thanks to Fred's note of April 4: that the group had been delayed by rebels in the Bamut area, and that they had been further delayed as they waited to be taken to Atchkoi-Martan. Coming up with the spy-list story could be seen as an attempt by the rebels to at least excuse their bad manners.

Except that Shirvani's account went a step further—a very big step. From what his contacts had learned, he told Craig, the counterintelligence commander in Atchkoi-Martan, Rizvan Elbiev, had not cleared the group—and they certainly had not set out on the road to Samashki on April 7. Rather, Elbiev had transferred his prisoners up the chain of command to the supreme counterintelligence commander for all rebel forces, General Abu Musayev, for a final determination. On April 14— and without the knowledge of Dudayev or General Maskhadov or any of the other Chechen commanders who knew Fred and might have intervened—Abu Musayev made his decision: it was to be death for all of them.

On that same afternoon, Shirvani said, a rebel execution squad entered the communications van where the three men—Fred, Andrei Sereda, and Sergei Makarov—were being held on the outskirts of a village near Orekhovo named Stari-Atchkoi. Two of the men were killed inside the van, while the third was dragged outside and killed in the yard; Galina Oleinik had apparently been taken and killed elsewhere. Their bodies were then buried in a mass grave in a nearby grove of trees.

Listening to Shirvani's account, Craig felt very mixed emotions. While the graphic details were painful to hear, there was also a kind of relief in them, for they held the ring of authenticity and conclusion to a story that had increasingly seemed destined for neither.

But it was not just the specificity and details that were so convincing. The existence of an FSB "black operation" such as Shirvani described could also explain the FSB's subsequent smear campaign, a smokescreen thrown up to cover its tracks. The few Chechens who had ever conceded even the remote possibility that Fred and the others had been murdered at Chechen hands had stoutly insisted that it could only have been done by bandits or renegades—at the very most, on the independent initiative of the low-level counterintelligence commander Rizvan Elbiev. Shirvani had not engaged in such damage control; instead, a Chechen who was loyal to the rebel cause, and who had never asked for a monetary reward, had now pointed the finger of culpability all the way to a member of the inner circle of the rebel leadership.

What's more, Craig and the other searchers had been suspicious of Abu Musayev for some time. Of all the Chechen rebel leaders, he had always been the most elusive, frequently promising to meet with them but never showing up. It had also been clear that a lot of the rebels didn't trust the counterintelligence commander—and a curious little detail on Musayev's résumé suggested both a reason for that distrust and for why he might have been so eager to embrace an FSB "black operation." In his prewar incarnation, Abu Musayev had been a high-ranking officer in the precursor to the FSB, the KGB.

Finally, Musayev's involvement may have explained why the searchers had never received any information from the rebels' Fred Cuny Search Committee. In a nice little touch of Caucasian irony, the chairman of that committee had been Abu Musayev.

That afternoon Craig returned to Ingushetia and made the difficult call to his uncle Chris back in Dallas. "Well," he said, "we've got some information, and it's not very good."

After Craig's call, Chris left work to tell his parents in Rockwall. By evening, everyone in the extended Cuny family had heard the news.

Beyond mere confirmation of his death, however, Fred's family wanted his body back. In this effort, Shirvani again offered his help, but he warned it would be a very high-risk undertaking.

Since any deal to recover the bodies would require the approval of Abu Musayev, Shirvani arranged for a meeting with the counterintelligence commander at a secluded spot in western Chechnya for the afternoon of Saturday, August 12. There, and with only one of Shirvani's field contacts to mediate, Craig and Eric Shutler would finally come face to face with the man identified as Fred's killer.

Arriving at the rendezvous site, Craig and Eric waited for several hours, but neither Shirvani's representative nor Abu Musayev showed. Feeling increasingly nervous, they returned to Sleptsovskaya and put a call through to Chris in Dallas.

"Man," Eric said, "we're right back into this same damned thing. We're getting hints down here that we're getting too close, and I'm not feeling good about this. Craig and I are starting to think it's time to pull out."

Chris agreed, but Craig and Eric then decided they would try to make contact with Abu Musayev one last time. The following day— Sunday, August 13—they sent word through one of Shirvani's representatives that they were still waiting and still wanted to meet with the counterintelligence commander. That same night, the search headquarters in Sleptsovskaya received four visitors.

. . .

"It was about nine o'clock," a man I'll call "Vorzhinski" recalled, "and we were sitting around in the living room talking. We heard one quick shout from outside and someone running across the courtyard. Then the door burst open and there was a guy standing there in a black ski mask and camouflage fatigues, pointing a Kalashnikov at us. Three more came in behind him."

"Vorzhinski" is a tall, dark-haired Greek-American in his early thirties, handsome in a broody sort of way. Having moved to Moscow to study Russian, he had occasionally worked as an interpreter for the Soros Foundation office there; in late July 1995 he had been asked if he wanted to take the place of Greg Smith on the Fred Cuny search effort in the North Caucasus. He arrived in Ingushetia, just in time for the mission's frightening denouement. Sitting in the tiny kitchen of his Moscow apartment, he chain-smoked Marlboros as he recalled that night.

"They shouted at us to put our hands on our heads and get on the ground. There must have been eight or nine of us stretched out there. They patted us all down and, as one or two kept their guns trained on us, the others started tearing the place apart."

By a stroke of good fortune, Craig Cuny was not in the living room at the time of the attack, but in the other building on the compound conversing with an Australian relief worker. Hearing the commotion outside, he and the relief worker managed to conceal themselves in a large dresser just as two of the gunmen burst in. Careful to make no sound, they listened as the raiders rummaged through the room. Within minutes they had grabbed up the search team's computer and satellite telephone, then vanished into the night.

It was only later that "Vorzhinski" would remember a curious detail of the attack. Other than the first command for everyone to get on the ground, the gunmen had barely spoken, instead communicating with one another through hand-signals.

"To me, it suggested two things. One, they knew exactly what they were doing and, two, they were worried we'd recognize their voices— either their accents or because we personally knew them."

The attack would serve as a fitting epitaph to the entire four-month search for answers in the Caucasus for, like everything else that had happened, its meaning was open to a great variety of interpretations and conspiracy theories—and highlighted yet again the impenetrable web of treachery that enveloped the region. Although the gunmen had been wearing Russian camouflage uniforms and carrying army-issue Kalashnikovs, most everyone was of the opinion that they were Chechens, especially the landlord's family, who believed they detected regional accents in the few words the attackers had spoken. Yet it was hard to imagine how four armed rebels could have come across the border and trolled the streets of Sleptsovskaya without having encountered either the Russian army or the Ingush police and soldiers who were everywhere in the frontier town. Almost certainly, then, the assault had been carried out with the complicity of the Ingush security forces, or perhaps even done by the Ingush acting on their own.

But this was one Caucasian riddle that Craig and Eric decided they hadn't the luxury to ponder. Concluding that the attack had been meant as a warning and an indication that they were getting uncomfortably close to the truth, they made plans to leave. On August 15 they flew to Moscow, the long and harrowing quest for Fred and his lost companions now at an end. That same day, Chris Cuny arrived in Moscow from Dallas, and on the morning of the seventeenth he and Craig held a press conference at the Moscow Radisson Slavjanskaya. Chris read a brief statement outlining their findings and laying blame for the murder of his brother on both Chechens and Russians in roughly equal parts.

"On or before March 3o, [Russian] intelligence operatives traveled to Bamut and spread disinformation about Fred, Galena [sic], and the two doctors. Multiple sources have told us and given written testimony that word was spread indicating that Fred was anti-Islamic and that one or more of the Russians were members of the FSB. It is likely that this information was spread due to Fred's outspoken criticism of the Russians' role in the war involving indiscriminate killing of civilians."

Chris then outlined the chronology of events they had established through the help of Shirvani, naming Abu Musayev as the rebel leader who, having believed the Russian disinformation campaign, ordered the group's execution on April 14. Toward the end of the statement Chris turned angry:

"We have been silent about our suspicions up until now due to concern that it would affect our search and our safety. This has proven futile and certainly doesn't seem to matter in light of the fact that we were shelled and shot at by Russian troops, extorted by Chechen soldiers and Ingush officials, and robbed at gunpoint in our quarters inside Ingushetia. . . . Let it be known to all nations and humanitarian organizations that Russia was responsible for the death of one of the world's great humanitarians."

The next day Chris, Craig, and Eric boarded a flight for Texas and a final end to their odyssey, but not before one last wrinkle of intrigue. Two days before the Cunys' press conference, Russian newspapers had cited an unnamed Russian intelligence source again making the assertion that Fred was alive and working as a CIA adviser to Dudayev. It appeared that someone in Russian intelligence had decided to float the story one more time as a way to cast doubt on the Cuny family's damaging account—but it raised the question of how they could have known the account would be damaging two days before the family's press conference. The apparent source of this story, as with so many similar stories in the past, was Major General Alexander Mikhailov of the FSB.

True to form, the intelligence spokesman scoffed at that accusation. Instead, he saw in the timing of the whole affair a conspiracy of a very different sort. In early August the FSB had detained a U.S. Army captain, Jason Lynch, and accused him of spying on a Russian nuclear facility. Lynch had been expelled a few days before the Cunys' press conference, but "the Lynch affair" was still the talk of Moscow diplomatic circles.

"To me, that is curious," Mikhailov said. "Why hold this press conference about Fred Cuny, why say these lies about the FSB, in the midst of the Lynch case? Could it be they were under orders, a way to divert attention from the Lynch matter?" The major general rolled a cigarette between his fingers, his glittery blue eyes scanning his desktop. "Curious. I find this very, very curious."

.   .   .

On the evening of September 19, 1995, a "celebration" of the life and work of Fred Cuny was held in an eighth-floor conference room of the Carnegie Endowment for International Peace headquarters in Washington, D.C. Officiating at the ceremony was Fred's old friend, Mort Abramowitz. In attendance were most of Fred's extended family, along with representatives of scores of humanitarian relief agencies, diplomats, State Department personnel, foreign ambassadors, even National Security Adviser Anthony Lake. After brief opening comments, a visibly shaken Abramowitz invited those in the audience to step to the podium and offer their own eulogies and tributes to Fred. The tributes—some humorous, some sad—continued for well over two hours.

Afterward Craig Cuny felt vaguely annoyed. He had sat through the hours of speeches, then graciously engaged in small talk with dozens of well-wishers, thanking them for their condolences. That night, as he wandered the quiet streets of nearby Georgetown, he felt his annoyance grow.

"I guess in a way I'm tired of it," he said. "It gets tiring to hear all these people talking about how much they loved my father, how great he was, when he spent his whole career butting heads with most of them and trying to get them to listen."

As that night wore on, Craig realized there was a deeper source to his irritation. Walking back over the P Street bridge above Rock Creek Park, he paused to gaze down at the cars passing beneath.

"I just really wanted to get his body back. And I know we don't have the whole story. In my heart, I know we still don't have the whole story."

PART FIVE

A Town Called Eternal

CHAPTER 11

CUNY AT TOP OF RELEASE LIST, PEACE NEGOTIATORS SAY. Top negotiators on both sides of the Chechen peace talks have assured Frederick Cuny's relatives that . . . [he] is at the top of the list of prisoners to be released. . . . But since neither side has told Cuny's relatives they are holding him, the statement has left them as confused as they have been throughout the four-month search.
—Moscow Times, August 5, 1995

ON THE MORNING of October 27, 1995, I drove out to Vnukovo Airport on the southern outskirts of Moscow. Accompanying me were Stanley Greene, a forty-five-year-old Paris-based photographer, and Ryan Chilcote, a twenty-two-year-old Southern Californian who had been living in Moscow and would serve as our interpreter. We were bound for the North Caucasus, to search for further clues into the disappearance of Fred Cuny and his companions.

In the ten weeks since the Cuny family's search had ended, no new information had come to light, and the war in Chechnya was beginning to heat up again. On October 6, General Anatoli Romanov, the supreme commander of Russian forces in the war zone, had been nearly killed in a bomb attack in a Grozny underpass and remained in a coma. Two days later helicopter gunships had swooped down on the Chechen village of Roshni-Chu and wiped out an entire street, killing at least sixteen civilians. Together, the two attacks had effectively ended the latest fledgling peace negotiations between the military and the rebels, and there were now reports of firefights throughout Chechnya; the deadliest had occurred three days earlier, October 24, when a Russian column traveling through a "pacified" zone had been ambushed, leaving at least seventeen soldiers dead. As the spokesman for Russian troops in Chechnya had stated the following evening, the situation "remained complex."

But, as was always the case with Chechnya, drawing clear lines of responsibility for most of these complexities was no easy matter. General Romanov, it turned out, had been on his way to a top-secret conference with a Chechen peace negotiator, a meeting known to only a handful of senior Russian officers; even officials in the Kremlin suspected the attempt on his life had been carried out not by the rebels but by hard-line officers trying to sabotage the peace process. Conversely, the Kremlin tried to deny their forces were responsible for either the gunship assault on Roshni-Chu or those on a number of other Chechen villages in recent weeks.

"Any air raids are forbidden," Oleg Lobov, Yeltsin's special envoy to Chechnya, explained blandly. "The territory in question is under rebel control, and that makes it difficult to say what has really happened there."

Instead, Russian officials hinted, the gunship assaults might have been the handiwork of the rebels themselves, or of marauders dispatched from the republic of Georgia. Just how the gunshipless rebels could have launched the attacks, or why the steadfastly neutral Georgians would want to, was left unclear. Even Boris Yeltsin seemed to be tiring of the Chechnya situation.

"Perhaps we could have pursued a different policy there," he opined on October 19, "in, how shall I put it, a more sophisticated, farsighted way . . ."

At the same time, the war had become even deadlier for outsiders. In August an American freelance photographer, Andrew Shumack, vanished in Russian-held Grozny, never to be seen again, the latest of at least a dozen journalists to have been killed or disappeared so far. Shortly after, two Russian Orthodox priests who had come to mediate a prisoner exchange were instead whisked away by a rebel commander who claimed they were spies; only one would eventually return alive. In late September the Grozny headquarters of a peace delegation from the Organization for Security and Cooperation in Europe (OSCE) had been virtually besieged by forces loyal to the Grozny mayor, with hand grenades thrown into their compound.

All of which had made my task of looking for clues to the disappearance of Fred Cuny and his companions quite a bit more difficult. Along with a series of bureaucratic hurdles, I had been held up in Moscow for almost two weeks simply trying to find an interpreter who would accompany Stanley and me to the North Caucasus. No one, it seemed, wanted to go to western Chechnya, the scene of some of the heaviest current fighting, and they certainly didn't want to go to investigate the Cuny story. After being rejected by a half dozen prospective interpreters, I had finally found Ryan.

Among other concerns, the delay in our departure led me to wonder just how punctilious the New York Times might be, should something untoward happen on the trip, in keeping to the terms of the death benefit I had signed back in New York. "Dear Scott," the letter from the Times business office had read, working off dates I had provided, "in the event of your death while on assignment for the New York Times Magazine in the region of Chechnya from the period beginning October 18, 1995, through October 30, 1995, we will provide $50,000 to the designated beneficiary named below." Since it was now the twenty-seventh, there was the chance only my first few days in Chechnya would be covered.

If, in fact, I got to Chechnya at all, for at Vnukovo Airport we discovered there might be a last-minute hitch to our travel plans. Rushing through a dank terminal room to board the Tupolev jet revving its engines on the tarmac outside, I asked Ryan to double-check with the gate guard, a stout, middle-aged woman in a blue uniform, that this was indeed the flight to Ingushetia.

She shrugged. "Perhaps."

I pressed the issue.

"Perhaps it will go there, but perhaps it will go somewhere else," the guard elaborated. "There has been some small problem at the airport in Ingushetia, so maybe the pilot will prefer to go somewhere else."

"What kind of somewhere else?" I asked.

The guard became annoyed with me. "That doesn't concern you," she spat, shooing us toward the waiting plane. "The pilot will decide in the air and inform you at the appropriate time."

Actually, I had a pretty good idea what the "small problem" at the Ingushetia airport was. Three days earlier, seven helicopter gunships had swooped down on the airport in early afternoon; while five gunships had hovered to provide air cover, two had landed to disgorge some thirty well-armed commandos. After spraying the parking lot with machine-gun fire, killing one civilian and wounding two others, the commandos had robbed the airport office and coffee shop, then clambered back aboard the gunships; within minutes, the flotilla had disappeared over the horizon.

In a pattern that was now familiar, the Russian government had first denied responsibility for the attack—and again implied it might be the handiwork of the Georgians. Finally the Defense Ministry had begrudgingly admitted the attackers were Russian commandos, offering that they had gone to the airport to "familiarize themselves with local developments" after hearing reports that Chechen rebels were gathering there. Precisely why the rebels would choose to congregate in broad daylight at an airport in a neutral country, or how they might have reached it without the knowledge of the thousands of Russian troops billeted nearby, was left open to speculation.

Our pilot evidently decided against a landing in Ingushetia—evidently, because he never bothered to inform anyone. Instead, as we descended into a fertile valley, the snow-capped Caucasus Mountains rising spectacularly in the distance, passengers peered down at the land and debated among themselves where we might be. Kabardino-Balkaria, it turned out, two republics over from Ingushetia. Somehow, it seemed a completely fitting introduction to the North Caucasus.

·   ·   ·

Sitting in his spacious office on the third floor of the Presidential Palace and dressed in Russian army camouflage fatigues, General Ruslan Aushev, the President of Ingushetia, explained the concept behind the amusement park.

"We thought to ourselves, 'In this time of great tension and misfortune for our people, what can we give to our youth that will lift their spirits, encourage them that things will become better?' This is how we came to discuss, with our humanitarian assistance friends, the creation of an amusement park."

There is something decidedly absurdist about Ingushetia, a place that would seem more likely to exist in the pages of a novel by Graham Greene at his most caustic than in the real world. A tiny, semiautonomous Russian republic nestled on the northern flanks of the Caucasus Mountains, it is about one quarter the size of neighboring Chechnya—or considerably smaller than Rhode Island—but beset with world-class problems. In 1992, 40,000 refugees were added to its population of approximately 150,000 after a disastrous war with its neighbor to the west, North Ossetia. By late 1995, Ingushetia's population had mushroomed once again, with some 70,000 Chechens fleeing the war to the east. The pretty countryside remains dotted with tent cities built by international relief agencies, while several thousand displaced persons have taken up semipermanent residence in old boxcars along the shunting lines of the Trans-Caucasus railroad.

This enormous refugee population, together with the shattered local economy and the periodic armed incursions onto its territory by others—the Russians, Chechens, and Ossetians all appear to take turns trying to drag Ingushetia into the region's conflicts—would seem to make the republic an unlikely tourist destination, but that appears to be President Aushev's ultimate goal. He has declared Ingushetia an economic "goodwill zone" and, with the help of a Slovakian relief organization, is overseeing the construction of a small entertainment hub in the capital of Nazran—a coffee shop, a small park, and the fabled amusement park—with plans to expand from there. On the drawing boards is an aquatic theme park on a nearby lake, a large luxury hotel, perhaps even a golf course.

Until this bold vision comes to fruition, Nazran remains a sleepy town of some 30,000, the only interruption on its somnolence taking the form of Aushev's presidential motorcade. About a half dozen times a day the motorcade—consisting of an armored black Mercedes limousine and a soldier-laden Humvee flanked by motorcycle outriders with flashing lights and loud sirens—races down the capital's one principal paved road at great speed. If the residents are annoyed by these constant sound-and-light shows, Aushev probably isn't too worried; after all, a man elected with 99.99% of the vote can afford to ruffle a few feathers.

Despite its preposterousness, any search for answers into the disappearance of Fred Cuny and his companions begins in Ingushetia; it is here that the Soros relief operation was based, and it was from here that the group left on that doomed journey into the mountains. It is also possible that it was here where their fate was sealed, for ever since the carnage in neighboring Chechnya began, the Ingush government has performed truly acrobatic feats of wartime duplicity.

Although officially neutral in the conflict, Ingushetia has served as both a back base and supply route for the Russian military and as a safe haven and supply route for the Chechen rebels. Both President Aushev and his Vice-President, Boris Agapov, are reported to be close friends of Dzhokhar Dudayev, even as Aushev remains a standing one-star general in the Russian air force and Agapov was until recently a lieutenant general in the KGB. According to popular rumor, the rebel leader has maintained those friendships with frequent visits to Nazran, driving over from Chechnya.

At first glance, the story seemed bizarre, since to reach the Ingush capital required Dudayev to pass through a number of Russian army checkpoints at a time when there was a bounty on his head, and Nazran itself swarmed with senior Russian officers. Then again, this was the Caucasus.

"Oh, yes, Dudayev comes here a lot. He and the President fought in Afghanistan together, so they have a special bond." The speaker was a young Ingush policeman whose main function, it appeared at first encounter, was to watch over the construction of the amusement park.

In defense of President Aushev, it wasn't as if he were trying to build a rival to Disney World. Rather, the completed park would consist of four small, traveling-carnival-type rides: a bumper car rink, a tilt-a-whirl, a fiberglass dragon that would hoist a passenger cage some twenty feet in the air. On this particular day progress seemed to have come to a standstill, a half dozen laborers sitting in the sun smoking cigarettes while two foreign supervisors stared at blueprints.

"They're working especially hard," the policeman offered, "because of the grand opening on Saturday. The President's fortieth birthday."

Actually, the policeman had double duties, as I discovered when crossing the short expanse of broken ground between the amusement park and the Presidential Guest House. The hotel consisted of three newly built, two-story brick buildings set behind a high brick wall, and it was from here that Fred and Galina had left that last morning of March 31. After walking me to the gate, the policeman abruptly stopped and leaned close to mutter under his breath:

"Be careful while you are here. This is a very dangerous place."

I thought he was referring to the Guest House, but then he added: "Ingushetia. All the Caucasus. You can't trust anyone here."

My confusion over the range of his warning was understandable given the number of Guest House clients who had vanished in recent months. Musa Gadaborshev, the stooped, rheumy-eyed old man who managed the hotel, could remember at least six.

"There were the [*Nevskoye Vremya*] journalists from St. Petersburg. There were two of them staying here for some time, and then one day they went into Chechnya and—" He fluttered a hand in the air. "And then there was Mr. Fred Cuny and Galina Oleinik, and then another reporter from St. Petersburg." Sitting in the Guest House lobby, Gadaborshev thought for a moment. "Maybe one or two others, I can't remember now."

I asked what he recalled of Fred and Galina.

"Excellent people," he said, "and great friends to the Ingush people. Galya was staying here for a long time and, of course, I knew Mr. Fred from his first trip. A great man, very friendly." Gadaborshev shook his head sadly. "And still to this day we don't know what became of them."

When pressed, the old man remembered an odd detail from that time.

"It was Galya," he said. "Normally, she was very friendly, robust, but in those last days she seemed a little different—worried, I would say. She was very anxious that Fred Cuny arrive soon, and always, when she would return from somewhere, she would ask if there was some message from him. And then Fred Cuny arrived, they were here a short time, and then they went to Chechnya."

According to Gadaborshev, neither Fred nor Galina told him where they were headed that day of March 31, only that they would be returning soon—perhaps that same evening, perhaps in a day or so. They were traveling light, having left most of their belongings in their rooms.

Given the mesh of intrigue in Ingushetia, the question of how much or how little Musa Gadaborshev may have known of Fred and Galina's travel plans was of more than academic interest; the Presidential Guest House is, in fact, an official branch of the Ingush government and Gadaborshev is a relative of President Aushev.

"I only answer to the President," the old man said proudly. "On all matters, I consult with him."

Four blocks away from the Guest House stands the Presidential Palace, a white three-story building about the size of a traditional county courthouse in the United States. In his office on the third floor, President Aushev, a small, dark-featured man in camouflage fatigues, was clearly preoccupied by the Russian gunship assault on his national airport earlier in the week.

"We can see in this the handiwork of political formations and power centers within the Russian Federation that have little objectivity, and who somehow believe that getting Ingushetia involved in this war might be used to their advantage."

"Who, specifically?" I asked.

"Certain elements within the power structures and central organizations."

When the conversation turned to the matter of Fred Cuny and his lost companions, the President became less obtuse. Leaping up from his desk, the general crossed to an enormous map of Ingushetia and Chechnya on his office wall, and deftly unfurled a telescoping pointer.

"We were very energetic in our search. We looked for him here, and here, and here," he said, jabbing at different points across the breadth of Chechnya. "We looked for him everywhere, and we heard many stories, but in the end . . ." He sighed, set the pointer against the wall. "Well, I think at this point we must assume he encountered some group involved in finances."

"Finances?"

"Finances and narcotics."

When asked if the financiers he now believed responsible were more likely to be Russian or Chechen, the President shrugged. "Impossible to say. But criminal. Certainly criminal. Operating beyond the scope of any authority."

Throughout the summer-long manhunt, President Aushev had given searchers a variety of mixed signals. While he had been solicitous in meeting with Cuny family members and dispatched a number of his Emergency Situations officials to assist them in the field, there had also been times when he seemed to block the investigation from pursuing certain leads. He had developed a habit of repeatedly telling searchers that news would be forthcoming soon—"two days," Chris Cuny said, "it was always going to happen in two days"—only to then explain that another delay had been encountered. There was also the curious matter of his role in the "body double" episode in May. According to several accounts, he had told a number of people that a body believed to be Fred's had been found outside the village of Gutingen, but he had done so several days before Peter Kozov relayed that information to Chris Cuny in Moscow—and possibly even before the body had been discovered.

In his office downstairs Vice-President Boris Agapov had arrived at a conclusion similar to Aushev's about the lost group's fate. There was a careful, rather unnerving smoothness to the former KGB general, a slightly portly, middle-aged man who preferred well-tailored business suits and homburg hats to the President's military regalia. Agapov was reputed to be the real power behind the scenes in Ingushetia and, with his opaque blue eyes and Cheshire cat smile, he certainly looked the part.

In February 1995 he had acted as mediator in peace talks between the Russians and Chechens, and it was during the course of those talks that he first met, and sought advice from, Fred Cuny.

"I liked him very much," Agapov said, "and he grasped very well the intricacies of the situation. That is why I personally took such interest in trying to find him."

Yet the Vice-President had also played a confusing role in the manhunt. It was he who had most forcefully dismissed Ruslan Muradov's account that had Dudayev congratulating his fighters in Bamut for capturing Fred and the other three "spies," and some believed it was he who had then caused Muradov to disappear from sight. After the searchers from Texas had arrived, Slava Miklayev, the Intertect assistant who had narrowly missed accompanying the lost group, claimed to have found a Chechen rebel with important information, but Agapov had immediately vetoed any meeting between the man and the Cuny family.

"I never understood why he did that," Slava said. "It was very curious to me."

Shortly after, when the Texas searchers began to suspect that Slava himself might be a Russian spy, the idea was actively promoted by Agapov's personal representative in the manhunt, the detective Peter Kozov. On yet another occasion Agapov told a Russian journalist that he had information Fred and the others were dead, a story that ran in a Russian newspaper in early June. But when Craig Cuny confronted the Vice-President about the story Agapov denied all knowledge.

In his office, Agapov would only concede that it had been a time of great confusion. "We were hearing so many different stories, and what the truth of them is we don't know. There's a great deal of information that his life ended tragically, although it's not excluded that maybe somewhere he is being held, or he is hiding. That is a hope we keep in the depth of our hearts, but at this late date I would have to say the news is probably tragic."

As to who might be responsible, the Vice-President would barely hazard a guess. "Probably a group with a tendency toward criminal activity. Beyond that, it's very difficult to predict. All this time and effort has passed, and still we know so little."

A similar opaqueness reigned at the Emergency Situations building in Sleptsovskaya, the agency that had arranged for Ruslan Muradov to act as guide and driver to Fred on that last trip. When approached, a group of idle drivers out front all said they knew Muradov, that he had once been an Emergency Situations driver, but that they had not seen him in a long time.

Evidently Muradov had made far less of an impression on Emergency Situations officials within the building; there, no one seemed to recall him at all.

"Muradov . . . Muradov," a minor functionary named Alitov Dreikov muttered, scanning his desktop as if in search of clues. "I'm sorry, but that name is not familiar to me. It's a very unusual name for this area."

Apparently Dreikov was working off a very narrow definition of "area" for, as I knew from other sources, Ruslan Muradov's sister worked in the room two doors down from his. On that day her office was empty and locked.

The difficulty in pursuing any of these various inconsistencies was that no point could be pressed too forcefully. Given the Ingush government's double-dealing role in the Chechen war—even a possible role in Fred's disappearance—all queries had to be couched in larger discussions of the current political situation, questions about Fred slipped in unobtrusively. We were searching for answers to a mystery we could never admit to being very interested in.

That Sunday, I returned to Nazran for the grand opening of the amusement park. A large, expectant crowd had gathered and, shortly after two o'clock, the capital's downtown resounded with the familiar wail of police sirens. Moments later President Aushev's motorcade, having raced the four blocks over from the palace, skidded to a halt in the dirt parking lot. Trailed by assorted government ministers, the President emerged from his Mercedes and, acknowledging the shouted birthday greetings of his countrymen with a smile and friendly wave, stepped forward to cut a large red ribbon, officially opening the park. It was just about then that things turned ugly.

Within seconds, all four rides had been overwhelmed by a sea of children. On the tilt-a-whirl, a semblance of order was only established by allowing up to four children to ride in each seat, far beyond the machine's weight limit. At the bumper car rink, the situation was hopeless. With each car laden under the weight of a half dozen passengers, they could do little more than nudge against the shins of others trying to climb aboard. Within the hour, four of the tilt-a-whirl carriages were broken and the dragon ride had been closed after an alarming crack had opened in its neck.

When I returned the next day the dragon had already been hauled away and the other three rides were in the process of being dismantled, the bumper cars and broken tilt-a-whirl modules being loaded onto flatbed trucks. The young policeman standing before the Presidential Guest House sauntered over to my side.

"End of the season," he explained. After a time he turned. "You should have been at the palace last night," he said softly. "Dudayev came over for the President's birthday party."

. . .

Not surprisingly, the fog of intrigue didn't clear once we crossed into Chechnya.

By November 1995 the country had been carved into a surreal patchwork quilt of control zones, rebel-held "liberated territory" merging into Russian-held "pacified territory" with no discernible pattern. In some areas a de facto cease-fire had been declared, heavily armed Chechens traveling freely or lolling about at outposts within sight of army garrisons. And then, in the blink of an eye, it could change, the rebels attacking a Russian checkpoint, or Russian gunships descending upon a village with machine guns and cannon blazing. In western Chechnya the shifting cycles of war and peace had taken on the form of grotesque ritual. The Russians had surrounded—"sealed," they called it—a number of towns and villages with tanks and artillery, but during the day residents could usually come and go with relative ease, passing by the encircling garrisons where the Russian soldiers lounged in boredom. At night these same garrisons might rake the town with tank or machine-gun fire, launch a half dozen artillery shells or two hundred, and in the morning the garrison commanders would stoutly maintain that their men had not fired a shot.

What did not change all along the front—if something so diffuse could be called a front—was the flourishing black market, the Russian soldiers selling their weapons or uniforms or boots to middlemen, or even directly to the rebels, for vodka or heroin or simple food. Often these transactions took place within sight of pitched battles. Often these transactions provided the means for the next battle. It all made Chechnya a very difficult land to try to maneuver through.

One place I was anxious to reach was Samashki, the agricultural town astride the Sunzha River where Russian soldiers had gone on a two-day killing spree in early April, and where persistent rumors had placed Fred and his companions. At the time of our arrival in early November, Samashki remained "sealed," off limits to all outsiders, but under the guise of delivering relief supplies—and traveling, coincidentally, in the same UAZ "Fredbulance" that Craig Cuny had used to scour the countryside—we managed to slip past the outlying army checkpoints.

Before the shattered schoolhouse in the center of town, the survivors of the April massacre had built a grim display of the military ordnance that had been strewn through their streets: unexploded shells, bullet casings, metal ammunition boxes. In one corner of the schoolyard they had amassed a rather large pile of empty medicine ampules and syringes. Before going into battle, Russian soldiers are issued first aid kits that contain ampules of Promedol, a narcotic anesthetic used to treat shock, and many survivors of the Samashki massacre reported the marauding soldiers had acted drugged; the pile of discarded vials seemed to support their claim. The town itself was a testament to the randomness of this war. Some streets were gutted, either by fire or shelling, while others remained largely unscathed; most all the homes, though, appeared to have been looted, the front gates shot away, the houses beyond stripped even of their window frames.

Within minutes a large group of residents, mostly middle-aged women, gathered on the schoolhouse steps to tell their own personal horror stories of the April attack and of how they were bracing for the next one; just that morning the Russians had lobbed several shells into the town.

When shown a photograph of Fred Cuny, several of the women

insisted they had seen him. "Just before the attack started," one elderly woman said. "He was here. A very big man, yes?"

At the small emergency clinic nearby, the resident doctor, a dark-haired woman in her mid-thirties, had the same photograph of Fred beneath the glass cover of her desk.

"I personally did not see him," she said, "but I met the search team when it came through here. They told me the story of him, and I asked if I could have a photograph." She glanced down at it. "I keep it as a reminder that there are good people out there who are trying to help us."

Over the ensuing months the doctor had shown the photo to all those who came to her clinic for treatment, and she now believed that Fred and his companions had, in fact, been in or near Samashki on April 7, the day the attack began; too many people had claimed to have seen him, she explained, for it not to be true. Some had reported encountering him in the town center, while others had spoken of seeing an empty ambulance a mile out of town, just beside the notorious Outpost No. 6 on the Trans-Caucasus Highway.

"If that report is true, it's very sad," she said, "because those soldiers were very violent. A lot of people were shot at that intersection."

But by November 1995, Outpost No. 6 was gone, its original garrison long since rotated out of the war zone.

That afternoon, going back through the same Russian checkpoint we had so easily cleared in the morning, we were briefly stopped. At first the young unshaven commander seemed angry that foreign journalists had breached the security net, but then he turned vaguely solicitous.

"Don't you know it's dangerous here?" he asked with a tone of incredulity. "You could die here. One American already has. His name was Fred Cuny, and he died right there." The commander pointed off to the low-slung buildings of Samashki, a mile back in the valley. "He was with the rebels and when the fighting started they killed him."

Behind him, his garrison was little more than a two-acre patch of torn ground surrounded by concertina wire, a warren of trenches and foxholes cut from the earth, a few tanks and artillery pieces. His men wore tattered remnants of different uniforms and most were sprawled on the open ground, smoking cigarettes and listening to music in the sunny afternoon. They all looked very young. The commander gazed over his grim fiefdom, nodded his chin at his soldiers.

"Or maybe he was killed in a place like this." He turned back and gave a wry smile. "This is Chechnya, after all, and anything can happen here."*

That observation was reinforced a few days later. Traveling along a "clear" road just inside the border with Ingushetia, we instead found ourselves driving directly onto the construction site of a new Russian encampment. The road had apparently been ordered sealed earlier that day, and since we had defied this unknown order we were automatically suspected of being rebel sympathizers. Ordered out of the car at gunpoint, we were made to stand in a field with our hands in the air as our documents were taken away to be inspected by the regimental colonel.

Left to guard us at the roadside were a half dozen young conscripts—seventeen and eighteen—and even though we were technically their captives they couldn't help but be somewhat awed by our presence; from small towns in Russia, none had actually seen an American in person before, let alone, in the case of Stanley, a black American. Before long the initial tension had dissipated, and the boys were earnestly peppering us with questions about New York City, Hollywood, and Disney World. Eventually one reached into the shoulder pocket of his uniform and drew out a small notebook to shyly ask us for our autographs; all his comrades quickly followed suit. To keep the friendly

* Many of the purported sightings of Fred Cuny in the Samashki area, it would eventually emerge, may have been a case of mistaken identity. Thomas Goltz, a middle-aged American journalist with at least a passing resemblance to Cuny, had spent much of February and March in Samashki, and had left just before the massacre took place. Many Samashki residents apparently confused the two.

rapport going, I provided them with a constant supply of American cigarettes.

One of the conscripts stood out. He was a sad-eyed boy of seventeen named Sergei who spoke very good English, having graduated from a language high school in his hometown of Vologda in southern Russia. Beyond his English, what struck me was that Sergei repeatedly turned down my offers of cigarettes, explaining simply that he didn't smoke. I made a joke of it, because he was the first Russian soldier I'd encountered who didn't smoke and, at the very least, he could have later used the American cigarettes as barter. Each time, though, Sergei politely refused.

After about an hour of waiting, a lieutenant came down the hill with several older soldiers and the mood quickly changed. The conscripts retreated a few paces, but already the officer—a powerfully built man of about thirty with a blond crew cut—had observed their chumminess with us, and he was not pleased. It would still be a few minutes before the document check was finished, the lieutenant explained, and since it had begun to rain, it might be better for us to wait in the car.

For some reason I couldn't immediately identify, this seemed like a bad idea.

"I'm fine," I replied.

"Get back in the car now," the lieutenant ordered. "All of you."

Leaving the older soldiers to stand guard over us, he shouted for the conscripts to follow him up the hill. Waiting in the car, listening to the rain pelt the roof and watching the windows fog up, I realized why my instinct had been to stay outside. In the car, we were anonymous, indistinct, easier to kill.

In a few minutes the garrison commander, a short, middle-aged colonel, came down from the command post. He was flanked by Sergei and the other conscripts who had first guarded us. I noticed that none of the boys were looking in our direction, but rather at the ground by their feet, and then I noticed Sergei was smoking a cigarette. The colonel stopped about ten yards in front of us, and the conscripts fanned out to form an arc on either side of him, their guns half raised, their gazes still averted to the ground. They appeared very somber, not at all the laughing, shy boys of a few minutes before, and it occurred to me then that they were mentally preparing themselves to shoot us.

Instead, the colonel began an angry interrogation of us, barking out his questions to be heard over the rain and the ten-yard separation. After a time, and seemingly just as angry as before, he turned and strode quickly back up the hill. Shortly after, the blond lieutenant reappeared, carrying our identification cards and passports. He was grinning.

"Good news, guys," he called. "You're going home."

Handing back our papers, he wished us a safe journey as the conscripts crowded in to shake each of our hands. As we drove away, they stood in the rain to wave goodbye, even the lieutenant, and I realized that the answer to the Fred Cuny mystery could have been just this simple: an unlucky encounter at a Russian checkpoint, some frightened soldiers or a brutal commander, and it all could have been over very quickly.

. . .

Not that matters were a whole lot better on the other side of the battlefield. Under the same pretense that had been employed to enter Samashki—a delivery of relief supplies—we decided to try and reach the rebel fortress of Bamut.

In the seven months since Fred's group had disappeared, the Russians had hurled tens of thousands of artillery and tank shells on Bamut, launched at least four major ground assaults, but still the rebels held fast. Now, in November 1995, the Russians unleashed a nightly artillery barrage on the town so intense that it shook the windows of the home where we were staying in Sleptsovskaya, eleven miles away. Early one morning I and four others—Stanley, Ryan, a Hungarian relief worker, and an Ingush driver—set out from Sleptsovskaya in a UAZ ambulance laden with boxes of antiseptic wash and gauze bandages.

On this journey there would be some uncomfortable parallels between ourselves and the lost party. We would travel the identical route they had taken: south through the Ingush foothills, east over the exposed mountain track, and into the back side of Bamut. Like them, we would be traveling in a gray UAZ ambulance filled with medical supplies and, like them, there would be five in our group.

By noon we had crossed the one-lane metal bridge over the Assa River and begun to climb the grinding mountain track into the high country of the Caucasus. Several times the ambulance sank up to its floorboards in the mud and once nearly tipped over on an incline, and I was struck by what an improbable route this would have been when Fred and the others chose it in late March; as bad as the track was in November, it must have been far worse in the rains and melting snow of early spring.

After an hour or so we came out onto the high plateau, skirting the ruins of an abandoned Russian fort. On the entire route we passed no cars, and only two small inhabited farms. By early afternoon we had reached the small village of Arshti and crossed into Chechnya. For the last three or four miles into Bamut the road was paved, heavily scarred with the starburst patterns of artillery shells and the gouges of machine-gun bullets. We had just reached the outskirts of Bamut when things began to go awry.

Stopped at the top end of the town by four rebels, we were angrily ordered out of the ambulance and into a small farmhouse that served as the Bamut commandant's headquarters. For some time we were treated fairly well, given tea and cigarettes, as the rebels questioned us on what we were doing, why we had come. Despite the cordiality, it was clear we were being detained until the commandant arrived.

After about an hour's wait he made his entrance, a dour, short man in his early forties wearing an imitation black leather jacket and strange black ankle boots. For several minutes he intently studied our identification papers, while quietly asking a few general questions. Finally he stared down at the concrete floor for a long moment, gave a tired sigh, and looked up.

"How do I know you're not spies?"

Not an easy thing to prove, of course, but for some time we tried.

We explained that we had come to donate medical supplies and to appraise the situation in Bamut, to see if there were wounded who needed medical care, or shortages of essential goods. This did little to ingratiate us with the commandant; in fact, we only seemed to be indicting ourselves further. At one point, one of the rebels turned to Alex, the Hungarian relief worker, and, pointing to the courtyard outside, asked if there was a particular wall he preferred to be shot against.

"This is a restricted area," the commandant said. "No one from the outside is allowed in here. By coming here when it is restricted, we have to assume you are spies."

Bamut was clearly not the town where you wanted to be saddled with this label. Quite aside from what may have happened to Fred and the others, the place had a fearsome reputation—and was adding to it all the time. The two journalists from the St. Petersburg newspaper *Nevskoye Vremya* had been missing since March, and there were persistent rumors that they had been buried alive. In July another Russian journalist had been detained there and accused of being a spy. According to newspaper accounts, the journalist had been made to dig his own grave, then was dragged out of his cell every morning for six days to be "executed"; after making him kneel before the grave, the rebels fired a shot behind his ear. In the end they had apparently decided he wasn't a spy after all, and the journalist was now reported to be in a Moscow sanitarium and quite mad. Then there was the case of Father Anatoly, the Russian Orthodox priest who had been grabbed two months earlier while trying to mediate a prisoner exchange. Brought to Bamut, he had supposedly been killed along with several other prisoners in the cross-fire of a Russian assault, but many believed the rebels had simply executed him. As *Izvestiya* had reported in July, the Chechens were now routinely accusing journalists of being FSB agents, and "among journalists today the Chechen village of Bamut is the most notorious."

All of which made the manner in which we extricated ourselves from the situation in the farmhouse quite astonishing.

"I can see this is not a good time to visit Bamut," I said with as much calm as I could muster, "but we have an appointment to meet with President Dudayev in a few days. If he gives us permission, may we come back here?"

It was a feeble attempt at reverse psychology and a monumental bluff born of desperation—and if the commandant decided to hold us until he could check out our fictitious Dudayev meeting, matters would only deteriorate. Instead, invoking Dudayev's name sparked an almost magical transformation.

"Okay," the commandant said at last, actually affording us the slender hint of a smile. "If the President approves, of course you can come back. You will be our honored guests."

And just like that, we were free.

Yet, as we drove away from Bamut that afternoon, along with supreme relief, I also felt the first stirrings of an insight. There was a very crucial difference between the two sides in this war, one that had been revealed in the various unpleasant incidents we had been a party to so far: Samashki, the "sealed" road with Sergei and the conscripts, Bamut. It was a difference that just might shed some light on the Fred Cuny mystery, and it had to do with discipline.

The Russian army—at least that portion of it that had been sent to Chechnya—ranked among the most thoroughly undisciplined fighting forces I had ever encountered in a war zone. The Chechen *boyaviki*, on the other hand, was undoubtedly the most disciplined rebel force I had ever encountered, a discipline that had shown itself not just in its periodic humiliations of the Russian forces but in the reaction of the Bamut commandant when I invoked his supreme commander's name. It didn't require a lot of deep thinking to figure out which of these two armies would be more likely to randomly murder four travelers who happened into their path.

Except this matter of discipline gave rise to another riddle. Put simply, disciplined soldiers hold secrets and undisciplined ones don't. In the episode with Sergei and the conscripts on the sealed road, for instance, I had no doubt that, if ordered, the boys would have opened fire, but I was just as certain that at least one of them would have felt tormented by it and eventually told someone—his mother, a friend, somebody. Taking into account the massive publicity that had surrounded Fred's disappearance, I was now convinced that, if he and the others had met their demise in such a way, some Russian conscript somewhere would have talked.

So that would seem to leave the Chechens, but here was the second part of the riddle. In Bamut we had invoked the name of Dzhokhar Dudayev one time and it had set us free. If Fred had run afoul of the rebels, he had not only Dudayev's name to invoke—and with far more legitimacy than I—but that of the rebel chief of staff, General Aslan Maskhadov, a man who knew Fred and considered him a friend of the Chechen people. Considering the extraordinary discipline and rigid chain of command of the *boyaviki*, what rebel commander would have taken it upon himself to kill Fred Cuny without checking with his superiors? Not the commandant in Bamut, I was quite certain.

After ten days in the Caucasus, then, I felt as if I were back facing the same conundrums that had plagued me—and everyone else who had looked for answers—from the outset. In fact, maybe further back, because now nothing seemed plausible.

It was just about then that Magomet appeared.

. . .

A stocky Chechen in his early thirties, Magomet was the war-wounded rebel who had attached himself to the Cuny family search team back in May, and who had provided them with some of their most reliable information. It was also Magomet who in June had arranged a meeting with the senior rebel officers in Bamut to gather more clues, only to see those clues vanish when the officers were incinerated by a Russian helicopter gunship en route. He appeared at the house where we were staying in Sleptsovskaya late one evening; in the mysterious way information traveled in the Caucasus, he had been in central Chechnya when he heard some foreigners in Ingushetia were interested in talking with him.

By Magomet's account, he had been initially drawn into the manhunt for Fred Cuny simply because it was a job—always a rarity in the region—but had gradually become emotionally invested in its outcome because of what he had learned of Fred and his work, and out of a sense of friendship with Craig. Even after Craig and the other searchers had left the region in August, Magomet said, he had continued looking for answers—and he had found them. Late into that night, the former Chechen fighter sat at a kitchen table in the Sleptsovskaya house and laid out his version of what had happened to Fred and the others.

In most ways his account closely matched the one given to Craig Cuny by "Shirvani," the Jordanian businessman, although with a bit more specificity. That was especially true when it came to the fabled FSB "black operation," the spy list that had supposedly circulated in the Bamut area just before Fred and the others arrived. According to Magomet, the point man in the operation had been a mysterious figure known only as Usman who had slipped out of Sleptsovskaya for Bamut on March 29. He carried with him a list of the four "spies"—Fred, Galina, Andrei, and Sergei—who would soon be on their way to the town, and he gave the list to the now deceased commandant of Bamut, Moli Astimirov.

"I myself saw this list only a month ago," Magomet said, "and it listed all their names, their vital statistics, their [spy] affiliations. It said Fred Cuny was an anti-Islamic spy, and the others were FSB."

Acting on the tip from Usman, Astimirov detained Fred's group when they showed up on the afternoon of March 31. Their release was only secured, Magomet reported, through the strenuous intervention of the Bamut deputy commandant, Ramzan Ferzuali.

"Ramzan was a good man," Magomet said, "a close friend of mine, and he knew at once that this was an FSB plot."

Allowed to leave Bamut, the group had continued east on the morning of April 1, only to run into the second group of rebels on the forest road outside Orekhovo.

"But these men were not regular *boyaviki*," Magomet said. "They were just some criminals who had attached themselves to the *boyaviki* cause. They robbed the group and held them hostage overnight in their bunker in the forest."

From there, Magomet's version followed the familiar course—that Fred and the others had been brought back to Bamut to await a meeting with the local counterintelligence commander, that they had set out for that meeting in Atchkoi-Martan on the morning of April 4—but then it began to diverge somewhat.

"They never made it to that meeting," he said, "because the man who was taking them, Shirvani Albakhov, was working with the criminals in the forest."

Albakhov was the rebel colonel who had supposedly first questioned Fred's group on March 31, and then overseen their detention in Bamut as they waited to be taken to Atchkoi-Martan. He was also, quite conveniently, one of the rebel commanders killed in the helicopter gunship attack in June.

"On April 4," Magomet continued, "Albakhov was supposed to bring the group to Atchkoi-Martan, but instead he returned them to the criminals at the forest bunker. Then, on the fourteenth of April, when the Russians were launching their first great storming of Bamut, these men panicked. Their bunker was near the front line, they were afraid, so they killed the group and fled." Magomet shook his head sadly. "This is a great disgrace to the Chechen people but, as I said, they were not real *boyaviki*—little more than criminals, and I would put Shirvani Albakhov in that category as well."

What was impressive about Magomet's version was its wealth of detail. He claimed to have met and interrogated one of the "criminals" in the forest bunker and even provided me with his name. He was quite precise on when and how the executions took place—shortly after 2 P.M. on April 14 by a six-man firing squad—and where the bodies were buried: in a clearing just down from the gang's bunker outside the village of Stari-Atchkoi. According to Magomet, Fred had been traveling with $8,000 in cash, and each of the men in the firing squad detail had been given $500 while their ringleader and Shirvani Albakhov split the rest.

What was far less impressive was the way his version contorted itself to avoid any blame falling on the "regular" *boyaviki*. In his telling, the much-touted spy list only served to explain why the group had initially come under rebel suspicion; their subsequent murders were completely separate, a purely criminal matter.

As criminals went, though, this gang in the forest seemed a most unusual bunch. As was made clear in the unconcerned tone of Fred's note of April 4, once the group was returned to Bamut from the forest bunker, they were under rebel supervision—and, evidenced by the fact that the note got out at all, supervision that was quite relaxed. If the band of outlaws had been intent on holding the group, why would they have returned them to Bamut? Once having released them—and presumably already having robbed them—what interest would they then have in recapturing them? Also odd was the idea that these panic-stricken bandits would take the time to organize a formal firing squad amid a ferocious Russian ground assault, then further delay their flight by digging graves.

From a strategic standpoint, however, it seemed a bad time to point out these inconsistencies to Magomet. Instead, I carefully walked him through the account again, pinning him down as to precisely where the forest bunker was, where the bodies were buried.

"So this was a purely criminal act," I asked, "with no involvement of the regular *boyaviki?*"

"Absolutely," he replied. "They are not to blame at all."

"And the criminals are now gone from this area?"

"Yes. They fled during the storming, and it is now under regular *boyaviki* control."

"Then it should be no problem for us to go to Stari-Atchkoi and collect the bodies."

Magomet didn't even blink. "No problem at all. We will go together."

And so began our strange, week-long odyssey with Magomet.

We had long since learned there was no such thing as a direct route to anywhere in Chechnya, but even by those standards our path to the bunker outside Stari-Atchkoi was remarkably circuitous. There were detours to Grozny, to several small towns in the "liberated territory" in the central plains, even a trek to the rebel stronghold of Vedeno in the southeast. Along the way were meetings with village elders, merchants, a variety of rebel commanders—and, along the way, Magomet's account began slowly to change.

The evolution followed a distinct pattern. Periodically, at cafés where we were eating or at farmhouses where we were staying, Magomet would suddenly rise and announce he had to go visit some "cousins." These visits could range from a few minutes to several hours, but each time Magomet returned, there was a little bit more to tell about the Fred Cuny mystery.

"Some new information has been received," he would intone cryptically, as if he had come by it telepathically.

The true source of these messages seemed clear enough: Magomet was checking in with rebel commanders, trying to figure out what more he was allowed to tell us. It placed him in an interesting bind. He was trying to help us, of that I was quite sure, but he was also trying to contain the story within acceptable limits. My task, it seemed, was to continually test those limits, and one way to do that was to keep on the pressure about getting to the bunker in Stari-Atchkoi.

One afternoon, after returning from another of his "cousin" get-togethers, Magomet allowed that there might, in fact, have been some "regular *boyaviki*" involvement in the murders after all, involvement that extended beyond that of the now dead colonel, Shirvani Albakhov.

"It looks like it was probably Rizvan Elbiev," he said, referring to the counterintelligence commander in Atchkoi-Martan. "Apparently the group did reach him, but he had a copy of the spy list from Bamut, and for some reason he believed it. Rizvan Elbiev was the one who ordered the executions."

In this newest incarnation of the story, it was Elbiev who had officiated over the murders in the forest and made off with the lion's share of stolen money, with the previously maligned Shirvani Albakhov reduced to a mere supporting role.

"So maybe it was for the money," Magomet said, "but the spy list gave Elbiev the excuse. He did it very quietly, giving some of the money to the killers so that no one higher up [in the rebel leadership] would learn the truth."

I had even more difficulty with this story than with the last one; I simply didn't believe that Rizvan Elbiev, or any other local rebel functionary, would have taken it upon himself to murder an American who was known to the seniormost rebel leadership. Again, though, I kept my doubts to myself.

"So, if it was just Elbiev acting alone," I pointed out, "it still shouldn't be a problem to get the bodies."

This time Magomet was a bit more hesitant. "No," he finally said, "it shouldn't be too much of a problem."

Meanwhile, though, we didn't appear to be getting any closer to Stari Atchkoi. Events began to quicken when Magomet led us into the main square of a small town in central Chechnya to meet with Omar Hadji, a commander from the southwestern front that encompassed Bamut.

With a long black beard and turbaned hat of brown fur, Hadji was an imposing figure, a portly man of forty-one tucked into brand-new Russian fatigues. A mullah, or Islamic priest, the most impressive feature of his outfit was the long broadsword—his "avenging knife," he called it—dangling from one hip. According to competing local rumors, Hadji had used the sword to decapitate either three of his own men who had violated Islamic law or three Russian prisoners of war. As about a dozen of his well-armed fighters gathered around, I began the interview, with Ryan standing by to translate.

To provide some measure of camouflage to my true area of interest, I'd made it a policy ever since arriving in the Caucasus to slip in my questions about Fred amid a broader discussion of the war. Recently I had made a further modification. I had noticed that even those

Russian speakers who didn't understand a word of English often recognized the name "Fred Cuny" when I relayed a question through Ryan, and the delay while that question was translated gave them more time to form a careful response. To avoid that, I'd devised a shorthand code with Ryan, dropping all references to Fred by name and simply referring to him as "our man."

"Okay," I said to Ryan after putting several generic questions to Omar Hadji, "now ask him about our man."

A quick flash of puzzlement rose in Hadji's eyes, and it suddenly occurred to me that the chubby swordsman might have a much better grasp of English than he had let on.

"I don't know anything about that personally," Hadji replied, his early joviality seeming to dissolve a little. "I know that many people were here looking for him, that apparently he came to a bad end on the Russian side. That is all I know."

I felt quite certain I had made a major blunder. As soon as the interview was over and we returned to the nearby farmhouse where we were staying, I told Magomet I wanted to get out of the area as quickly as possible.

"Very good," he said. "I just need to go and talk with some of my cousins."

"There's no time," I replied. "We have to go now."

"Five minutes," Magomet said. "Ten at most."

All argument was to no avail; Magomet got in the car and drove off. It was two hours before he returned. "Okay," he said, "let's go."

Jumping into the car, we got a hundred yards down the road when a Mercedes full of *boyaviki* cut us off; they explained that the supreme commander of the southwest front, General Ruslan Gilayev, had agreed to my request for an interview. I couldn't recall having made such a request but it seemed pretty obvious this wasn't an invitation that could be turned down gracefully.

Followed by carloads of *boyaviki* in front and back, we made for a foothill town a few miles away. I noticed that Magomet, usually quite gregarious, had become very quiet, nervously tapping his fingers on the steering wheel. Pulling to a stop before the metal gate of a large farm-house compound, he turned and gave a sheepish grin.

"I think maybe I'll wait out here."

Walking through the gate, I saw there were about fifteen or twenty rebels milling about in the courtyard, including Omar Hadji. He gave a great smile at the sight of us. As I knelt down to undo my shoes before going into the house, a Caucasian tradition, he came alongside to pat me on the back. "Don't worry," he said in English. "Everything's gonna be fine."

We waited in the living room of the house for twenty minutes before General Gilayev entered. He was thirty-two years old but appeared much older, with the cold, thousand-yard stare of the combat veteran in his unblinking gray eyes. Once again, I feigned interest in a whole array of topics, only getting around to my Fred questions—but without the foolish "our man" business—late in the interview. Even so, I noticed that Gilayev's voice dropped slightly, seemed to take on a more careful tone.

"This was a very sad episode, and even to this day we don't know what happened. But you must remember that the Russians have killed so many here, what is one or four more to them? And of course they wanted to kill Fred Cuny because he was a great friend of the Chechen people. Anyone who is a friend to us, they are ready to kill."

Whatever the terms of the test, we apparently passed. After an hour or so Gilayev announced he had to go fight a battle—"every day is a working day," he explained—and we were ushered out to our car.

"Good interview?" Magomet asked innocently, sitting behind the steering wheel.*

---

* On a subsequent assignment in Chechnya, Stanley Greene, the photographer, learned further details about this incident. A senior Chechen commander informed Greene that General Gilayev had ordered our executions and that the rebels gathered at the farmhouse had been summoned there to serve as our firing squad. It was Omar Hadji, by this account, who interceded with Gilayev to spare our lives; if true, my sincere apologies to Hadji for commenting on his weight.

That night we stayed in a bomb-damaged house on the southern outskirts of Grozny. Earlier shelling had collapsed about half the ceiling, and it appeared the rest might go very soon; throughout that night a firefight raged about a half mile away, the concussion of artillery rattling the remaining rafters and sprinkling us with masonry dust as we slept.

Early the next morning Magomet sat at the small kitchen table, drinking tea and smoking cigarettes. He appeared distracted. "Where would you like to go today?" he asked.

We'd had this little exchange every morning for the past week, and I always gave the same answer. "Stari-Atchkoi. I want to find the bodies."

"We cannot go to Stari-Atchkoi," he said. "The Russians are attacking again."

I became irritated. I reminded Magomet that there was a back road into Stari-Atchkoi that was protected from Russian shelling—a road that I had first learned about from him, in fact, during those early optimistic days when he had waxed about how easy our journey to the bunker would be. To this, Magomet only stared down at the table.

"You will be killed," he whispered finally. "If not by the Russians, then by the *boyaviki*. If we try to get to Stari-Atchkoi, we will all be killed." He lit another cigarette. "Some new information has been received."

In Magomet's latest update, the finger of blame now traveled up the chain of rebel command, the murders not just the free-lance initiative of the Atchkoi-Martan commander, Rizvan Elbiev, but extending all the way to Abu Musayev, the supreme counterintelligence commander of all rebel forces.

"It is such a great disgrace to the Chechen people," Magomet said, becoming visibly upset. "This was Musayev's doing, but it was because of that spy list. So that is why you cannot go to Stari-Atchkoi, because of Musayev's involvement. It is too much a disgrace that he and all the others were fooled by that list."

Frankly, I'd had it with the spy list. We had now arrived at almost precisely the same story that the Cuny family had heard from Shirvani, the Jordanian businessman. Since I now saw that we would never get to Stari-Atchkoi and that it wasn't going to be safe for us to stay in Chechnya much longer, I decided to lay out to Magomet precisely why the spy-list story—and with it, the whole rationale of an FSB black operation—couldn't possibly be true.

From the very outset, that black operation had seemed a remarkable feat for an organization as utterly disorganized and incompetent as the FSB had become. At one point during that summer's search effort, the chief FSB investigator in Ingushetia had shown up for a meeting with American Embassy officers so drunk that the Americans had actually disarmed him as a safety precaution, the investigator not even noticing as his gun was slipped from its holster. Yet, by the spy-list account, this was the same organization that had managed to find out ahead of time exactly who would be in the UAZ ambulance, compile all their vital information, and get an agent up to Bamut in advance to spread the word. What's more, a couple of key points pushed that feat from the realm of the improbable into that of the fantastic.

One detail that few seemed to have pondered—even the Cuny family had overlooked it to an extent—was that the two Soros-sponsored projects in the North Caucasus—the mobile trauma unit at the Sleptsovskaya hospital, and Fred and Galina's disaster assessment mission—were very separate entities, one supported by the International Science Foundation but answering to the Russian Red Cross, and the other, Fred's, operating under the aegis of the Open Society Institute. Not only did Fred have absolutely no authority over Andrei Sereda and Sergei Makarov, he hadn't even met them before the morning of March 30, the day after the shadowy "Usman"—the FSB double agent who allegedly carried the spy list—supposedly showed up in Bamut. While it was plausible, even likely, that the four would end up traveling together—after all, Galina had often accompanied the doctors into the field—there was little reason to automatically assume they would, and certainly no reason to assume it with such definitiveness as to put all four of their names—and only their four names—on a spy-list manifest.

Given the ad hoc nature of disaster relief, changes in the group's composition could have occurred up to the very moment they left Sleptsovskaya, another doctor from the trauma unit deciding to join them on the trip at the last minute, or Sereda and Makarov suddenly called away on an emergency.

The spy list was even harder to imagine given another small detail. In the wake of the incident at the Assinovskaya checkpoint, the overall supervisor of the mobile trauma unit in Ingushetia, Misha Panormov, had expressly forbidden Andrei Sereda and Sergei Makarov to venture into Chechnya. Obviously, the doctors had disobeyed that dictate once Fred arrived on the scene, but how could Usman—or anyone else—have predicted that?

The great irony in all this was that those details had been very easy to overlook—and the FSB spy-list story very easy to believe—because of the FSB's own smear campaign against Fred in the wake of the disappearances. By constantly floating rumors that Fred was alive and operating as a CIA operative in the Chechen hills, the FSB had seemed to go out of its way both to suggest it had been watching Fred and to draw suspicion on itself.

But rather than proof of their involvement, I now saw the FSB's clumsy smear campaign as a peculiar blend of ignorance and panic. They truly didn't know what had happened to Fred and the others, I believed, but the ominous circumstances of the disappearances in Chechnya sounded precisely like the sort of thing their loosely supervised agents in the field were capable of. Suspecting their own men had probably murdered the group, the FSB had quickly launched a public relations counteroffensive to "prove" their innocence, and the more that counteroffensive backfired, the more shrill and outlandish it became. In short, the FSB had not only outsmarted itself, but its guilty behavior had served to lend further legitimacy to the spy-list fable.

"But I saw the list with my own eyes," Magomet argued, and he did so with such vehemence that I believed him.

"Then it was a fake," I said. "It was put together afterward to shift some of the blame onto the Russians."

Magomet was not particularly happy to hear any of this, but he was even less pleased with what came next.

Because if the FSB spy-list fiction was removed from the equation, it meant the rebels had killed Fred and the others completely of their own volition: no black operation, no byzantine double-cross, just their own cold reasons. And since our own close encounter in Bamut had left me more convinced than ever that a lower-level rebel commander wouldn't have taken it upon himself to murder a friend of the chief of staff, General Maskhadov—not Colonel Rizvan Elbiev and, even less likely, a member of the inner circle like General Abu Musayev—the most logical explanation was that the kill order had come from someone higher up than Maskhadov. The only person who fit that bill was President Dzhokhar Dudayev.

Here, again, there was the thread of a clue— ironically, one of the very first to come to light and one of the most vigorously discredited. It was Ruslan Muradov's account that had Dudayev in Bamut on the morning of April 9 congratulating his fighters for capturing the four foreign spies. "We arrived in Bamut around 5 P.M.," Muradov had written.

> I was immediately informed that at noon Dudayev had been in Bamut, both in upper and lower [communities of] Bamut. Guys who I knew well from Bamut said that the people who I had been escorting were staff of the FSB . . . Dzhokhar [Dudayev] pointed to the "coerced statements" taken from the four people. He didn't read the statements, but he counted off the last and first names of all four. At this he announced his gratitude to all who had taken part in the detention of the Fred Cuny group. What he was planning to do with them, he didn't say.

Rather lost between Vice-President Boris Agapov's stirring denunciation of the story and Muradov's own lack of credibility was the elemental question of why the driver would have ever made up such an account. Ruslan Muradov was a Chechen patriot and a supporter of the rebel cause; why would he concoct a lie that cast aspersions on his own leader? Perhaps most salient of all, why make up a story that could very easily get him killed?

Rather than a possible conspirator, it seemed clear to me that Ruslan Muradov had been the one person—and perhaps the only person—who had told the truth all along. He had walked for ten hours through a battlefield to deliver Fred's note to Sleptsovskaya. He had stayed on the scene for nearly a month after the disappearances, and had made repeated trips into the war zone looking for his missing charges. Those were simply not the actions of a guilty man.

Instead, I believed, Ruslan Muradov had slipped from sight because he saw that his words were coming back to haunt him. He had vanished not because he was fearful of being unmasked as a conspirator but because, by relating what he had heard in Bamut, he had unwittingly identified the chief conspirator in the murders, Dzhokhar Dudayev. What's more, he had first related that story to the one man who was probably the least interested in hearing it: the Vice-President of Ingushetia, Boris Agapov.

"Having stayed in Bamut until April 10th," Muradov had written at the end of his statement, "I returned to Sleptsovsk[aya] where I met with Agapov and [Peter] Kozov and told them in detail what happened."

When the manhunt became very high-profile, when foreigners and government officials began showing up to investigate—and, not least, when Boris Agapov denounced him as a liar—Ruslan undoubtedly figured out his life expectancy was going to be very short if he stayed around.

As to why Dudayev would order Fred's murder, one possibility was fairly simple. Since the very beginning of the war Dudayev had fed his countrymen a steady diet of paranoid propaganda about the myriad ways the Russians were trying to kill him, tales of a veritable horde of Russian spies and assassination squads roaming the country posing as journalists and relief workers as they tried to get the President in their rifle sights. Interestingly, these claims seemed to have increased in direct proportion to Dudayev's fall in popularity as the war ground on.

Yet there had always been curiously few concrete signs that the Russians were actually trying to kill Dudayev. Rather, he seemed able to pass through their checkpoints, conduct interviews within sight of their garrisons —even cross over frontiers to attend birthday parties in neighboring republics, apparently—virtually at will. By November 1995 about the only indication that Dudayev was being ruthlessly hunted down were his own persistent claims that it was so, and a lot of rebel commanders were becoming openly suspicious of the ease with which their President managed to so consistently slide past Russian authorities; some were even suggesting that Dudayev was in some byzantine collusion with the Russians. By holding Fred Cuny and the others up as spies, the little general may have seen it as a cheap and easy way to bolster his claims of being a fugitive, on the run from devious and well-disguised trackers.

For a long time that morning at the kitchen table in Grozny, I outlined my theory to Magomet. At the end of it, he simply gazed off for a while. Then he did something very unexpected; he began to cry.

"If it's true," he explained between his sobs, "then we didn't deserve him. Fred came here to help us, and instead we killed him. Chechnya doesn't deserve a man like that."

.   .   .

But there was a second possible explanation for why Dudayev, as I believe, ordered the group's murder, one that I chose not to tell Magomet. It had to do with the peculiar significance of the town of Bamut, of what might be hidden away there.

.   .   .

On the afternoon of November 1, 1993, on the second anniversary of the declaration of Chechen independence and with war still a year away, Dzhokhar Dudayev stood on the steps of his Presidential Palace in Grozny and watched as his "national army" marched past in review. The highlight of the parade, trundling slowly by on the beds of enormous transport trucks, were the casings of two SS-20 nuclear warheads. About ten minutes later, spectators saw two more SS-20s roll past and, after another ten minutes, two more. Eventually, most observers realized they were seeing the same two missiles over and over again, that President Dudayev, evidently so thrilled at their sight, had simply ordered the truckdrivers to keep circling the block.

Despite the farcical aspect of the spectacle, the sight of those two missiles in downtown Grozny would underscore one of the most convoluted—and little reported—shadow dances of the Chechen conflict: the complex machinations set in motion around the world over the question of whether Dudayev had somehow got his hands on nuclear warheads.

When the Soviet Union collapsed in 1991 its nuclear arsenal was scattered across four of the former Soviet republics: Russia, Ukraine, Kazakhstan, and Belarus. Over the next four years, and largely through a combination of extraordinary arm twisting and financial incentives from the United States, all three of the latter republics ceded control of the nuclear weapons on their soil, with the warheads either destroyed or transported to Russian territory.

At least, that was the official story. The problem was that in the chaos accompanying the disintegration of the Soviet Union and the speed with which the former Red Army had abandoned the field, no one outside the inner circle of the Kremlin and the former Soviet military elite could be absolutely certain that all the missiles had been collected. In fact, there were ample indications that even the elite may not have known—and nowhere was that doubt more in evidence than in their reaction to Chechnya and to Dudayev's trail of cryptic comments on the topic.

As early as 1992, Dudayev and several of his senior aides were darkly hinting that they possessed nuclear warheads and were willing to use them if Russia didn't recognize Chechnya's sovereignty. After the SS-20 parade in November 1993, those hints grew steadily more overt as the threat of war drew nearer. In the summer of 1994, with the Russians' destabilization effort against Dudayev in full swing, the

Chechen economic minister appealed for UN peacekeepers to be sent to the republic; to sweeten the deal, he suggested such a force could take control of Chechnya's unspecified "nuclear objects." In mid-December 1994, amid last-minute negotiations to forestall all-out war, General Maskhadov was asked by a journalist if his rebel forces possessed a nuclear bomb. "That is a secret," the Chechen chief of staff replied tersely. When asked point-blank by a *Time* reporter in March 1996 if he had "weapons of mass destruction," Dudayev enigmatically replied: "We won't use them, unless Russia uses nuclear weapons."

Officially, the Russian government and military dismissed the whole notion of there being nuclear warheads in Chechnya, pointing out that the SS-20s in Grozny were clearly just empty casings. Once the war began, however, Dudayev's veiled claims found some curious advocates: the ultranationalist and virulently anti-Dudayev media in Moscow. These were the same newspapers and magazines that had carried out the smear campaign against the Soros Foundation—and would soon do so against Fred Cuny—and, as in those other campaigns, their primary sources for the nukes-in-Chechnya story appeared to be intelligence agents from the FSB and war hawks in the Russian government.

A motive for the FSB and Kremlin hawks to promote the story was not hard to find: surely, nothing was more likely to keep the United States and Western Europe on Moscow's side in the war than the terrifying prospect that the "mad little general" in Grozny had his hands on nuclear warheads. In this way, the war hawks in Moscow may have simply latched on to a disinformation plot by Dudayev and turned it to their advantage.

But, of course, a disinformation plot can only work if there is some plausible basis for believing it—and there is substantial evidence that a lot of people, in both the Russian and American governments, took the nukes-in-Chechnya story quite seriously.

Over a series of trips to Moscow during the war, Tim Thomas, an analyst at the Foreign Military Studies Office at Fort Leavenworth, raised the issue with a number of senior Russian military officials.

"Officially, they would say, 'No way, it's not possible,' " Thomas recalled, "but, hell, you can read body language, you can read eyes, and it was obvious they were concerned."

According to Andrew and Leslie Cockburn in their book, *One Point Safe*, the American government deemed the threat so credible that they dispatched a CIA team to Chechnya in 1994 in an unsuccessful attempt to inspect two warheads purportedly in Dudayev's hands. For its part, the CIA refused to either confirm or deny that report. "I don't know that we ever took the idea that seriously," a spokesman said.

Another American official involved in tracking nuclear weapons in Russia, and who spoke on condition of anonymity, disagreed.

"I don't know anything about this particular [Cockburn] claim," the official said, "but I certainly think that, with all the rumors floating around about [nuclear weapons in] Chechnya, the CIA would have at least been concerned enough to check it out. Given the chaotic state of affairs in Russia, if some kiosk girl in Murmansk said she had a warhead buried in her backyard, we'd probably check it out."

Scott Parrish, a researcher at the Monterey Institute's Center for Nonproliferation Studies, the world's preeminent clearinghouse for public information on nuclear weapons, held a similar view.

"I think the Americans would have to have been concerned," Parrish said. "On the one hand, in all the research we've done over the years, we've never been able to confirm a report of a missing Russian [nuclear] weapon—and I think that with all the documentation we've gathered, we would have heard about it. On the other hand, the Russians are extremely defensive on this topic. If something had gone missing, they would probably try very hard to keep it secret."

But in the strange reverse logic that is inherent in the arena of nuclear weaponry, the question of whether or not there were live warheads in Chechnya is curiously beside the point. For Dudayev, it was enough that the Russians feared he might have them, and in stoking that fear he had a powerful tool: the old nuclear missile base in the small mountain village of Bamut.

Designed to house a new generation of intermediate-range nuclear missiles, the SS-4, the base in Bamut was constructed in the 1960s at the relatively flat northern edge of the town. Its operation was rather short-lived; by terms of the Intermediate-Range Nuclear Forces treaty (INF), the installation was deactivated in 1987 and its SS-4s removed, to be either destroyed or redeployed to other missile bases. In the estimation of Scott Parrish at the Monterey Institute, it is unlikely that any of those missiles could have been left behind since, under the terms of the INF treaty, someone from the Pentagon's On-Site Inspection Agency should have eyewitnessed their removal.

What was not mandated by the INF treaty, however, was the destruction of the installation itself, a vast warren of underground bunkers and missile silos protected by a massive overlay of steel and reinforced concrete. It remained as a perfect repository for nuclear missiles in the future and, in fact, the only such potential repository in all of Chechnya. In essence, if the Russians were truly worried that the Chechen rebels had their hands on warheads, the first place they would come looking for them was Bamut—and getting the Russians to come to Bamut may have been Dudayev's primary goal all along.

Dudayev may well have been crazy, but he was crazy like the proverbial fox, and if he could lure the Russian army into concentrating a sizable portion of its forces in a campaign to take Bamut, it would not only relieve pressure on his fighters elsewhere, it would draw his enemy into attacking the most impregnable part of his line. If that was his goal, it certainly worked.

For some fifteen months the Russians pounded Bamut with every weapon in their arsenal and launched repeated ground assaults that cost hundreds of soldiers' lives. The sheer tonnage of explosives dropped on the little town probably surpassed that used to "pacify" all of Grozny; in fact, Bamut may well have the distinction of being the most heavily bombed patch of earth in military history. As Anatol Lieven rhapsodizes in his book, *Chechnya:*

"For the defenders of Bamut, in the Caucasus foothills, who defended their village for *fifteen months* in the face of a bombardment to which they could make no reply, their performance places them in the ranks of the great epic defenders of history, alongside the men of Verdun and Masada."

Well, maybe not quite. Clearly, one huge reason the rebels were able to withstand the assault was that the missile base's network of tunnels and underground silos made them virtually immune to whatever the Russians threw at them.

Ultimately, then, a belief that there might be nuclear warheads in Bamut emerges as one of the only plausible explanations for why the Russian army wasted so much matériel and so many lives in trying to take the town, rather than merely cordoning it off. (Of course, another plausible explanation is sheer idiocy, something that can never be fully discounted in analyzing the Russian conduct of the war.) The Chechens' motive for so stoutly defending Bamut is a bit more obvious: the more Russian shells that fell harmlessly on the reinforced concrete of Bamut, the less would fall elsewhere in Chechnya, and the more Russian ground assaults on Bamut, the more Russian soldiers they could kill.

But the interesting thing about bluffs—and virtually all analysts now believe Dudayev *was* bluffing about his warheads—is that they have to be even more closely protected than the real thing. If someone from the outside were able to get to Bamut and firmly establish that the warheads didn't exist, then the bluff was over. This may have explained why so many uninvited outsiders who ventured into Bamut were never seen again—and it may have explained why Dudayev decided that Fred Cuny and his companions had to die.

According to Ruslan Muradov, Dudayev arrived in Bamut on the morning of April 9. At that point his forces had been holding Fred's group for over a week. In that time they had been shuttled about the area quite a bit—to Atchkoi-Martan to meet with the counterintelligence commander, to the bunker on the forest road outside Stari-Atchkoi—but, perhaps most crucially, they had spent at least three days and three nights at the Muradov home in Bamut during which they had been very loosely supervised.

By April 9, Dudayev surely knew that Fred Cuny was a friend of his chief of staff, General Maskhadov, and that Fred was considered a friend of the Chechen people. But perhaps he also suspected Fred or one of his companions of having a hidden agenda in coming to Bamut, to sniff out just what was inside the missile silos at the base of town. Or perhaps he simply decided he couldn't take that chance. For whatever reason—if, in fact, the missile base was the reason—Dudayev decided they all had to die. Taken back to the forest bunker outside Stari-Atchkoi—no doubt for more interrogation and more torture—his orders were finally carried out on the afternoon of April 14.

. . .

There is, obviously, one last question in all this. Is it possible that Fred or one of his companions actually was a spy?

In the cases of Galina Oleinik, Andrei Sereda, and Sergei Makarov, it is theoretically possible. Both doctors were ethnic Russians, while Galina was an Ossete, an ethnic group seen as enemies of the Chechens. All three were affiliated with organizations or professions that had a long history of being riddled with KGB agents. On the other hand, it's hard to imagine why any of these three "spies" would have so repeatedly risked their lives in order to save Chechen civilians from Russian bullets on earlier occasions, and why they would have done so in corners of the battlefield that had little strategic, or spying, value.

Naturally, as leader of the lost group, the uncomfortable question most firmly attaches to Fred Cuny.

Even before the international manhunt for him got under way, there was speculation that the reason for Fred's return to Chechnya was that he had embarked on an intelligence-gathering mission on the Russian military for the United States government. That certainly seemed to be the suspicion of the FSB in launching its subsequent smear campaign, and it was a suspicion that Fred himself had, however inadvertently, helped fuel by his actions in the month just prior to his return to the battlefield.

Several times in March, Fred had gone to Washington for meetings on Chechnya with high-level government officials, including the

Undersecretary of Defense for Policy, the President's special assistant for Russian affairs, and Deputy Secretary of State Strobe Talbott. He had also met with officials of the CIA, the Defense Intelligence Agency, and senior Russian policymakers at State. Later, when news of these meetings became known, they would serve as the cornerstone of the Fred-as-spy theory.

At first glance, the reaction Fred encountered at those meetings would seem to quickly demolish any theory of an intelligence-gathering mission to Chechnya. With the Clinton administration so steadfastly committed to turning a blind eye to the brutal Russian military campaign that even Talbott, the second-highest-ranking official of the State Department, could be "stunned" by Fred's eyewitness account, it would seem the last thing anyone in the American government wanted was any more information about Russian misdeeds in the field.

On the other hand, so determined was the Administration's head-in-the-sand posture on Chechnya that it suggested the possibility of an intelligence-gathering mission of a diametrically opposite sort, one directed not against the Russians but against the Chechens. Not only might such a mission help justify the Administration's continued support of Russia in the war—a position that was growing more morally indefensible by the day—but it might also gather evidence on two matters that had to be of concern to the American government: the rumors of nuclear weapons in Chechnya and the rumors of growing Iranian influence.

Ironically, it may well have been Fred Cuny who most fueled this latter fear during his meetings in Washington that March, as he recounted details of his first trip to the war zone. One source familiar with what Fred told the State Department could not even bring himself to utter the most explosive revelation aloud. Instead, the source took up a pencil and wrote on a piece of notepaper, "He saw Iranians there," then carefully erased the four words.

But if it wanted to track down these alarming rumors, the American government was in something of a bind. Chechnya was simply too dangerous to send a bona fide intelligence agent into the field, and the handful of journalists and academics who styled themselves "Caucasus experts" were largely regarded as unreliable, apologists for one side or the other, or given to wild exaggeration. A solution of sorts may have presented itself in the form of Fred Cuny. Who better to ask for such a favor than a noted disaster relief expert who was about to return to the war zone, who had already displayed his willingness to share information with the American government, and who was on friendly terms with the highest-ranking officers in the rebel army? And who better to ask than a man who could be appealed to on grounds of patriotism and duty, who was enamored of his newfound respect within the American foreign policy establishment and—not least—who had always displayed a fascination with cloak-and-dagger exploits? In just this way, and in conjunction with his aboveboard disaster relief effort, Fred may have simply viewed a detour through Bamut as a kind of civic duty, one that both his respect for officialdom and his own self-importance could not allow him to decline.

"If it happened," Craig Cuny said, "I think it would have been done very informally. [A government official might have said], 'Look, you're going back to Chechnya, you've got good relations with the rebel leadership, and we're concerned about what's going on in Bamut; would you mind going through there and just seeing what you see?' " Craig considered for a moment, then added, "Actually, they wouldn't have even had to come out and ask that directly. Knowing Fred, if he caught wind that there was something weird going on in Bamut, he would've gone up there anyway."

A State Department official, as usual insisting on anonymity, expressed shock at the very idea that anyone in the American government might have prompted Fred to take the Bamut road. "I just find that inconceivable," he said. "I can't imagine any official being so indifferent that they'd deliberately put an innocent person's life at risk like that."

Of course, this was one of the same officials who had so perfected indifference at the Russians' slaughter of innocent life in Chechnya that he could be "shocked" to learn of it from Fred Cuny.

Whether used or not, whether their decision to take the Bamut road was a purely innocent miscalculation or one with an ulterior motive, Fred, Galina, Andrei, and Sergei set off on a journey that they knew might cost them their lives. On that last morning Fred had called his assistant and told her in a hushed, frightened voice that he was going back onto the battlefield.

"Just think about me," he had whispered, and then he had climbed aboard the ambulance and set off for the lonely, windswept track through the mountains. In that act, the world lost a man who had dedicated his life to saving others, a man it could not afford to lose.

. . .

Shortly after returning to Moscow from Chechnya, one fleeting moment in a long conversation suggested to me that I might just be right about my theory on Bamut. Then again, having just spent two weeks in Chechnya being steeped in conspiracy theories of all kinds, I might well have imagined its importance.

Hearing that I was back in town, Ambassador Pickering asked to speak with me. For over ninety minutes we sat in his office on the seventh floor of the American Embassy, his secretary holding all his calls, as he peppered me with questions about what I'd learned of Fred's disappearance. At some point in my long narrative I briefly mentioned that I and several others had gone to Bamut, and it was a detail the ambassador returned to a few minutes later.

"So, what did you see in Bamut?" he asked. "A lot of heavy weaponry?"

I replied that we had been stopped at the outskirts of the town, that we'd never reached or even seen the main battlefield down by the missile base. The ambassador gave a sharp nod, and the conversation quickly moved on to other things.

EPILOGUE

IN JULY 1996 the streets of downtown Sarajevo were clogged with the Land Cruisers and Cherokee Chiefs of scores of humanitarian aid organizations. Since the signing of the Dayton Accord peace settlement six months earlier, relief groups had flooded the Bosnian capital, as well as much of the countryside, and started up relief programs in every sphere from housing reconstruction to small-business capitalization seminars to psychological trauma assessments of school-age children. One of the most immediate problems Bosnia faced, it seemed, was simply how it might handle all the foreign assistance suddenly pouring in. In his office by the Miljacka River, John Fawcett, the International Rescue Committee director who had worked with Fred on the water filtration project, mused about his lost friend.

"I've heard so many people here in the last six months say, 'Damn, I wish Fred was here, because he'd get this thing organized.' " Fawcett smiled. "But I seriously doubt Fred would be caught anywhere near this place now—too many do-gooders around. Fred needed that buzz of being out there where no one else was, where he could stand out and make up the rules as he went along."

At the Carnegie Endowment in Washington, Morton Abramowitz took a longer view. "You know, I look at what happened in Rwanda—what's happening now in Zaire—and I can't help but think how much better things would be if Fred were still there. The other side to this tragedy is that there weren't just four victims out there in Chechnya. Over the next decade there's going to be thousands—probably tens of thousands—of people whose lives will be ruined or lost because Fred isn't around."

In death, Fred has achieved some of the recognition and appreciation he sought in life. In 1995, with his fate in Chechnya still unknown, he was awarded a MacArthur "genius" grant. In 1997 he was posthumously awarded a medal of valor by the Bosnian government. A number of his old colleagues, including Mort Abramowitz, Rick Hill, Don Krumm, and Julia Taft, started the Frederick C. Cuny Memorial Fund, designed to provide educational grants for disaster relief workers around the world.

At the same time, the old rumors of Fred's intelligence connections continue to be recycled and expanded upon. In his 1998 memoir, Michael Rose, the British general who had commanded UN troops in Sarajevo and attempted to blame the marketplace bombing on the Bosnians only to be undermined by Fred, described his dead nemesis as a "shadowy," ex–U.S. Marine officer. "We assumed he was working for the CIA," Rose wrote.

For Fred's family, the hardest part has been the lingering questions, of not knowing precisely what happened in those mountains and, worse, that last flicker of hope—a hope that is also a kind of torture—that he might yet be alive. In the four years since Fred's disappearance, his parents, Charlotte and Gene, have aged considerably. Of his three brothers, it is the youngest, Chris, who seems most deeply affected. For the first couple of years he tried to keep Intertect going under the Cuny family name, becoming its director and hustling for contracts, but finally accepted that it was impossible. Today, Fred's company has been absorbed by the International Resources Group, a global environmental consulting firm based in Washington, under the directorship of Rick Hill, Fred's former deputy.

For Craig Cuny, the family member who looked longest for Fred in Chechnya, the adjustment has been fairly smooth—at least, so he says. Now running a successful video production company in Austin, he recently remarried and plans to begin producing promotional videos for disaster relief agencies on their overseas projects. With a gregarious and carefree manner, he rarely talks about his father or what happened in Chechnya to acquaintances or even close friends; when he does, it is usually with a kind of carefully honed detachment.

"As time has gone on," he said to me one day, "I've realized that this is just the way Fred would have wanted to go out. A big drama, all these people wondering what happened, all these mysteries and questions left over." He laughed. "If Fred had been able to script his own death, it's exactly the way he would have done it."

Every once in a while, however, a flash of bitterness seeps through.

"You know what I'd like to see?" he said late one night in April 1996 as we drove through downtown Austin. "I'd really like to see Dudayev dead."

The sentiment was very out of keeping with Craig's character and apropos of nothing we had been discussing, but that's the way our few conversations about Chechnya tended to happen. We had developed a close bond, cemented in part by our both having gone to Chechnya to look for Fred and having survived, but neither of us ever felt much of an urge to talk about it.

By odd coincidence, we discovered the next morning that Craig's angry wish had come true. On the afternoon of April 21, 1996, Dudayev and a coterie of bodyguards had driven a short distance out of the village of Gekhi-Chu in central Chechnya so that the President could make calls on his satellite phone. While talking with a contact in Moscow, a "smart bomb" keyed to his telephone frequency was fired from a nearby Russian plane, killing Dudayev and two of his bodyguards. At least that was the official story. There were rumors that Dudayev had actually been set up by some of his own men who had tired of his erratic ways and his posture in pursuing negotiations with Boris Yeltsin—either his obstructionism or his appeasement, pick one.

With and without Dudayev, the capricious brutality that had always typified the war in Chechnya continued. In January 1996, Major General Alexander Mikhailov, the FSB press spokesman who had been an architect of the Fred Cuny smear campaign, was finally done in by his penchant for spreading misinformation. After another Budyennovsk-style raid into Dagestan had gone awry, a large force of Chechen rebels found themselves surrounded with some 150 civilian hostages in the little village of Pervomayskaya. After several days of intermittent skirmishing and tense standoff, General Mikhailov arrived from Moscow and the shooting quickly intensified. "We are not counting them in terms of corpses," Mikhailov said with obvious satisfaction as Russian shells pounded the village. "We are counting them in terms of arms and legs." The next day, he announced he had information that all the hostages had been executed and, "Now we will destroy the bandits."

As the massed Russian artillery reduced the village to rubble, the remaining rebels somehow slipped out of the encirclement—as they had done so many times in the past. It was then discovered the civilian hostages had not been executed, although the Russian bombardment had succeeded in killing quite a few of them. Forced to admit he had lied about the purported executions, Mikhailov was quietly dismissed from his job. In trying to arrive at a motive for his actions in both the Fred Cuny case and the tragic events in Pervomayskaya, one is left with the unsatisfying conclusion that two factors in the major general's psyche—a visceral hatred for "southerners," a love of mischief-making—had combined to bewildering—and in the second case, lethal—effect.

Soon after Dudayev's death in April 1996, President Boris Yeltsin suddenly moved toward peace with great dispatch. The reason for the haste was obvious enough; with presidential elections just two months away, he badly needed a boost in the polls. By late May the peace accord had been finalized and the acting Chechen President, Zelimkhan Yandarbiyev, summoned to the Kremlin for its formal signing.

But as with the war, there would be a powerful element of farce in the peace. When Yandarbiyev held up a treaty paper he apparently hadn't seen before and asked its import, an irritated Yeltsin waved a hand at him in disgust.

"Don't worry about what it says. Just sign it."

Yandarbiyev did so.

Within days of winning the presidential election—greatly aided by both American "democracy advisers" and the new Russian oligarchy that had profited so handsomely from his misrule—Yeltsin had apparently forgotten all about the peace treaty, his troops escalating their attacks in Chechnya once more. In response, the rebels took the war back into the "pacified" ruins of Grozny, pinning down thousands of Russian troops and shattering the myth of Russian control once again. Faced with the specter of a truly monumental military disaster, Yeltsin finally looked for an exit, dispatching the new chief of his security council, former army general Alexander Lebed, to secure a new peace settlement with General Aslan Maskhadov. With remarkable speed and amity, the two military men did so, cobbling together a settlement that simply put off the thorny question of Chechnya's status within the Russian Federation for five more years. As his reward for achieving in a few days what Yeltsin had failed to achieve in five years, Lebed was soundly denounced by government hard-liners as a traitor who had "lost" Chechnya, and was soon dismissed from the Russian cabinet.

Not that the Chechnya fiasco has been bad for everyone's career, of course. With each new setback, Boris Yeltsin had sought to fix blame on some of his closest political advisers and generals, and angrily dismissed them from their posts; almost all were eventually reinstated, and in most cases promoted. One of the most improbable success stories has been that of Ingush Vice-President Boris Agapov, the former KGB general who maintained a friendship with Dzhokhar Dudayev throughout the conflict and who may have played a role in covering up Fred Cuny's murder. In June 1997, Agapov was appointed deputy secretary of the Russian Security Council; appropriately enough, he was put in charge of crisis management.

In January 1997, General Aslan Maskhadov was elected Chechnya's President. Regarded by both sides as perhaps the only military commander to have acted honorably during the war, there were hopes that Maskhadov might be able to restore some measure of order. Those hopes were soon dashed. Instead, the general busied himself with a number of laws designed to refashion Chechnya as an Islamic republic—surely the most absurd was an initiative to erect signs in Arabic, a language that virtually no Chechens read or spoke—even as the country descended deeper into chaos. By the middle of that year there was really no government to speak of and Chechnya was rapidly resembling the nest-of-thieves caricature of old Russian propaganda, the rebel bands that had defeated the Russians now turning their weapons on each other, or whatever foreigners happened into their path.

The general climate of lawlessness and terror had been given obscene punctuation in December 1996 when six foreign Red Cross workers were murdered at a hospital in central Chechnya, shot in the head with silencers as they slept; it continued to worsen in "independent Ichikeriya." By June 1997 at least thirty journalists and relief workers had disappeared in Chechnya, some presumably murdered, others held for ransom by the various armed factions that roamed the land. By the beginning of 1998 that number had risen to seventy, and virtually all relief agencies and media sources had abandoned the region. In almost any measure, the tiny republic in the North Caucasus had become—and still remains—one of the most dangerous places on earth.

.   .   .

As for Fred Cuny's ultimate legacy, it is—like the man—a complicated one. In the 1990s he had finally found his niche in the murky confluence of humanitarian aid, diplomacy, intelligence, and military action, but in that confluence were forces he could not predict or control. He had become a living example of his theory of converting chaos into opportunity, finding his moment to shine in the massive upheavals that accompanied the end of the Cold War, but in the end that chaos had taken his life.

His death also served as a reminder of a grim new feature of modern war: no one is safe. In the wake of his disappearance, and the deaths of so many other relief workers in the four years since, even the most activist-oriented of humanitarian aid organizations have begun to reappraise their charters, pondering whether the new barbarism that reigns on the world's battlefields allows them to operate as they have in the past. If they decide they cannot—and each new slaughter of relief workers brings them closer to that decision—then the murderers win. It suits their purpose to have no witnesses to their crimes.

On our last morning together Magomet, the former Chechen fighter, had said that Chechnya didn't deserve Fred Cuny. On one level, he was right. Certainly the men who started that war didn't deserve him, nor did most of those who waged it. But there were, in fact, people enough in Chechnya who did deserve him: the elderly ethnic Russians trapped in their shattered Grozny homes, the hundreds of thousands of Chechen refugees left to wander their devastated homeland. It was for them that he went back.

. . .

In August 1996 a bloodstained skirt was found tucked inside an asbestos pipe in a bomb-destroyed house in the village of Stari-Atchkoi. Wrapped inside the skirt were the passports and identity papers of Fred, Galina, Sergei, and Andrei; they too were bloodstained.

Along with the passports was a note to General Aslan Maskhadov from Galina Oleinik. It had been written in a desperate, barely legible scrawl.

> *Esteemed Aslan—We tried to come to you, with the medicines and the two doctors we promised. Fred Cuny is with me, the American whom you already know—who came in order to hold the meeting which did not happen last time. I ask you to*

*confirm that you are aware of us and our mission. With
respect. Galina Oleinik—Soros Foundation.*

The note was final proof of where Fred and the others had been
headed on that doomed journey, and of where that journey had ended.

. . .

In the winter of 1998 the FBI Overseas Terrorism Section took a
new interest in the case of Fred Cuny. Through information provided
by the Cuny family, myself, and others, they now feel they have a strong
idea of where his body might be located. Recovering his remains, however, is likely to be a long and difficult process, one that will require at
least a partial lifting of the murderous fog that still cloaks Chechnya.

"Hopefully, there'll come a day when we can try it," said Jerrold
Bamel, the head of the Foreign Assassinations office. "Fred Cuny did a
lot for this country and for the world, and the least we can do is try to
bring him home again."

AFTERWORD TO THE
ANCHOR EDITION

IN THE TWELVE MONTHS since the hardcover publication of *The Man Who Tried to Save the World*, there have been new developments in the story of Fred Cuny's disappearance, and on the Chechen landscape where that disappearance occurred. Unfortunately, in this corner of the world, developments do not necessarily translate into either illumination or progress.

In the spring of 1999, several different Chechen "businessmen" began making anonymous approaches to the American embassy in Moscow, to the Cuny family in Texas, and to myself, claiming they had located Fred's remains and could arrange their return. In light of such myriad "offers" made in the past, these overtures were regarded with skepticism—until one group produced a photograph of the same metal brace that had been surgically implanted in Fred's left leg back in 1966. In response, two of Fred's brothers, Chris and Phil, flew to Paris to meet with the businessmen, only to be told that recovering the remains would cost them $7 million. While the outrageous price tag made the point somewhat moot, the Cuny brothers reasoned that even trying to negotiate would further endanger other hostages then being held for ransom in Chechnya, and they returned to Texas empty-handed. The Cuny family's refusal to pay blood money for Fred's return did not, however, bring an end to the sales pitches: through the autumn of 1999, Craig Cuny continued to receive E-mail messages and faxes from anonymous sources in Russia and Chechnya claiming firsthand knowledge of his father's whereabouts, often accompanied by amateurishly doctored photographs of Fred.

Nineteen ninety-nine also saw an eerie reprise of the horrific slaughter that had befallen Chechnya in the middle of the decade. This second Chechen war, while sparked by a sequence of events as puzzling as the first, seems destined to have far more lasting and profound consequences.

After largely ignoring Chechnya for three years—ever since the August 1996 peace settlement that allowed the defeated Russian army to withdraw from Grozny and gave the breakaway republic de facto independence—Russian President Boris Yeltsin suddenly returned his attention to the "bandit state" in the summer of 1999. Although the ostensible pretext was an attack by Chechen-based Islamic militants on neighboring Dagestan, more cynical observers suggested Yeltsin was once again looking for a "small, victorious war" to deflect attention from a series of scandals implicating his family and closest cronies in the financial raping of Russia. In August, Yeltsin abruptly fired Sergei Stepashin, his fifth prime minister since 1991, and replaced him with Vladimir Putin, a virtually unknown former KGB spy chief. Putin immediately set about to prove his mettle. After first ordering the villages held by the Islamic militants in Dagestan to be pounded into rubble, he capitalized on a spate of mysterious apartment bombings in Moscow that killed some three hundred civilians by ordering a military incursion into Chechnya itself.

Initially, the incursion was advertised as a limited operation to set up a "cordon sanitaire" in northern Chechnya, but as the Russian military juggernaut rolled over the northern steppes, the mission quickly expanded to one of complete "pacification." Avoiding the armored frontal attacks that had cost them so dearly in the first war, the

Russian army instead pounded Chechnya with air strikes and massive artillery bombardments, quickly killing an estimated four thousand civilians and sending a quarter-million Chechens—perhaps half of the republic's depleted population—fleeing for their lives to neighboring Ingushetia. In contrast to the first Chechen war, this one proved wildly popular with the Russian people. Galvanized by both their visceral hatred of the Caucasian "blacks" and a sense of national humiliation at the ruination of their country over the past decade, Russians seemed only too willing to believe the army's steady reports of virtually casualty-free victories over the "terrorists," and increasingly looked to Putin as the national savior. By the parliamentary elections of mid-December, every major Russian political party had jumped on the war bandwagon, and Putin had emerged as the odds-on favorite to succeed Yeltsin in the upcoming June presidential elections.

No one seemed to much care that the reality on the Chechen battlefield was very different. Despite their talk of "precision strikes" on rebel encampments, the Russian military was primarily killing civilians—and also taking far more casualties from the highly mobile Chechen fighter units than they had let on. By late December, with their scorched-earth campaign finally reaching the outskirts of Grozny, Russian generals were once again proudly boasting that the capital would fall within a matter of days. Instead—and just as in 1994—the Chechens turned Grozny into a death zone for the ill-prepared Russian forces, finally compelling the Russian army to "liberate" the city by razing it street by street in January 2000.

By then, however, the most dramatic result of the second Chechen war had already occurred. On New Year's Eve, Boris Yeltsin stunned the world by announcing his resignation and naming Vladimir Putin as acting president. With the timetable for presidential elections now moved up to March—hardly enough time for the full extent of the fiasco in Chechnya to be apparent to the Russian people—Putin's ascension to full power was all but assured. If there was any question that a backroom deal had been made, it was answered quickly: one of Putin's first decrees as acting president was to grant a blanket amnesty to Yeltsin

364

and his family for any and all crimes they had committed over the nine years of his rule.

The similarities to the first Chechen war extended tragically to the international arena. After initially deeming the Russian incursion into Chechnya as justified in order to maintain Russian territorial sovereignty and combat terrorism, the Clinton administration was finally compelled to return to its hand-wringing stance of the past when the full brutality of the invasion became clear. The American government's plaintive protests to the Kremlin did not suggest, however, that it intended to take any real action to end the humanitarian catastrophe; rather, it was clear to all that the plight of the Chechen people would once again be secondary to larger geopolitical concerns. At the same time, the West may soon wish it hadn't been so acquiescent to the Chechen slaughter this time around. With Boris Yeltsin gone, the West will now likely have to deal with Vladimir Putin for many years to come, an extremely cunning leader whose popularity with the Russian people stems in equal parts from having perpetrated that slaughter and from thumbing his nose at the West's feeble protests over it.

. . .

As of this writing, the fighting in Chechnya continues with the Russian leadership still maintaining that the complete pacification of Chechnya will be achieved "soon," even as the death toll escalates by the day. Ultimately, of course, it will be discovered that no such pacification is possible, and another back-room deal will be made—perhaps shortly after the March elections that will complete Putin's rise to power. Until then, it is only a question of how many more Chechens and Russians—as well as aid workers like Fred Cuny who make it their mission to clean up the folly of generals—will be sacrificed.

ACKNOWLEDGMENTS

Among the many people to whom I'm indebted for this book coming to pass, there are clearly two I must thank most of all: my companions in Chechnya, Stanley Greene and Ryan Chilcote. Both Stanley and Ryan showed extraordinary bravery and resourcefulness, and more than once were responsible for extricating us from bad situations stemming from my bad decisions. My gratitude to them is of a depth and nature that perhaps only they can fully appreciate.

In any biography, which this book is at least in part, there is an element of conceit; ultimately, no other person's life is truly knowable. When that person is the victim of a mysterious and unsolved crime, the element of conceit is joined by one of unfairness. Fred Cuny saved many thousands of lives during his lifetime and certainly deserved to have a book written about him if he had died of old age or—perhaps the likeliest scenario—in a small-plane crash in some Third World country. Because of the circumstances of his disappearance in Chechnya, however, any such book must also raise questions and explore aspects of his personality and of his past that his loved ones might prefer left alone. The Cuny family knew that this book would probably contain material they found objectionable or overly intimate, and yet all were extraordinarily generous and forthcoming, as well as gracious at my constant intrusions during one of the most painful periods in their lives. My heartfelt thanks to all the Cuny family—and especially Gene, Charlotte, Chris, and my very good friend, Craig—for both their tolerance and their kindness.

This book cannot hope to be a definitive account of Fred Cuny nor of the international disaster relief system. Nevertheless, I would like to thank all of Fred's many friends and colleagues around the world who gave so freely of their time to help me draw a portrait of this most complex man and of his work: Rita Baker, Mike Huston, Rick Hill, Damir Lulo, Beth Rabren, Don Stevenson, Henry "Steve" Stevenson, Carol Streatfeild, Emily Young (Texas); Morton Abramowitz, Ken Anderson, Franca Brilliant, Paul Goble, Tex Harris, Don Krumm, Jean "Jinx" Parker, Lionel Rosenblatt, Julia Taft, Vic Tanner (Washington); Aryeh Neier, Elisabeth Socolow (New York); John Fawcett, Mike Hess, Hazim Kasic, Kenan Logo, Samantha Power, Ognen Samardcic, Sead Sirbabulo, Brian Steers, Sonja Vukotic (Bosnia); and Veronica O'Sullivan (San Diego). That Fred Cuny had so many good friends around the globe—and I undoubtedly met with a mere fraction of them—is certainly a powerful testament to his way with people.

I also want to extend my thanks to those in various branches of the American government who helped me gain an understanding both of the government's policy in regard to Chechnya, and of the efforts made to find Fred Cuny. Among those I can name are Anne Johnson at the State Department, Jerrold Bamel at the FBI, and at the American Embassy in Moscow, Ambassador Thomas Pickering, Michael Gofeller, and Gabe Escobar. To all those who spoke or met with me on condition of anonymity at the State Department, the Pentagon, and the CIA, I am also deeply grateful; I suspect most knew that my analysis of American policy in Chechnya would not be a favorable one, and yet were forthcoming and cooperative anyway.

There were also a great number of journalists, Soros Foundation officials, outside experts, and search-team members who greatly assisted me in various aspects of this story: Heidi Bradner; Chris Buchanan and Sherry Jones of PBS *Frontline*; John Colarusso of McMaster University; Thomas Goltz (sorry about the mix-up!); Scott Parrish of the Monterey Institute's Center for Nonproliferation Studies; John Pomfret of the *Washington Post*; Joe Rogers, formerly of the Soros Foundation; Kurt Schork of Reuters; Greg Smith of the Cotton Club in Shanghai; and Timothy Thomas at the Foreign Military Studies Office. Within this category I would especially like to thank the staff of the *New York Times* office in Moscow, especially Steve Erlanger for his remarkable forbearance at my pestiness, and my good friends Alessandra Stanley and Michael Specter. In helping track down the numerous loose threads that remained in the frantic last days, I would have been lost without the superb researching skills of Jesse Moss and Sarah Richards.

At Doubleday, Calvin Chu and Maria Carella have earned my eternal gratitude for making this book look so good—as has, of course, Deborah "Kool Kat" Cowell, for so cheerfully tolerating my endless phone calls and favor-seeking.

Penultimately—since book acknowledgment pages are about the only place one can get away with using the word—I would like to thank my family and my many friends who both endured my whining when the book was not going well and who tolerated my long silences when it was. As she well knows, Nanette bore the worst of this, and I'm most appreciative of the many pleasant conversations we had along the way. To Benjamin Anastas, Paul Albanese, Walid Bitar, Bex Brian, Sue Clark, Melinda Farrell, John "Pinkie" Faherty, Maura Fritz, Francisco Goldman, Tom and Jody Grimes, Colin Harrison, Rex Henderson, Sebastian Junger, Barrie Kessler, Guy Lawson, Pete Manno, Amy Margolis, Pearson Marx, Janet McGowan, Tom and Lee Montgomery, Michael Morse, Jerry "Le Jeré" Renek, Frances Richardson, Ellen Ryder, Chuck Siebert, John and Mary Tintori, and Wilson Van Law: sorry; I'm really going to try to be a much better friend in the future.

Finally, I owe a very special thanks to my agents, Deborah Schneider and Patty Detroit, and to the two editors and friends who saw a unique tale in the Fred Cuny story even before I did. Without the superb editing and constant encouragement of Gerry Marzorati at the

New York Times Magazine and Bill "Chivato Jefe" Thomas at Doubleday neither the original article nor this book would have been written. At different times, I put both of them through hell as I tried to fashion this story, and yet both remained resolutely confident—at least so they claimed—in my ability to do so.

INDEX

380